THE TENSIONS BETWEEN
CULTURE AND HUMAN RIGHTS

AFRICA: MISSING VOICES SERIES

Timothy Stapleton, Professor, History, University of Calgary

ISSN 1703-1826 (Print) ISSN 1925-5675 (Online)

This series addresses issues and topics that have been overlooked in political, social, and historical discussions about Africa.

No. 1 · *Grassroots Governance?: Chiefs in Africa and the Afro-Caribbean*
Edited by D.I. Ray and P.S. Reddy · Copublished with the International Association of Schools and Institutes of Administration (IASIA)

No. 2 · *The African Diaspora in Canada: Negotiating Identity and Belonging*
Edited by Wisdom Tettey and Korbla Puplampu

No. 3 · *A Common Hunger: Land Rights in Canada and South Africa*
By Joan G. Fairweather

No. 4 · *New Directions in African Education: Challenges and Possibilities*
Edited by S. Nombuso Dlamini

No. 5 · *Shrines in Africa: History, Politics, and Society*
Edited by Allan Charles Dawson

No. 6 · *The Land Has Changed: History, Society and Gender in Colonial Eastern Nigeria*
By Chima J. Korieh

No. 7 · *African Wars: A Defense Intelligence Perspective*
By William G. Thom

No. 8 · *Reinventing African Chieftaincy in the Age of AIDS, Gender, Governance, and Development*
Edited by Donald I. Ray, Tim Quinlan, Keshav Sharma, and Tacita A.O. Clarke

No. 9 · *The Politics of Access: University Education and Nation-Building in Nigeria, 1948–2000*
By Ogechi Emmanuel Anyanwu

No. 10· *Social Work in Africa: Exploring Culturally Relevant Education and Practice in Ghana*
By Linda Kreitzer

No. 11· *Secession and Separatist Conflicts in Postcolonial Africa*
By Charles G. Thomas and Toyin Falola

No. 12· *The Tensions between Culture and Human Rights: Emancipatory Social Work and Afrocentricity in a Global World*
Edited by Vishanthie Sewpaul, Linda Kreitzer, and Tanusha Raniga

UNIVERSITY OF CALGARY
Press

The Tensions Between Culture and Human Rights

Emancipatory Social Work and Afrocentricity in a Global World

EDITED BY

Vishanthie Sewpaul,
Linda Kreitzer, and
Tanusha Raniga

Africa: Missing Voices Series
ISSN 1703-1826 (Print) ISSN 1925-5675 (Online)

University of Calgary Press
2500 University Drive NW
Calgary, Alberta
Canada T2N 1N4
press.ucalgary.ca

LIBRARY AND ARCHIVES CANADA CATALOGUING IN PUBLICATION

Title: The tensions between culture and human rights : emancipatory social work and Afrocentricity in a global world / edited by Vishanthie Sewpaul, Linda Kreitzer, and Tanusha Raniga.
Names: Sewpaul, Vishanthie, editor. | Kreitzer, Linda, 1955- editor. | Raniga, Tanusha, editor.
Series: Africa, missing voices series ; no. 12.
Description: Series statement: Africa, missing voices series ; no. 12 | Includes bibliographical references and index.
Identifiers: Canadiana (print) 20210134569 | Canadiana (ebook) 20210141018 | ISBN 9781773851822 (softcover) | ISBN 9781773851877 (international hardcover) | ISBN 9781773851839 (open access PDF) | ISBN 9781773851846 (PDF) | ISBN 9781773851853 (EPUB) | ISBN 9781773851860 (Kindle)
Subjects: LCSH: Human rights—Africa. | LCSH: Africa—Social life and customs. | LCSH: Ethnology—Africa. | LCSH: Social service—Africa. | LCSH: Afrocentrism.
Classification: LCC JC599.A35 T46 2021 | DDC 323.096—dc23

The University of Calgary Press acknowledges the support of the Government of Alberta through the Alberta Media Fund for our publications. We acknowledge the financial support of the Government of Canada. We acknowledge the financial support of the Canada Council for the Arts for our publishing program.

The editors acknowledge the financial contribution of the Association of Schools of Social Work in Africa and the International Association of Schools of Social Work towards the publication of this book.

Copyediting by Peter Enman
Cover design, page design, and typesetting by Melina Cusano

TABLE OF CONTENTS

Introduction: Culture, Human Rights, and Social Work: 1
      Colonialism, Eurocentricism, and Afrocentricity
            Vishanthie Sewpaul and Linda Kreitzer

1   Disrupting Popular Discourses on Ilobolo: The Role of   25
      Emancipatory Social Work in Engendering Human Rights
      and Social Justice
            Vishanthie Sewpaul, Manqoba Victor Mdamba, and
            Boitumelo Seepamore

2   Nigerian Marital Cultural Practices and Implications for   47
      Human Rights
            Augusta Yetunde Olaore, Julie Drolet, and Israel
            Bamidele Olaore

3   Socio-Cultural Constructions of Intensive Mothering   67
      and Othermothering: Domestic Workers' Experiences
      of Distance Parenting and their Conceptualization of
      Motherhood
            Boitumelo Seepamore and Vishanthie Sewpaul

4   Misrecognition of the Rights of People with Epilepsy in   85
      Zimbabwe: A Social Justice Perspective
            Jacob Rugare Mugumbate and Mel Gray

5   Harmful Cultural Practices against Women and Girls in   105
      Ghana: Implications for Human Rights and Social Work
            Alice Boateng and Cynthia A. Sottie

6   The Intersection of Culture, Religion (Islam), and Women's   125
      Human Rights in Ethiopia: Private Lives in Focus
            Yania Seid-Mekiye and Linda Kreitzer

7   The Implications of a Patriarchal Culture for Women's   147
    Access to "Formal" Human Rights in South Africa: A Case
    Study of Domestic Violence Survivors
        Shahana Rasool

8   Child Marriage among the Apostolic Sects in Zimbabwe: 165
    Implications for Social Work Practice
        Munyaradzi Muchacha, Abel Blessing Matsika, and
        Tatenda Nhapi

9   "Everybody Here Knows This, If You Want to Go to School   183
    then You Must Be Prepared to Work": Children's Rights
    and the Role of Social Work in Ghana
        Ziblim Abukari

10 Human Rights and Medicalization of FGM/C in Sudan   209
        Paul Bukuluki

11 Cultural Dimensions of HIV/AIDS and Gender-Based   237
    Violence: A Case Study of Alur and Tieng Adhola Cultural
    Institutions in Uganda
        Paul Bukuluki, Ronard Mukuye, Ronald Luwangula,
        Aloysious Nnyombi, Juliana Naumo Akoryo, and
        Eunice Tumwebaze

12 When National Law and Culture Coalesce: Challenges for   255
    Children's Rights in Botswana with Specific Reference to
    Corporal Punishment
        Poloko Nuggert Ntshwarang and Vishanthie Sewpaul

Conclusion: Emancipatory Social Work, *Ubuntu*, and   273
    Afrocentricity: Antidotes to Human Rights Violations
        Vishanthie Sewpaul and Linda Kreitzer

List of Contributors   297
Index   301
    Author Index   301
    Subject Index   306

Culture, Human Rights, and Social Work: Colonialism, Eurocentricism, and Afrocentricity

Vishanthie Sewpaul and Linda Kreitzer

> We stand at the thick of human experience, in the space of human problems, in the real-life local places where people live in the face of dangers, grave and minor, real and imagined. Here is where fear and aspiration, desire and obligation, mesh in the close encounters of ordinary men and women with the pain and disaster and with the infrapolitics of power that apportion those threats unequally and distribute responses to them unfairly across social fault lines in actual worlds.
>
> —Kleinman, 1998, p. 376.

We begin with the above quotation by Kleinman (1998), whose treatise on human suffering bears direct relevance for social work. At the heart of our concern is the human suffering and consequences born out of cultural practices—spaces within which people breathe, live, learn, marry, work, play, and become mothers and fathers; daughters; sons; brothers; sisters; friends and colleagues—in the face of "grave and minor, real and imagined" threats and dangers. The threats and dangers relate as much to the consequences of pernicious cultural practices as they do to the

1

possible threats and dangers of giving up customs, traditions, and norms that have come to be inscribed as parts of core identities and entangled with socio-economic realities. Such understanding bears important implications for how we deal with the vexing issues of diversities and human rights that are discussed in the various chapters in this book, and which are consolidated and detailed in the conclusion in relation to socio-economic and political governance, and to social work education, research, and practice.

Culture has been variously defined through different disciplinary lenses. Generally, it incorporates elements of the arts, values, beliefs, symbols, customs, traditions, and practices of groups of persons, with an emphasis on the intergenerational and contemporaneous transmission of these. We accept the definition of Spencer-Oatey (2008), as it addresses the ambiguities inherent in culture; embraces the formal and informal dimensions of culture; addresses intersubjectivity and the role of the individual within the group; and speaks to both culture's constraints and the agency that people possess, and can exercise, in the face of such constraints.

> Culture is a fuzzy set of basic assumptions and values, orientations to life, beliefs, policies, procedures and behavioral conventions that are shared by a group of people, and that influence (but do not determine) each member's behaviour and his/her interpretations of the 'meaning' of other people's behaviour. (p. 3)

Culture does not exist in isolation. It is interlinked with histories and socio-economic and political structures and can contribute to the development and flourishing of humanity or the curtailment of human freedoms. Culture is learned and is not static or cast in stone; in its various facets it is forever changing. It is the specific elements of customs and traditions of culture, that may or may not be linked with broader cultural epistemologies, that we are particularly concerned with. Frantz Fanon (1963), one of the most eminent of post-colonial intellectuals, cogently posited that:

> Culture has never the translucidity of custom; it abhors all simplifications. In its essence it is opposed to custom, for

custom is always the deterioration of culture. The desire to attach oneself to tradition or bring abandoned traditions to life again does not only mean going against the current of history but also opposing one's people. (p. 180)

As we discuss in this chapter, there is a richness and value to African philosophical world views that, if abided by, would prevent the reproduction of customs and traditions that violate human rights. In a globalizing world, there are numerous factors at multi-systemic levels that influence local customs and traditions. However, the power of intersubjectivity, the interpersonal and immediate group affiliations at the local level cannot be underestimated in the reproduction of culture. But the subjectivities of human beings are not fixed; neither are the social circumstances or the moral reasoning of people (Kleinman, 1998), and it is these that the authors of the various chapters of this book invoke in their call for a retention of the affirming aspects of African cultures, and a repudiation of those aspects that depreciate and violate human dignity and human rights. As in other parts of the world, in "African societies . . . there are multiple universes of discourses" that include the "commonsensical, the scientific, and the religious" (Hallen, 2002, p. 42).

The salient issues discussed in each of the chapters are by no means intended to convey the message that human rights violations occur in the name of culture on the African continent only. Such violations occur on a global level. But our focus of interest is Africa, and we argue that an authentic commitment to Afrocentricity must serve as a guiding principle in stemming the abuse of human rights in the name of culture. Interrogating the intersection of political economy, culture, and human rights in Africa, with country-specific examples and the kinds of pedagogical and practice strategies that social work students, educators, researchers, and practitioners might use, holds promise for interventions in other contexts.

Africa is not homogenous; it comprises 54 countries, each with its varying levels of socio-economic development, forms of socio-political governance, unique languages, cultures, histories, and liberation struggles. Like many other colonized societies, countries across Africa have reflected a strong culture of anti-colonial resistance, which has been its source of strength and development. As much as there are diversities across countries in Africa, there are in-country differences as well, and we must not essentialize the cultural norms and practices within countries. A discussion on culture and human rights would be invalid if we did not locate contemporary Africa in the context of its colonial legacies and the impacts of Eurocentrism. It is this that we turn our attention to in the following section.

Colonialism, Eurocentricism, and Afrocentrism

There is widespread acceptance that colonialism has imposed an indelible footprint on colonized peoples across the world. The effects of colonialism in Africa in respect of the denigration of African people—reducing them to the level of non-beings; the cultural annihilation through assimilation into the languages, religion, and cultures of the colonized; the dispossession of African peoples of their lands; the fragmentation of their families; and the deliberate retention of the colonized in slave-like working conditions in abject poverty—have been widely documented. Through colonialism and missionization a Western or Eurocentric hegemony has come to characterize education, research, and practice in the humanities, and the social and natural sciences broadly (Asante, 2014a; Biko, 1978; Dei, 1994; Dei, 2012; Fanon, 1963; Hallen, 2002; Kumah-Abiwu, 2016) and in social work in particular (Harms Smith & Nathane, 2018; Midgley, 1981; Mwansa & Kreitzer, 2012; Sewpaul, 2014). Unfortunately, in a rapidly and intensely globalizing world, various forms of imperialism continue to exist that materially disadvantage people in the Global South, and archetypes of the presumed superiority of the West and the presumed inferiority of the rest of the world abound, which do impact the self-conceptualization of people (Asante, 2014a; Biko, 1978; Fanon, 1963; Hallen, 2002; Sewpaul, 2016). In addition, new forms of imperialism, in the face of neoliberal capitalist expansion, influence life choices, which have become increasingly commodified, as seen, for instance, in changing *ilobolo* practices. Apart from ideological beliefs, growing inequality and poverty caused by free market ideologies constrain choices, and may contribute to violations of human rights, as, for example, lack of employment opportunities may induce women to remain as active agents as they perform female genital mutilation.

Colonialism changed Africa's religious, cultural, economic, and political landscapes. Contemporary intercountry and intra-country, inter-ethnic and inter-religious forms of violence, rooted in a colonial history, are major contributors to human rights violations in Africa, with poverty being a precursor to and a consequence of conflicts and human rights violations (Adejumobi, 2006; Annan, 2006; Fanon, 1963). In the words of Fanon (1963), "the poverty of the people, national oppression and the inhibition of culture are one and the same thing" (p. 191). The colonialists denied people their local languages and cultures and created arbitrary borders that cut across national territories, forcing in some instances people of different ethnicities to live together and in other instances separating ethnic groups and sowing seeds of division, fear, suspicion, and prejudice (Mwansa & Kreitzer, 2012). This did not augur well for democracy, development, respect for human rights, or shared values and identities.

Africans have been, for centuries, the subject of colonial denigration, and with ongoing forms of imperialism, continue to live in the gaze of the colonizer (Fanon, 1963). That Africans must resist colonial domination is beyond dispute. But should Africans do this at their own peril by holding on to customs and traditions that work against their own peoples? The often-cited refrain is: "It's in our culture. The West must not tell us what to do." We agree! Our argument is that we must do it for ourselves, by ourselves. Detailing colonial Europe's assault on humanity, Fanon (1963) asserted: "Humanity is waiting for something other from us than such an imitation [of Europe], which would be almost an obscene caricature," and in his conclusion beseeches: "For Europe, for ourselves and for humanity . . . we must turn over a new leaf, we must work out new concepts, and try to set afoot a new man [sic]" (p. 255). Afrocentricity, which according to Chukwuokolo (2009), is *a resolute attempt to put the records right* by historicizing African peoples in Africa and across the African diaspora and by acknowledging the "contributions of Africans in all areas of civilization be reflected in world history" (p. 33, emphasis added), has been one response to such a call. This was the major pursuit of Steve Biko (see Biko, 1978), the champion of the Black Consciousness Movement in South Africa (who was beaten to death in prison at the age of 31), who dedicated his life to the transformation of the thinking of black people, and to the alteration of their material conditions of life.

Asante's (2014a; 2014b) seminal writings on Afrocentricity have informed many academic disciplines, including social work, with their emphasis on the agency, rather than the subjugation of African peoples; centring African identities and experiences in relation to location and place; and conceptualizing Africans as subjects rather than as objects of history (Asante, 2014a). According to Asante (2014b):

> Afrocentricity seeks a mature relationship to other cultures, neither imposing nor seeking to advance its own material advantage. By centering their culture and claiming it as a valuable part of humanity, African people own or assume agency within their own contexts, thereby fulfilling their roles as legitimate partners in multicultural discourse, something constructed together. Such an idea is fundamentally more about humanity than materialism, winning, and domination. (p. 1)

At the centre of Afrocentricity are the humanism and humanistic ethics needed to deal with the multiple problems of Africa, with social solidarity and deepened people-centred social democracy being the lifeblood of societies (Asante, 2014a; Biko, 1978; Hallen, 2002; Fanon, 1963; Fashina, 1989). According to Fashina (1989), "the only justified institutions and practices are those which promote concern and respect for all, tend to minimize pain and suffering, and recognize the moral claim of everyone, irrespective of social class, status or race" (p. 182). To this we add the categories of gender, age, sexual identity and sexual orientation, religion, language, ethnicity, marital status, family type, disability, and illness.

Afrocentricity is not anti-white. It is anti-oppression; it seeks to rectify distorted Eurocentric histories and archetypical constructions and reconstructions of Africa. It does not seek to replace Eurocentrism—it is a countering of Western hegemony, an epitome of resistance politics. Given the internalization of Western archetypes by African peoples, and the subsequent interiorizing of inferiority by African peoples (Asante, 2014a, 2014b; Biko, 1978; Chawane, 2016; Fanon, 1963; Hallen, 2002; Sewpaul, 2016), Afrocentricity—with its validations of African identities—is not just desirable, but a necessity. Authentic multicultural relations and dialogue cannot happen without inclusion of all the world's population. Afrocentricity benefits Europe (by offering the Western world alternative perspectives) as much as it does Africa and the African diaspora (Asante, 2014a, 2014b; Chawane, 2016, Fanon, 1973; Hallen, 2002). It affirms the co-existence of all cultures and examines how power and privilege are played out in global political, economic, and multicultural arenas.

Ubuntu, which roughly translates into "humanity" or "African humanism," has several derivates such as *bomoto* (Congo), *gimuntu* (Angola), *botho* (Botswana), *umunthu* (Malawi), *bumuntu* (Tanzania), *umuntu* (Uganda), and *hunu* among the Shona majority of Zimbabwe. However, *Ubuntu* has come to be seen as a Pan-African philosophical framework (Mupedziswa et al., 2019). *Ubuntu*, signifying the aphorism of "umuntu ngumuntu ngabantu," meaning "a person is a person through other persons," is an Afrocentric ideal that has become post-apartheid South Africa's national ethos. *Ubuntu* played a major role in the Truth and Reconciliation Commission, as it embraced the virtues of forgive-ness, compassion, the interconnectedness of humanity, and restorative justice. Given the atrocities inflicted on Blacks[1] during apartheid, South Africa could have easily decompensated into civil war. It was the spirit of *Ubuntu* that allowed for a peaceful transition into a non-racial democracy (Barnard, 2014; Sewpaul, 2015; Stengel, 2012). Mandela (1994), who is the epitome of *Ubuntu*, wrote of his mission to liberate both the oppressed and the oppressor, saying that "a man who takes away another man's free-dom is a prisoner of hatred; is locked behind the bars of prejudice and narrow-mindedness" (p. 544).

The seven principles of Kwanzaa[2] (InterExchange, 2019) represent core Afrocentric principles, which are:

1. Umoja (Unity): To strive for and maintain unity in the family, community, nation, and race.

2. Kujichagulia (Self-Determination): To define ourselves, name ourselves, create for ourselves, and speak for ourselves.

3. Ujima (Collective Work and Responsibility): To build and maintain our community together and make our

brothers' and sisters' problems our problems and solve them together.

4. Ujamaa (Cooperative Economics): To build and maintain our own stores, shops, and other businesses and to profit from them together.

5. Nia (Purpose): To make our collective vocation the building and developing of our community to restore our people to their traditional greatness.

6. Kuumba (Creativity): To do always as much as we can, in the way we can, to leave our community more beautiful and beneficial than we inherited it.

7. Imani (Faith): To believe with all our heart in our people, our parents, our teachers, our leaders, and the righteousness and victory of our struggle. (para. 4)

These principles, developed in the United States by African-Americans to acknowledge and uphold their African heritage, have significant implications for socio-economic and political governance systems—a discussion that we take up in the concluding chapter—and for human rights discourses.

There are undoubted virtues to *Ubuntu*, whatever structures of society it is made manifest in, and the emphasis on collective responsibility and communal caring, as seen in extended family systems of caring for the elderly and children in Africa, must be celebrated. But unfortunately, with the romanticization and idealization of traditional communities and of *Ubuntu*, their potential downsides have often been overlooked. *Ubuntu* has become corrupted in some instances to privilege one's family or tribal group over others, thus contributing to nepotism, has been used to subjugate some groups of persons and to hinder the progress of individuals who must not be seen to be above the group or community. Pawar and Cox (2004, p. 256) wrote about the "mean spirited, superstitious, religious, constraining and backward" characteristics of traditional communities that need to be eradicated. As in the Asian context, it is the often the "specialness" of African values, traditions, respect for authority, and group identification that are used as justification for suppression of civil and political rights and freedom (Adejumobi, 2006; Sewpaul, 2016), with Adejumobi (2006) warning about the dangers of group and ethnic identification, which can become "exclusionary and bifurcated" (p. 255), as evident in the genocide of Rwanda. Sono (1994) asserted that the emphasis on group solidarity, consensus, and community could degenerate into a "total communalism" (p. xiii), and eloquently articulated that the group could be

> overwhelming, totalistic, even totalitarian. Group psychology, though parochially and narrowly based . . . nonetheless pretends universality. . . . Discursive rationality is overwhelmed by emotional identity. . . . To agree is more important than to disagree; conformity is cherished more than innovation. Tradition is venerated, continuity revered, change feared and difference shunned. Heresies [i.e., the innovative creations of intellectual individuals, or refusal to participate in communalism] are not tolerated in such communities. (Sono, 1994, p. 7, square brackets in original)

It is these aspects of traditional communities that the various chapters in this book challenge. The prevalence of human rights' abuses on the continent, and across the globe, speaks to the gap between rhetoric and reality. Sadly, on a global level the moral arc is not bending toward greater equality, inclusion, justice, emancipation, and protection and promotion of human rights. On the one hand, there are the ideals of democratic participation, unity, collective caring, and respect for diversities while, on the other hand, we have seen the erosion of *Ubuntu*—the most inhumane and atrocious violations, especially against women and children, justified mainly on the basis of culture. Human rights violations cannot be condoned within traditional African value systems that hold human dignity to be inviolable, and where respect, restraint, and collective responsibility (Cobbah, 1987) are exalted. Indeed, as previously pointed out by Sewpaul (2016), genuine adherence to these cultural precepts can serve to stem abuses in the political and personal spheres of people's lives.

Of salience to our deliberations is the often dichotomous relationship constructed between the West and the rest of the world. Afrocentricity, as discussed above, is not intended to replace Eurocentrism. While African cultures do represent collectivism and respect for family, and embody unifying and holistic principles, this does not mean these are non-existent in the West. Makgoba and Seepe (2004) call for a replacement of the Eurocentric with the Afrocentric, asserting that the Afrocentric is "emancipatory and liberatory," compared with that which is "authoritarian, patriarchal and Eurocentric" (p. 14). In the Chinese context, Chung and Haynes (1993) emphasize the concepts of "love, humanity, perfect virtue and benevolence," and they dichotomize Western culture as "low context culture" that is "left-minded" and Eastern culture as "relatively high context" and "right-minded" (p. 38), while Cobbah (1987) claimed that the we-centredness of the African marks a self-conception that is different from the Western conception. Repudiating claims such as these, Sewpaul (2016) concluded that "there are inherent dangers in trying to substitute one form of domination with another, and as with the cultural conceit of the West, the arrogance of the Rest is unbecoming" (p. 34). Zeleza (2006) challenged such dichotomies, asserting that "communality in Africa is often as exaggerated as individuality is in Europe. . . . In both contexts . . . individuals and community are mutually constituting and the practice of rights claiming, consuming or constraining them—entail a social context" (p. 47).

The chapters in this book challenge such dichotomies and the notion of an essentialist or monolithic African or Western culture, both of which preclude the wide range of cultural diversities within these contexts. Given the impact of colonialism in undermining the intellectuality and self-confidence of colonized peoples and destroying local traditions and cultures, one can understand the rarefication of African cultures. Perhaps as a reactionary measure, tradition gets to be upheld as the core of an authentic indigenous culture, an emancipatory alternative to a hegemonic Western culture (Sewpaul, 2016). The various chapters in this book engage with the complex relationships between culture and human rights, and their concomitants—democracy and socio-economic development—and the implications of these for social work practice, research, education, and social policy. While the chapters do not specifically use the concept

Afrocentricity, almost all of them invoke indigenous African values and practices to contribute to individual, family, and community well-being, and to stem human rights abuses. In this chapter and in the conclusion, we consolidate the discussion, and more specifically the recommendations, within the Afrocentric and emancipatory theoretical frameworks.

The economic exploitation of Africa, and its underdevelopment, cannot be used as an argument that freedom from want and hunger must prevail over political and civil liberties. Sen (1999), a development economist and a Nobel Laureate, provides ample evidence to demonstrate the interdependence among the different types of rights, asserting that agency and freedom are central to addressing social, economic, and cultural deprivations. As with the debate about the applicability of civil and political rights in Africa, there are dissenting views on culture and human rights. Notwithstanding the popular critique that universal human rights instruments are rooted in a Western, individualistically framed ideology, the African (Banjul) Charter on Human and People's Rights, adopted in 1981 by the Organization of African Unity (now the African Union), embraces civil and political rights, socio-economic and cultural rights, and environmental rights (Organization of African Unity [OAU], 1981). Like other regional declarations, it tries to marry universal human rights with culturally specific norms, with emphasis on the collective, the family, and community, and on duties and responsibilities.

The West has not always been the carrier and transmitter of democratic ideals and practices. History reflects that in some instances African and Asian countries were ahead of Western countries in embracing diversities and human rights (Sen, 2005). We need to reclaim those positive parts of our histories and, as Fanon (1963) points out, reject those traditions that are in violation of human rights. Our anti-colonial stance must work for Africa! There is a difference between challenging the cultural conceit of the West and a defensive approach where we withdraw into practices that are contrary to the core values that we hold as Africans. African world views place a ubiquitous importance on human dignity, recognizing our common humanity, and doing no harm. This fundamental, we-centred approach is inconsistent with some traditional cultural practices that violate the rights of women, men, and children and that social workers have a moral and ethical obligation to engage with, challenge, and change.

Culture, Human Rights, and Social Work

Social work's respect for cultural diversity is one of its most unifying, constitutive aspects, and debates around universal human rights and cultural specificity abound in the literature (Hugman, 2013; Ife, 2008; Ife & Fiske, 2016; Sewpaul, 2016). Issues that are central to human rights, as reflected in various international and national declarations and conventions, are crucial to social work. From its inception social work has been regarded as a human rights profession. In 1936, Bertha Reynolds, an American social worker with radical Marxist leanings who lost her job as associate dean at Smith College on account of her attempt to unionize workers (NASW Foundation, 2004), warned: "If they [social workers] do not stand courageously for all human rights, they will lose their own, including the right to practice their profession as a high and honorable calling" (p. 12). Drawing on the ethical leadership of Nelson Mandela, Sewpaul (2015) asserted that, if imbued with the values of *Ubuntu* and an emancipatory focus, social work is politics with soul. The Global Social Work Statement of Ethical Principles (GSWSEP) (IASSW, 2018), the Global Definition of Social Work (IASSW/IFSW, 2014), the Global Standards on Social Work Education and Training (Sewpaul & Jones, 2004), and the Global Agenda for Social Work and Social Development (IASSW/ICSW/IFSW, 2012) all affirm that commitment to social justice and human rights grants social work its legitimacy. These core global documents are discussed in the concluding chapter.

Social work's commitments to respecting cultural diversity and doing no harm are accepted on global, regional, and local levels. While these are noble ideals, and on the surface may appear to be unproblematic, the reality is that the values of respect for cultural diversity and doing no harm may often reflect competing and conflicting interests. These over-arching principles are subject to political and cultural context-specific interpretations, which engender relativistic discourses and practices that do often inflict harm and violate human rights. While communities might hold doing no harm as a prized value, the problem with this principle is that when one is socialized into a culture, one often does not see the harm induced by certain cultural practices; they become naturalized and normalized (Sewpaul, 2016). It is the countering of such normalization and naturalization that is at the heart of emancipatory social work, which is discussed in the concluding chapter. A critical question, previously posed by Sewpaul (2016), "how far do we stretch the boundaries of moral relativism" (p. 35) in the name of cultural diversity, bears relevance.

Brown (as cited in Ife, 2008) asserted that "arguments about cultural difference represent perhaps the strongest criticisms of the idea of human rights, and for many they are the most difficult" (p. 68). Given the pre-eminence placed on respect for cultural diversity, it is not surprising that some social workers choose to remain neutral and not make pronouncements on violations that occur in the name of culture. But no culture must be regarded as sacrosanct and above criticism. The pre-eminence placed on respect for cultural diversity is such that, in response to such a principle in the Global Social Work Statement of Ethical Principles (GSWSEP) (IASSW, 2018) reading as

> "recognizing that culture often serves as a disguise to violate human rights, social workers serve as cultural mediators to enable consensus building, to find an appropriate balance between competing human rights, and to advocate for the rights of marginalized, stigmatized, excluded and oppressed individuals and groups of persons," one global social work organization responded with: "regarding the first part of the sentence. . . . members have questioned whether the statement is judgmental and/or lacks cultural sensitivity that is key to social work practice" (e-mail communication).

The debates around cultural relativism and universal human rights warrant specific consideration. Many countries have policies and legislation opposing human rights violations. This does help, but legislation alone is insufficient to protect people against human rights violations that occur in the name of culture, where in almost all instances, as the various chapters in this book reflect, children and women are on the receiving end of such violations. Social workers must challenge the violations of basic rights to bodily integrity, to security, and to life that occur in the guise of culture.

We concede that the issues around culture and human rights are extremely complex, which places great demands on one's ethical reasoning, and in a world of ethical plurality one must make choices. While these choices might be well reasoned, they are often not neutral. Similarly, writing is not neutral; it reflects the subject location and the world views of the writer. As human beings we use empirical data—and sometimes not-so-empirical data—and at times rely on outright superstition, myths, blind faith, and commonsensical taken-for-granted assumptions to assert our truths. While the authors of the various chapters in this book strengthen their arguments with logic, reasoning, and empirical data, they do adopt standpoints in the interests of human rights and social justice. We acknowledge alternative interpretations and experiences in relation to all of the human rights issues discussed, and the controversies surrounding them. The very framing of female genital mutilation, for example, has been critiqued as a Western imposition, which is acknowledged by Alice Boateng and Cynthia A. Sottie in chapter 5 and by Paul Bukuluki in chapter 10. Some defenders of the practice, such as Fuambai Ahmadu, call for the use of female genital cutting/circumcision, and for an affirmation and validation of the practice, which they claim has aesthetic, cultural, and medical benefits (Tierney, 2008; Wax, 2006).

Outline of the Book

The book includes 12 chapters, written by social work authors from various parts of Africa. We wanted a continental diversity of voices and experiences that speak to culture, human rights, and social work in Africa. Many of the chapters are research based, where the authors use empirical data to support their arguments. The reader will note that there are similarities of cultural values, beliefs, and practices across Ghana, Ethiopia, Uganda, and Zimbabwe in relation to, for example, wife inheritance, property rights, and widowhood rites.

Chapter 1 begins with a look at the custom of *ilobolo* (bride wealth) in South Africa that is practised widely by isiZulu-speaking people in the province of Kwa Zulu Natal. The three South African writers, Vishanthie Sewpaul, Manqoba Victor Mdamba, and Boitumelo Seepamore, are concerned with the detrimental effects of ilobolo on women, men, and children. Through research, voices of community members, and student discussion forums, involving both women and men, it becomes clear there are different views on this cultural practice in relation to human rights. For some, it is an oppressive, patriarchal practice that should be modified or abolished, and for others it is a way for men and women to value each other's role in their marriage and is constructed as the essence of the identity of isiZulu-speaking people. Consequent upon neoliberal capitalism, the costs of ilobolo are rising, thus blocking opportunities for people to marry, and it accentuates poverty. The authors conclude with the difficulties that social workers face in relation to the compromising of civil and socio-economic rights on account of traditional norms. They identify emancipatory educational and practice strategies, including critical reflexivity and reflexive dialogue, as ways that social workers can begin to engage with communities in thinking differently about this cultural tradition that does undermine people's human rights.

Chapter 2 takes the reader to Nigeria, where marital cultural practices are critiqued in relation to human rights. The authors, Augusta Yetunde Olaore, Julie Drolet, and Israel Bamidele Olaore, begin by acknowledging the strong role culture plays in Nigerian life. They present research findings from a study concerning how indigenous, Afrocentric social care practices contribute to child and family well-being in Nigeria. This chapter specifically looks at widowhood cultural practices, inheritance and property rights, and marital infidelity. Following an explanation of each of these cultural practices, the authors discuss them in light of the African Charter on Human and Peoples' Rights (ACHPR) (OAU, 1981) and the Universal Declaration of Human Rights (UN, 1948). They conclude that these practices violate women's rights and freedoms and work against the above-mentioned international instruments that are designed to protect all people. Recommendations for eliminating the discriminatory practices and human rights infringements, inherent in the marital cultural practices, are discussed.

Chapter 3 takes us back to South Africa, looking at domestic workers' experience of distance parenting and their conceptualization of motherhood. Boitumelo Seepamore and Vishanthie Sewpaul discuss research completed on mothering, othermothering, and distance mothering, whereby women are forced through economic necessity to parent from a distance, and question whether this practice is in the best interests of the child. This qualitative research was conducted in the eThekwini

Metropolitan Municipality, to understand the experiences of female domestic workers who parent from a distance, and the meanings that participants attach to motherhood. Their discussion centres around four interrelated themes concerning distance mothering and its effect on the mother's own self-worth and the child's experience of having a mother who parents from a distance. Patriarchy and colonialist attitudes feed into a negative view of women who have no choice but to work away from home. The focus is on the intersection of race, class, and gender in connection with women who parent from a distance and the effect this has on them and their children's human rights. The chapter concludes by calling for a shift from the discourse on intensive mothering to intensive parenting, and ways in which social workers can effect change through consciousness raising.

The misrecognition of rights of people with epilepsy takes the reader, in chapter 4, to Zimbabwe, where authors' Jacob Rugare Mugumbate and Mel Gray discuss this growing issue worldwide. Through Nancy Fraser's social justice lens, they discuss the misrepresentation of this medical condition in relation to human rights. The qualitative research was conducted in Harare to identify social injustices arising from misrecognition of the rights of people with epilepsy. Their findings suggest that lack of educational and vocational support services, lack of medical health services, lack of public social welfare and disability services, lack of employment opportunities, and lack of recourse to justice in the workplace are factors that violate the human rights of people with epilepsy. They conclude with a proposed integrated model of epilepsy management that would address injustices experienced by people with epilepsy.

Chapter 5 looks at harmful cultural practices directed against women and children in Ghana. These are practices that are usually justified on grounds of religion or culture but violate international human rights. The traditions discussed are widowhood rites, widow inheritance, female genital mutilation/cutting (FGM/C), female ritual bondage (trokosi), and early marriage. Alice Boateng and Cynthia A. Sottie provide backgrounds to each of the cultural traditions and examine how patriarchy and oppressive relationships are upheld through these traditions. Conflict within the family, unequal access to resources, health risks, and child exploitation are consequences of these negative cultural traditions. There is a conflict between knowing that there is an infringement of human rights and, on the other hand, wanting to preserve cultural traditions. The authors advocate for social workers to educate communities about the harmful effects of these practices and work together to adopt a less punitive stance and to engage with custodians of traditional and religious practices to gain a deeper understanding of the beliefs behind these practices. Together, communities can brainstorm ways in which such beliefs and practices can be expressed and acted upon without any harmful effects on women and children.

Chapter 6 looks at the intersection between culture, religion (Islam), and women's rights in Ethiopia. Yania Seid-Mekiye and Linda Kreitzer explore the human rights instruments that uphold women's rights in a country where men hold more socio-economic and political power than women and exercise authority over women both in the home and in the public sphere. This research study looks at the intersection of culture and Islam in relation to marital relationships and argues that the present interpretation of the Quran favours men and limits women's human rights in family relationships. Three of the themes explored show the influence of patriarchy over Islamic women: (1) marital relationships generally; (2) polygamous practices; and (3) property and inheritance rights. The interpretation of the Quran that supports patriarchy is challenged by Islamic female scholars who refute these interpretations and offer a different interpretation of the more controversial Quranic scriptures in relation to the three areas mentioned above. The voices of Islamic women interviewed in the research also add to the argument that the Quran is used by men to subjugate and oppress Islamic wives in their marital relationships. The authors conclude that social workers are change agents and need to advocate for women's human rights. They need to work for the establishment of a system to abolish or reinterpret the unjust readings/understandings/interpretations of Islam's scriptures, and educate Muslims to understand how to maintain balanced, fair, and just relationships.

Chapter 7 looks at the patriarchal culture in South Africa, which permeates marital relationships in the form of domestic violence. Shahana Rasool conducted research to understand the help-seeking patterns of abused women. Her findings are supported by international and continental human rights instruments along with the voices of the women who were interviewed. Her study analyzed the theme of curtailments through the headings of freedom of expression and association and freedom of movement. Her findings show that women do not readily seek help to protect themselves from violence in the home. Her conclusion is that unless patriarchy is addressed at the deepest level, in the private, public, and political domains, not much will change for these women in terms of having the courage to address or walk out of the relationship. The way in which men exert power and control over women in abusive relationships challenges the constitutional rights of women, including their right to dignity, equality, bodily integrity, and freedom of expression, association, and movement. She concludes by challenging all social workers and citizens to support women in violent relationships in navigating their way out of abusive relationships, and to educate women about their rights as well as the different resources available to help them.

Chapter 8 introduces the issue of child marriages in the Apostolic sect in Zimbabwe. Munyaradzi Muchacha, Abel Blessing Matsika, and Tatenda Nhapi set the context in relation to human rights instruments that consider child marriage as a major violation of child rights. In exploring this conflictual cultural tradition through those who advocate for child marriage and those who consider that it violates the precepts of human rights instruments, the authors critically look at the different factors that have favoured child marriages and the reasons why this practice remains, including the role of poverty. More broadly, the authors argue that child marriages are underpinned by patriarchy and gender relations that marginalize and restrict opportunities for girls and women. The authors argue that legally prohibiting child marriage does not necessarily eliminate the practice in communities. Any attempt to change behaviours must be promoted and implemented in a manner that appreciates the local socio-economic, religious, and cultural circumstances. They argue that the role of social workers is to dialogue and engage with sect leaders by promoting active participation, mutual learning, and collective decision making with the community. More importantly, social workers need to continue to be involved with poverty reduction policies and urge the Zimbabwean government to implement a social safety net.

Chapter 9 looks at child protection in Ghana. Ziblim Abukari examines the present child protection laws in Ghana by briefly explaining these laws and how they compare to the Convention on the Rights of the Child (UN, 1989) and the African Charter on the Rights and Welfare of the Child (OAU, 1990). Traditional beliefs about the notion of the child and childhood are explained, and how vulnerable children were protected before colonization through a fostering system. He then concentrates on Ghanaian child laws concerning the education of the child and child labour. He concludes by offering ways that social workers can advocate for social protection of the child by educating themselves about the relevance of children's rights to their work in the field, and he identifies the need for human rights to be front and centre of social work education. Children and their families and communities should also be educated about the rights of the child. Finally, social workers need to be involved in policy making to ensure children are treated with the dignity and respect that human rights instruments advocate for.

Chapter 10 takes the reader to Sudan and the issue of female genital mutilation/cutting (FGM/C). Paul Bukuluki shares the findings from his phenomenological study on FGM/C using document analysis plus consultative meetings in the form of focus group discussions (FGDs) with health workers, particularly midwives, in Khartoum, Sudan. He lays out the background of FGM/C and the controversy surrounding this practice in relation to human rights. Themes from the study discussed in this chapter include the magnitude of FGM/C in Sudan, medicalization of FGM/C, health consequences of FGM/C, the violation of health rights, and negotiations with society's values and policies. He identifies a need for a health-system and multi-sectoral response to FGM/C, including poverty alleviation and strengthening accountability frameworks for health workers. The development of training tools that, from the onset, conceptualizes FGM/C and its medicalization as a violation of human rights is needed. Health professionals and social workers can use education to highlight the risks of FGM/C through collaboration with leaders and community members to develop alternatives to this practice which have proven successful in other parts of Africa.

Bukuluki and colleagues, in chapter 11, take the reader to Uganda, to discuss HIV/AIDS and gender-based violence (GBV). They conducted qualitative research to document the socio-cultural norms, values, and beliefs that impact on HIV/AIDS and GBV; to document good community practices in responding to HIV/AIDS and GBV, based on Afrocentric values; and to synthesize community-proposed recommendations for positive change. They argue that there is a link between culture and HIV/AIDS and gender-based violence. Human behaviour is influenced by culture, and positive cultural resources can be tapped into to decrease the prevalence of HIV/AIDS and gender-based violence. Their research findings showed practices and beliefs related to death and widow inheritance, practices related to healing and body beautification, and practices related to sexuality as factors in the perpetuation of HIV/AIDS and GBV. They conclude by giving recommendations of positive Afrocentric cultural values that can be used to address HIV/AIDS and GBV.

Chapter 12 looks at the challenge of children's human rights in relation to corporal punishment (CP) in Botswana. Poloko Nuggert Ntshwarang and Vishanthie Sewpaul begin with a brief literature review concerning CP and its meaning in Botswana in relation to human rights instruments. They detail a qualitative phenomenological study of women parenting children in Selebi Phikwe town in Botswana. Their aim was to understand the parenting practices of women with children in single female–parent families where the female is working, two-parent families where both parents are working, and two-parent families where the female is not working and the male is employed. The results of the study indicate that the entrenchment of CP in Botswana is deep, and it cuts across different family structures and socio-economic status, with most families having used CP as a form of discipline. They suggest that legal reform is needed to abolish CP and that the Convention on the Rights of the Child be upheld. Recognizing that it is difficult to change cultural behaviours, they advocate for educators and social workers to educate themselves on the effects of CP on children, and to advocate for conscious positive parenting, and alternate ways to parent children that do not use violence as a disciplinary measure.

The Conclusion features a discussion of emancipatory social work and Afrocentricity and their importance to social work in Africa in a world that is powered by neoliberalism and ethnocentricity, and where human rights and culture clash in the everyday lives of people. It brings together the salient themes of this book, which offers important knowledge to social workers around the world and in particular those social workers in Africa.

NOTES

1   Used in the political sense as in the Black Consciousness Movement to refer to all people of colour, which in South Africa included African Blacks, Coloureds and Indians.

2   Kwanzaa was developed by Maulana Karenga (who was a professor of Africana Studies at California State University, Long Beach) and was first celebrated in 1966/7 in the USA to honor the African heritage of African American culture. It is usually celebrated annually in late December and has spread from the USA to places like Jamaica, London, Ghana, South Africa, Toronto and Paris.

REFERENCES

Adejumobi, S. (2006). Citizenship, rights, and the problem of conflicts and civil wars in Africa. In C. Heyns & K. Stefiszyn (Eds.), *Human rights, peace and justice in Africa: A reader* (pp. 250–271). Pretoria, ZA: Pretoria University Law Press.

Annan, K. (2006). The causes of conflict and the promotion of durable peace and sustainable development in Africa. In C. Heyns & K. Stefiszyn (Eds.), *Human rights, peace and justice in Africa: A reader* (pp. 239–243). Pretoria, ZA: Pretoria University Law Press.

Asante, M. K. (2014a). Afrocentricity: Toward a new understanding of African thought in the world. In M. K. Asante, Y. Miike, & J. Yin (Eds.), *The global intercultural communication reader* (2nd ed., pp. 101–110). New York, NY: Routledge.

Asante, M. K. (2014b). *Afrocentricity: Key concepts in intercultural dialogue.* No. 23(1). Center for Intercultural Dialogue. Retrieved September 2020 from https://centerforinterculturaldialogue.files.wordpress.com/2014/07/key-concept-afrocentricity.pdf

Barnard, R. (2014). 'Introduction.' In R. Barnard (Ed.), *The Cambridge companion to Nelson Mandela* (pp 1–25). New York, NY: Cambridge University Press.

Biko, N. M. (1978). *I write what I like* (A. Stubbs, Ed.). Johannesburg, ZA: Heinemann.

Chawane, M. (2016). The development of Afrocentricity: An historical survey. *Yesterday and Today, 16,* 78–99.

Chukwuokolo, J. C. (2009). Afrocentrism or Eurocentrism: The dilemma of African development. *New Journal of African Studies, 6,* 24–39.

Chung, D. K., & Haynes, A. W. (1993). Confucian welfare philosophy and social change technology: An integrated approach for international social development. *International Social Welfare, 36,* 37–46.

Cobbah, J. A. M. (1987). African values and the human rights debate: An African perspective. *Human Rights Quarterly, 9*(3), 309–331.

Dei, G. S. (1994). Afrocentricity: A cornerstone of pedagogy. *Anthropology & Education Quarterly, 25*(1), 3–28.

Dei, G. S. (2012). Reclaiming our Africanness in the diasporized context: The challenges of asserting a critical African personality. *Journal of Pan African Studies, 4*(10), 42–57.

Fanon, F. (1963). *The wretched of the earth*. Harmondsworth, UK: Penguin.

Fashina, O. (1989). Frantz Fanon and the ethical justification of anti-colonial violence. *Social Theory and Practice, 15*(2), 179–212.

Hallen, B. (2002). *A short history of African philosophy*. Bloomington, IN: Indiana University Press.

Harms Smith, L., & Nathane, M. (2018). Not domestication, not indigenization: Decoloniality in social work education. *Southern African Journal of Social Work and Social Development, 30*(1),1–18. https://doi.org/10.25159/2415-5829/2400

Hugman, R. (2013). *Culture, values and ethics in social work: Embracing diversity*. London, UK: Routledge.

Ife, J. (2008). *Human rights and social work: Towards rights-based practice*. New York, NY: Cambridge University Press.

Ife, J., & Fiske, L. (2016). Human rights and community work: Complementary theories and practices, *International Social Work, 49*(3), 297–308.

InterExchange. (2019). *The history, principles and symbols of Kwanzaa*. https://www.interexchange.org/articles/career-training-usa/history-principles-and-symbols-of-kwanzaa/

IASSW. (2018). *Global social work statement of ethical principles*. https://www.iassw-aiets.org/2018/04/18/global-social-work-statement-of-ethical-principles-iassw/

IASSW/IFSW. (2014). *Global definition of social work*. https://www.iassw-aiets.org/global-definition-of-social-work-review-of-the-global-definition/

IASSW/IFSW/ICSW. (2012). *Global agenda for social work and social development.* Retrieved February 2019 from https://www.iassw-aiets.org/wp-content/uploads/2017/01/Global-Agenda-English.pdf in

Kleinman, A. (1998, April 13–16). *Experience and its moral modes: Culture, human conditions, and disorder*. The Tanner lectures on human values. Stanford University, Palo Alto, CA.

Kumah-Abiwu, F. (2016). Beyond intellectual construct to policy ideas: The case of the Afrocentric paradigm. *Journal of Pan African Studies, 9*(2), 7–27.

Makgoba, M., & Seepe, S. (2004). Knowledge and identity: An African vision of higher education transformation. In S. Seepe (Ed.), *Towards an African Identity in Higher Education* (pp. 13–57). Pretoria, ZA: Vista University.

Mandela, N. (1994). *Long walk to freedom*. London, UK: Little, Brown.

Midgley, J. (1981). *Professional imperialism: Social work in the Third World*. London, UK: Ashgate.

Mupedziswa, R., Rankopo, M., & Mwansa, L. K. (2019). *Ubuntu* as a Pan-African philosophical framework for social work in Africa. In J. M. Twikirize & H. Spitzer

(Eds.), *Social work practice in Africa: Indigenous and innovative approaches* (pp. 21–38). Kampala, UG: Fountain.

Mwansa, L. K., & Kreitzer, L. (2012). Social work in Africa. In K. Lyons, T. Hokenstad, M. Pawar, N. Huegler, & N. Hall (Eds.), *The Sage handbook of international social work* (pp. 393–406). London, UK: Sage.

NASW Foundation (2004). Bertha Capen Reynolds (1885–1978)—*Social worker, author and professor of social work. Social Welfare History Project*. https://socialwelfare. library.vcu.edu/people/reynolds-bertha-capen/

Organization of African Unity (OAU). (1981). African (Banjul) Charter on Human and Peoples' Rights. Addis Ababa, ET: Author.

Organization of African Unity (OAU). (1990). African Charter on the Rights and Welfare of the Child. Addis Ababa, ET: Author.

Pawar, M., & Cox, D. (2004). *Community informal care and welfare systems: A training manual*. Centre for Rural Social Research, Charles Sturt University, New South Wales, AU.

Reynolds, B. C. (1936). Social case work: What is it? What is its place in the world today? *Child and Family Welfare, 11*(6), 12.

Sen, A. (1999). *Development as freedom*. Oxford, UK: Oxford University Press.

Sen, A. (2005). *The argumentative Indian: Writings on Indian culture, history and identity*. London, UK: Penguin.

Sewpaul, V. (2014). Social work education: Current trends and future directions. In C. Noble, H. Strauss, & B. Littlechild (Eds.), *Global social work: Crossing borders, blurring boundaries* (pp. 353–367). Sydney, AU: Sydney University Press.

Sewpaul, V. (2015). Politics with soul: Social work and the legacy of Nelson Mandela. *International Social Work, 59*(6), 697–708. https://doi. org/10.1177/0020872815594226.

Sewpaul, V. (2016). The West and the Rest divide: Culture, human rights and social work. *Journal of Human Rights and Social Work, 1,* 30–39.

Sewpaul, V., & Jones, D. (2004). Global standards for social work education and training. *Social Work Education, 23*(5), 493–513.

Sono, T. (1994). *Dilemmas of African intellectuals in South Africa*. Pretoria, ZA: UNISA.

Spencer-Oatey, H. (2008). *Culturally speaking: Culture, communication and politeness theory* (2nd ed.). London, UK: Continuum Books.

Stengel, R. (2012). *Nelson Mandela 1918-2013: Portrait of an extraordinary man*. Croydon, UK: Virgin Books.

Tierney, J. (2008). *A compromise on female "circumcision*. https://tierneylab.blogs.nytimes. com/2008/03/19/a-compromise-on-female-circumcision/

UN. (1948). Universal Declaration of Human Rights. Paris, FR: Author.

UN. (1989). Convention on the Rights of the Child. Paris, FR: Author.

Wax, D. (2006). Female genital cutting, sexuality and anti-FGC advocacy. https://www.academia.edu/1622829/Female_Genital_Cutting_Sexuality_and_Anti-FGC_Advocacy

Zeleza, P. T. (2006). The Struggle for human rights in Africa. In C. Heyns & K. Stefiszyn (Eds.), *Human rights, peace and justice in Africa: A reader* (pp. 42–48). Pretoria, ZA: Pretoria University Law Press.

Disrupting Popular Discourses on Ilobolo: The Role of Emancipatory Social Work in Engendering Human Rights and Social Justice

Vishanthie Sewpaul, Manqoba Victor Mdamba, and Boitumelo Seepamore

Informed by critical emancipatory theory, this chapter discusses *ilobolo* (bride wealth), which is widely practised among isiZulu speaking people in the province of KwaZulu-Natal (KZN) in South Africa. The practice is common in South Africa, and other parts of southern Africa, such as Lesotho, where it is known as *bohali*, and among the Ndebele and Shona people of Zimbabwe, where it is referred to as *lobola* and *roora*, respectively (Ansell, 2011). The South African Recognition of Customary Marriages Act 120 (1998), defines *ilobolo*, and in doing so lists its various terminologies:

> Lobolo means the property in cash or in kind, wheth-er known as *ilobolo, bogadi, bohali, xuma, lumalo, thaka, ikhazi, magadi, emabheka* or by any other name, which a prospective husband or the head of his family undertakes to give to the head of the prospective wife's family in consideration of a customary marriage. (p. 1)

For the purposes of this chapter, we use ilobolo, as is widely used among isiZulu speaking people in the province of KZN.

Charting historical influences, we discuss how ilobolo, which is practised throughout southern Africa, has changed over the years to become more commodified. Ilobolo, we argue, perpetuates poverty, women's oppression, and human rights violations, all of which are of central concern for social work. Among the challenges linked to the practice of ilobolo are: (1) children born out of wedlock; (2) single mothers; (3) absent fathers; (4) delayed marriages; and (5) men's inability to afford the high costs of ilobolo. Despite the drawbacks, the practice has become normalized and taken for granted, and calls for its modification are met with resistance. While some see ilobolo as a barrier to Africa's, and particularly women's development and emancipation (Mupotsa, 2014; Nkosi, 2011; Tsanga, 1999; Wagner, 1999), with Mazrui (1998) arguing that it promotes a *malignant sexism* (p. 45), others view ilobolo as positive and central to Black African cultural identity (Marewe & Marewe, 2010; Thorpe, 1991).

Ilobolo: Shifting and Contested Discourses and Practices

Ilobolo occupies a contested space, with multiple explanations for its practice. One main function that many seem to agree on is the bond the practice is believed to create between the families of the groom and the bride-to-be (Nkosi, 2011; Posel et al., 2011; Yarbrough, 2017). Another idealized notion lies in the centrality of ilobolo to the African cultural identity (Mupotsa, 2014; Nkosi, 2011; Rudwick & Posel, 2014). In addition to socio-economic considerations, Rudwick and Posel (2014) concluded that ilobolo symbolizes "cultural, gender and spiritual identities," where appeasing the ancestors is important, and that it is "widely regarded as unassailable due to its roots in Zulu cultural or ethnic consciousness" (p. 15). Murray (1981) discussed ilobolo serving the functions of conferring rights to a woman's child-bearing capacity, rights to her sexual and domestic services, and permanent rights over her children.

The contestations around ilobolo stem from the gap between its idealized notions and its actual consequences; from the tendency to commercialize its practice and from the challenge of discerning its actual functions in contemporary society. Traditionally, paying ilobolo was viewed as a transaction of reciprocal rights and duties between families. Furthermore, ilobolo was always paid to the woman's family in cattle, the amount determined by affordability. While cattle remain a valued commodity, shifts have occurred, particularly in urban areas, to cash payments. Ilobolo was also paid in cattle in instalments, with the first payment being before the couple was married and the remaining paid after the birth of the first child (Yates, as cited in Posel et al., 2011). However, in current practice it is now mostly paid off before the wedding. Conditions of the practice were that if the wife was infertile, her younger sister had to bear children for her, or the family of her husband had the right to ask for return of the cattle—a practice that has lost some of its salience. However, some do report that women fear leaving abusive relationships as they might have to return the payments made in respect of ilobolo (Nkosi, 2011; Rudwick & Posel, 2014). As discussed below, there are arguments that some of these shifts are linked to colonialism and modernity.

Colonialism, Modernity, and Ilobolo

The changes in ilobolo practices are partly associated with the influences of colonialism and modernity, and, in the South African context, the impact of apartheid. While acknowledging the socially constructed nature of history, Said (1993) cogently discusses the power of the past, asserting that "there is no just way in which the past can be quarantined from the present. Past and present inform each other, each implies the other and, . . . co-exists with the other" (p. 4). Colonialism and contemporary forms of imperialism have had profound impacts on the socio-economic and cultural landscapes of colonized people.

Historically, in KwaZulu-Natal, ilobolo did not have stipulations as to the number of cattle to be paid, and during the early 1800s, ilobolo rarely exceeded five cattle (Posel et al., 2011). Theophilus Shepstone, secretary for native affairs in KwaZulu-Natal, linked ilobolo to social status. Under his colonial administration, Shepstone formalized ilobolo to 11 cows for ordinary individuals, 15 cows for relatives of chiefs and 20-plus cows for daughters of a chief. Thus, in the mid-1800s ilobolo increased and some ilobolo prices went up to 100 cows (Posel et al., 2011). Shepstone's role in the pricing of ilobolo from commoner to relatives of the chief and to the chief's family indirectly introduced a social classification system in a Black African community where collectivism was seen to be the norm. In pre-colonial times, the groom's father helped with ilobolo payments. However, with colonial dispossession of the lands of Black African people, fathers no longer had the means to provide this support, and this contributed to the alteration of the practice to an individualistic one (Hunter, 2010).

The system of social classification and stratification was further entrenched during apartheid, with ilobolo practices reflecting more commodified relationships, which deepened the structural, racial fissures that were designed to maintain Black African people in poor and excluded positions, with apartheid laws that deliberately split families. Separate development and influx control laws, and migrant labour, undermined "the ability of men and women to form long-term relationships" (Hunter 2006, p. 103), and migrant men often established other families in the urban areas where they lived and worked.

Ilobolo adds to the already burdened Black African family, and further entrenches a range of social problems such as unmarried motherhood, absent fathers, domestic violence, and poverty. However, the social convention of ilobolo has become so normalized that even those who acknowledge its negative consequences argue for its continuity. Part of the argument for its retention resides in its anti-colonial and anti-modernist stances. As a reactionary measure, there is a tendency to protect certain practices that are "in our culture" against Western influence. Writing about the negative effects of modernity on the Shona culture in Zimbabwe, Mawere and Mawere (2010) write: "Consequently there is a resentment of the traditional subordination of women to their husbands in the modern Shona society especially among some learned and urbanized women" (p. 229). In this discourse the "traditional subordination of women" is celebrated as it rejects the "impositions" of colonialism and modernity, which they claim support "unbridled freedom" (p. 229). Obbo and Bledsoe (as cited in Marewe & Marewe, 2010) valorize the following: "In traditional bride wealth marriages, husbands have authority; husbands expect their wives to be obedient, and they tend to make claims on their wives' labour and income" (p. 229). The relegation of women to inferior, childlike status, and access to women's free and unpaid labour, remain unscrutinized in this discourse. Indeed, Marewe and Marewe (2010) go on to place the blame for moral degradation and social problems, such as the spread of HIV/AIDS, squarely on the shoulders of urban, educated women whose "children grow up calling father to all the boyfriends the mother brings home" (p. 229).

While the need to repudiate colonial legacies, "cultural conceit" of the West, and "imperial tyranny" (Sen, 2005, p. 107) is undeniable, such repudiation—as evident in the textual discourse of Mawere and Mawere—is at times absurd. Sen (2005) posits that "the so-called 'post-colonial critique' can be significantly constructive when it is dialectically engaged—and thus strongly interactive—rather than defensively withdrawn and barriered" (p. 85). Sewpaul (2014, 2016) argues that while there are merits to collective responsibility and communal caring, the virtues of the collective have often been abused to condone human rights violations. She calls for the need to "desist from idealizing African cultures based on collectivism, respect for family, and as embodying unifying and holistic principles as opposed to Western culture, which is represented as fragmented, individualized and reductionist" (Sewpaul, 2016, p. 34) and appeals for a recognition of the complexities and diversities within these contexts.

While condemning the Western appropriation of human rights, Zeleza (2006) claims: "These dichotomies fly in the face of the fact that communality in Africa is often as exaggerated as individuality is in Europe. . . . In both contexts. . . . individuals and community are mutually constituting and the practice of rights claiming, consuming or constraining them—entail a social context" (p. 47). Although to varying degrees, conservative, authoritarian, liberal, and radical views co-exist in the North, South, East, and West, differences within and across groups on a global level "must be celebrated insofar as such differences are not harmful to any group of persons" (Sewpaul, 2016, p. 34). Warning against the essentializing of Zulu culture, Rudwick and Posel (2014) assert that "there are no concrete and monolithic properties distinguishing members of one culture from those of another" (p. 6). Furthermore, Mupotsa (2014) questions the claim that ilobolo accords one a uniquely African identity, as "parallel practices exist in many cultures and national domains" (p. 226), but such logic is ignored in the face of the normalized and naturalized discourses around its practice.

Ilobolo: A Normalized and Naturalized Discourse and Practice

Discourse is a mode of social practice wherein there is a dialectical relationship between social structure and language. Language is embedded in social conventions and structures and is reproduced to retain and maintain various forms of power, privileges and/or oppressions in society, with women being at the bottom of the social ladder. Ideology—the taken-for-granted assumptions that people hold—is reflected in language, and social conventions and structures. Fairclough (1989) contends that "control over orders of discourse by institutional and societal power-holders is one factor in the maintenance of their power" (p. 37). Reflecting on the reproduction of gender and racial stereotypes, Sewpaul (2013) states that "the ideologies that we hold are reflected in, and reinforced by, activities in the home and school, cultural norms and practices, religion, politics, and the media. Our thinking, in turn, shapes social policies and social structures, reflecting a circular and dialectical relationship between structure and agency" (p. 119). Although ideology is false consciousness, it is, according to Althusser (1971), about the only consciousness we have. As products of our world, "those who are in ideology believe themselves by definition outside ideology" (p. 175); thus, we rarely recognize our own collusion in reproducing prejudices, stereotypes, inequalities, and oppressions.

A discourse with a 48-year-old, isiZulu-speaking woman—Thando (not her real name)—a domestic worker, with two adult daughters, and who was unmarried, as the late father of her children could not pay ilobolo, said that "when a man pays ilobolo, he like puts the woman in a jail, and controls her." She recalled her own experiences as an unmarried woman who suffered under the weight of raising her children single-handedly. As a single mother she will get an uncle to represent her at the ilobolo negotiations of her daughter, asserting that "in my culture women cannot talk." When asked why, she—who is a robust woman who usually speaks her mind—responded with: "I don't know. It's from old, old times. That is what we are told. If you want to change it, people will say this and that, and there will be too much problems." She could not see it any other way, and despite the apparent contradiction, asserted that if the man does not pay ilobolo, it will show that "he is not a man," and that the woman has no value. Thando's is not a single, isolated voice. Our numerous informal discussions with isiZulu-speaking people of KwaZulu-Natal (communities among which we live and work), the Facebook postings of friends and students, classroom online discussion forums, and empirical research with both males and females reflect that her experience and views resonate those of Black South Africans who, despite a cognitive awareness of ilobolo's drawbacks, support its continuity.

Women are strong defenders of ilobolo (Hunter, 2010; Nkosi, 2011; Rudwick & Posel, 2014; Yarborough, 2017). Nkosi (2011), who investigated the views of male and female university students toward ilobolo, found that females were more in support of ilobolo than males. A male participant in Nkosi's (2011) study ventured to propose a disruption in the dominant practice by suggesting that with greater emphasis on gender equality, perhaps ilobolo should constitute a reciprocal exchange (rather than payment from the man to the woman only), but his immediate retort to this was: "I'd probably be persecuted for making such [a suggestion]" (p. 90). Mupotsa (2014) detailed her experience of being chastised and labelled a "modern feminist" (p. 9) because of her critiques of ilobolo, and in her thought-provoking thesis reflected on "the ways tradition, even religion and consumption, and modernity are invoked in discussions of wedding work around particular subjects that both open and close off the possibilities for a liberatory agenda" (p. 11).

In a study of 45 university students' attitudes toward ilobolo in Zimbabwe, Chireshe and Chireshe (2010) found that 60 percent of students (64 percent of whom were females) saw ilobolo as contributing to women's oppression, 64 percent claimed that ilobolo forced women to stay in abusive relationships, and 76 percent believed that ilobolo promoted gender inequality. However, only 24 percent saw it as degrading of women, and an overwhelming majority (76 percent) expressed the view that the payment of ilobolo showed that the man valued his wife. The orthodoxies around its conceptualization and practices, as embedded in male and female subjectivities that have become "conterminous with the idea of a customary identity" (Mupotsa, 2014, p. 263), ensure the retention of its practice despite such identity being "invented, rehearsed, failed and reconstituted" (p. 263). The element of its validation of women allows the practice to continue, as women believe that they will be—and they indeed are—undervalued and undermined in the eyes of their husbands, families, and communities if ilobolo has not been paid for them, so much so that even men and women who assert that they do not believe in the practice acquiesce to it (Nkosi, 2011; Rudwick & Posel, 2014). Although there are contested discourses and practices between the ideal representations of ilobolo and its consequences, ilobolo remains an "authoritative" (Yarbrough, 2017, p. 16) discourse and a "*primary* legitimating institution over marriage" (p. 17) even in contemporary times.

Mupotsa (2014) has detailed how, despite ilobolo being "contested, invented, reinvented and debated," we have "become protagonists within a scripted fantasy" (p. 263), where within the dominant discourses "we are invited to perform our traditions and cultural identities in these processes in languages that attempt to make claims at primordial essences" (pp. 16–17). The claims to such *primordial essences*, and the construction of ilobolo as a "timeless or static tradition" (Rudwick & Posel, 2014, p. 8), fly in the face of the fact that ilobolo practices have been changing, according to the exigencies of socio-economic circumstances, the most prominent change being the shift from cattle to cash payments, as communities have become more urbanized. These naturalized discourses persist despite research evidence that details the consequences of the practice.

Unmarried Motherhood, Unemployment, and Poverty

Although most people wish to get married, many cannot afford the costs of ilololo. The 2005 South African Social Attitudes Survey (SASAS) (as cited in Posel et al., 2011) results reflect that from a national survey of 3,000 participants, 82 percent of never-married Black African adults either agreed or strongly agreed that they wished to marry. Posel et al. (2011) asserted that although marriage was highly prized, it was the high costs of ilobolo that inhibited marriage, a view supported by Yarborough (2017), who, through a study with the residents of the village of Maqongqo in KwaZulu-Natal, concluded that while marriage was a central pillar, ilobolo served as its greatest obstacle.

Several studies reflect the primary economic imperatives associated with ilobolo where families use it for material advancement (Ansell, 2011;

Hunter, 2006; Shope, 2006). With the commercialization and individualization of ilobolo, rising costs of living, and increased unemployment, men cannot afford ilobolo. Thus, many Black African women remain unmarried, while they bear children from their partners. Drawing from the results of the SASAS, Posel et al. (2011) reported that ilobolo was identified by half of all never-married respondents as the main reason for couples not marrying, and by over 60 percent of isiZulu-speaking male respondents. This finding was corroborated in their interviews, with one woman asserting: "Our daughters are getting old, having unclaimed children at home. I would not have had my baby at home if this *ilobolo* thing was not there" (p. 17), while another said that "the reason we are not married, and we get old in our mothers' homes is because of *ilobolo*. I wish it can be stopped—but they will never do that because it is culture" (p. 18).

The taken-for-granted assumptions of fertility defining femininity, and the celebration of fertility and motherhood in most communities, which authors such as Walker (1995) claim have greater salience for Black South African women within lineage and kinship structures, do place Black African women in invidious positions. They are demonized if they fall pregnant before marriage (Gilbert & Sewpaul, 2015), are denied the prospects of timely marriage on account of ilobolo, and they are simultaneously expected to prove their fertility by a certain age. There are, at the same time, taboos against cohabitation, so relatively few African couples live together before marriage (Posel & Casale, 2013; Yarbrough, 2017), often resulting in women raising children alone.

Unmarried motherhood and female-headed households bring with them their own socio-psychological and economic problems. According to Statistics South Africa (2017a) only 29 percent of Black African children had both parents living in the same household compared to the 75.6 percent among Whites, 74.8 percent among Indians/Asian, and 52.6 percent among Coloureds in 2015. The survey also reflected that 39.4 percent of Black African children grew up in female-headed households, compared with 28.1 percent of Coloured, 14.4 percent of Indian/Asian, and 16.2 percent of White children. These differences must be considered against the complex historical, socio-economic, and cultural factors that have resulted in particularly Black African men living apart from their children, thus becoming absent fathers. The gendered and racialized dimensions of poverty and inequality in South Africa can be seen in the fact that male-headed households earn higher average incomes than female-headed households, and that men earned almost twice what women earned from work in 2014/2015. White-headed households had an income roughly 4.5 times larger than Black African–headed households and three times larger than the average national income in 2014/2015 (Statistics South Africa, 2017b).

While the father role goes far beyond the provider role to influence a range of biopsychosocial dimensions of children's lives, Johnson (as cited in Richter, 2006) argues that "fiscal support and the fulfillment of the provider role by males have the typical effect of lifting children out of or preventing their descent into poverty" (p. 56). Children who grow up in two-parent families are more likely to dedicate their time to studying, rather than combine studying with household chores and economic activities outside the home (Statistics South Africa, 2017a), and they are more likely to enjoy better quality of education. These factors influence educational outcomes, which are an important indicator of income and quality of life, with poor education and its concomitant poor educational outcomes being significant factors in perpetuating intergenerational cycles of poverty (Sewpaul, 2015).

Given the evidence of the consequences of unmarried motherhood and absent fathers, and that research indicates that ilobolo is an important factor in preventing or delaying marriages, it makes sense to question some of the taken-for-granted assumptions surrounding its practice. Our arguments are based on sociological, empirical evidence reflecting that: (1) the majority of people express the desire to marry; (2) the costs of ilobolo thwart this aspiration; (3) cohabitation is frowned upon from a Zulu cultural point of view; (4) many children, particularly within Black African communities, grow up in mother-headed families with absent fathers, which has several biopsychosocial consequences; and (5) the high rates of poverty among female-headed households jeopardize the life chances of children. The ideological stances toward ilobolo, and its pragmatic and instantiated effects, must be the focus of dialogue and debate for any change to be effected. Unfortunately, the orthodoxies surrounding ilobolo often prohibit rational debate and dialogue. Apart from the psychosocial issues elucidated here, of serious concern is the gendered dimension of ilobolo.

Ilobolo, Gender Inequality and Oppression

Mupotsa (2014), challenging the dichotomy between the "modern" white wedding and the "traditional," points out that both contain traditions and rituals that reproduce patriarchal relations of power. Writing about the consumptive and gendered characteristics of both types of marriages, she concludes that these "place women at the centre of ritualized transfer in kinship mergers and exchanges" (p. 258), but Nkosi (2011) argues that marriages appear to be "worse for women married within the lobola system" (p. 32).

There are several aspects to ilobolo that disadvantage both women and men. The gendered dimension of the ilobolo transaction is but only one element of sexist discrimination. The ilobolo negotiations are generally determined by senior men in the family, with women being silenced and treated as minors in the process. Yarbrough (2017) discusses the attempts on the part of some women to exercise agency by engaging in behind-the-scenes negotiation with men, generally to bring down the price of ilobolo, but concludes by reflecting on the "profoundly gendered disadvantage that constrains this agency's hope" (p. 54).

Nkosi (2011) questions the relevance of ilobolo considering South Africa's goals of gender equality, and the assumption of shared productive and reproductive responsibilities. With ilobolo, traditionally paid in cattle, a woman's productive and reproductive capacities are transferred to her husband, and children born out of the marriage belong to the husband and his family. Thus, women give up control over their sexual and reproductive rights and share no rights in relation to children that they give birth to. In a study conducted by the Commission on Gender Equality (CGE, 2005) many participants perceived married men who had paid ilobolo to be always deserving of sexual intercourse, which wives must always submit to. Mupotsa (2014) argues that "the ritualized exchange of women for cattle is presumed more innocent than the present exchanges in cash and other consumer goods" (p. 11) and discusses how ilobolo is a site for the "contestation between men and women so the invented or 'rediscovered' traditions related to its practice emphasize the control of women in the name of custom. The emphasis on domesticity is then also firmly planted to the process of lobola and part of what is expected of a wife" (p. 18).

While such discourses are generally more nuanced, couched in the language of respect, value, obligations, and responsibilities—defining a "good wife" and a "good mother"—the totally crude affirmation of such control and domesticity is reflected in the views of Marewe and Marewe (2010) discussed above. Ilobolo entraps women in the homemaker role, even though they might be employed and adopting provider roles. A female participant in Nkosi's (2011) study elucidated what she believed ilobolo ought to be and how it is conceptualized:

> I don't believe hore [that] lobola was meant for that, to say you're buying someone and you're buying them as a slave mara [but] most men use that thing in that way ya hore [that] she's your slave now, you bought her and she has to cook for you, wash for you and do whatever and whatever. If she doesn't then you have the right to claim your money back. (p. 78)

The text of one of Nkosi's (2011) male participants reflects the relationship between monetary transaction, power, and possession: "When you have . . . the idea behind money, you exchange money to receive something that will be your possession" (p. 74). Several factors, including the level of education of the woman, whether she is a virgin, whether she has a child before marriage, and whether the child is the offspring of the intended spouse, influence the market value of the woman. Thus, women become tradable commodities, with there being identifiable markers of the commodity price. Some authors have discussed how ilobolo might render women more open to domestic violence and abuse (Mazrui, 1998; Nkosi, 2011; Wagner, 1999).

The discourse on power, possession, and violence brings us to the realm of HIV/AIDS, which disproportionately affects populations of southern African countries. There is an extensive body of literature that details the devastating impacts of HIV/AIDS at all societal levels. In their edited UNESCO publication, Klot and Nguyen (2009) elucidate how "gender organizes relational interactions within families, communities and institutions in everyday life" (p. 16) and explain "the mutually reinforcing ways that sociocultural, political and economic factors interact and influence physiological susceptibility to HIV" (p. 16).

Despite the dire consequences of gender role stereotypes, women are complicit in their reproduction on a global scale (Opoku, 2016; Sewpaul, 2013) and, within certain cultural practices such as ilobolo, in their own commodification, reflecting complex relations of power that challenge the binary of men as oppressors and women as victims. Mwamwenda and Monyooe (1997) argue that in patriarchal societies, where men are more valued than women, the payment of ilobolo might signify, for women, respect and value that they might not otherwise enjoy. Theorizing around the relationships between men and women in Somalia, where family honour is paramount, where the majority of women are subject to female genital mutilation/cutting, and where bride wealth is common, Barnes and Brody (1995) offer uncommon insights into gendered power dynamics, claiming that voluntary submission might indicate an assertion of power. They proclaim that women "partially resolve the contradiction between their acceptance of the ideals of honour, and their incomplete ability to realize them, by deferring to those in authority voluntarily" (p. 317). They quote Lila Abu-Lughod, who avers that "what is voluntary is by nature free and is thus also a sign of independence. Voluntary deference is therefore the honourable mode of dependency" (Barnes & Brody, 1995, p. 317). While this might exemplify a strategic mode of being in the face of authority and oppression, it more likely supports the thesis of our becoming "subjected beings" (Althusser, 1971, p. 182), trapped in common-sense, taken-for-granted assumptions (Gramsci, 1971), or the "voluntary intellectual imprisonment of the free subject" (Sewpaul, 2013, p. 120), where oppression is internalized and normalized (Freire, 1970; 1973).

The financial burden that ilobolo imposes on men, together with the dominant, essentialist construction of masculinity in terms of the provider role, wherein ilobolo is seen as a rite of passage into manhood, all against a background of increasing unemployment where men are unable to meet societal expectations, produces a crisis for men (Hunter, 2006; Morrell, 1998; Nkosi, 2011), *fathers without power*, as the title of Hunter's (2006) article suggests, and an "ambiguous fatherhood" (p. 101). Kometsi (2004) argues that threats to masculine identity may contribute to undue assertion of power and control, and to abuse. Some men see the gendered pattern of ilobolo as an injustice and as an oppression of them. In Nkosi's (2011) study one of the male participants was reported to have said that "it does seem unfair. . . . You pay ilobola and again you're expected to provide for your family. . . . You have to pay this certain amount and have your pockets empty and still again you have to manje [now] find a house together and so forth. . . . It's more pressure on the guy" (p. 72). When both partners in a relationship are economically productive, the principle of reciprocity can be used, as was suggested by the participant in Nkosi's study cited earlier on. With laws, policies, and social conventions overtly (there are hidden agendas to social conventions!) supporting gender equality, one might legitimately ask, if one of the functions of ilobolo is compensation to the parents for the costs of raising their daughters (Ansell, 2011; Rudwick & Posel, 2014), why should parents not be compensated for raising their sons? All the foregoing discussions have enormous implications for social work.

Implications for Social Work

The practice of ilobolo may seem innocuous compared with other cultural practices that violate human dignity and human security, and that constitute a threat to life, but the dynamics of its gendered practice are reflective of similar social conventions that underscore dominant discourses on femininities and masculinities within patriarchal societies. Opoku (2016), for example, describes the normalization of practices such as female genital mutilation/cutting, widow cleansing (where a woman has to have unprotected sex with a man upon the death of her husband), and circumstances where older women pay bride wealth, "marry," and often abuse poor younger women who can bear them sons (a practice called *Nyumba Ntobhu*), among certain ethnic groups in Tanzania. The normalization is such that it is women who are the "the 'torchbearers' of customary rites [who] choose to preserve these practices" (Opoku, 2016, p. 15). One of the challenges facing social work across the globe is the compromising of civil and socio-economic rights on account of culture. While principles such as doing no harm, self-determination, and respect for human dignity are held as sacrosanct in social work, these are often violated as culture trumps legislation, policy, and national and international human rights instruments (Sewpaul, 2014, 2016). The Global Standards for Social Work Education and Training specifically call for social work students to be schooled in a basic human rights approach (Sewpaul & Jones, 2005, p. 223), with the following footnote accompanying this standard:

> Such an approach might facilitate constructive confronta-
> tion and change where certain cultural beliefs, values and
> traditions violate people's basic human rights. As culture
> is socially constructed and dynamic, it is subject to decon-
> struction and change. Such constructive confrontation, de-
> construction and change may be facilitated through a tun-
> ing into, and an understanding of particular values, beliefs
> and traditions and via critical and reflective dialogue with
> members of that cultural group vis-à-vis broader human
> rights issues (p. 228).

Sewpaul (2013, 2014) earlier called for more critical and emancipatory approaches to underscore social work education, research, and practice and for social workers to adopt the role of cultural mediators by facili-tating intercultural dialogue, debate, and constructive confrontation when necessary. Emancipatory social work is directed at a heightening of awareness of external sources of oppression and/or privilege that holds the possibility of increasing self-esteem and courage to confront structural sources of poverty, inequality, marginalization, oppression, and exclusion (Sewpaul & Larsen, 2014). These strategies work for professionals as much as they do for the people social workers engage with. As it is difficult to think outside the box, conventional forms of community education are, in themselves, inadequate to address the complex challenges of culture and human rights. Emancipatory theorists have argued that critical awareness can contribute to developing alternative paradigms and to rad-ical change. Social workers can benefit from the theses of Freire (1970), Giroux (1997), Gramsci (1971), and Hall (1985) that speak to the power of emancipatory pedagogical strategies as catalysts in engendering human agency. Informed by emancipatory theorists, we appreciate that the claim to the *primordial essence* of ilobolo can be challenged and changed, as "we are not entirely stitched into place in our relation to the complex field of historically-situated ideological discourses. . . . We remain open to be positioned and situated in different ways, at different moments throughout our existence" (Hall, 1985. p. 103).

Gramsci (1971) argued that on account of ideological hegemony and our common-sense assumptions, change could not come from the masses, at least not at the beginning, except through the mediation of intellectuals—thus, the important role of social workers as public intellectuals in community education and of social work educators who use emancipatory strategies. The role of ideology becomes critical to the extent that it has the potential to reveal truths by deconstructing historically conditioned social forces or to reinforce the concealing function of common sense. It is thus vital that common sense be subject to critical interrogation (Gramsci, 1971), so we can shift from being the "subjected being" to a subject that is the "author of and responsible for its actions" (Althusser, 1971, p. 182). As social workers, we are products of our socio-political, economic, and cultural worlds, and we are subject to their dominant ideologies. But we also reproduce our worlds. It is, therefore, critical that we become aware of cultural, political, and capitalist ideological hegemony and appreciate how we can use our heightened consciousness and voices to contribute to socio-economic, political, and cultural change and development.

Such critical interrogation must begin in our classrooms where, by adopting critical, emancipatory approaches, we can help students to appreciate the structural determinants of life and to confront and transform their own taken-for-granted assumptions. Education must remain student-centred and simultaneously emphasize human agency and the impacts of structural factors and social conventions on our lives, and the relationship between freedom and responsibility (Sewpaul, 2013). As social work educators, we can adopt a critical multiculturalism (Giroux, 1997) to help students to examine how various forms of oppressions, rooted in "race," culture, gender, class, geographic location, sexual orientation, etc., get reproduced historically and institutionally, and in doing so, we must consistently reject essentialist and stereotypical views.

Conclusion

Discourses on ilobolo intersect with discourses on culture, economics, gender, human rights, and social justice. Because language plays a powerful role in maintaining ideological hegemony, we must analyze and deconstruct language—and deconstruct stereotypes and attributes attached to certain categories (Giroux, 1997; Hall, 1985; Sewpaul 2013). As Hall (1985) emphasized, "Ideological struggle actually consists of attempting to win some new set of meanings for an existing term or category, of dis-articulating it from its place in a signifying structure" (p. 112). The signifying structures within which ilobolo is placed—its *primordial essence*; its socio-cultural constructions of ideal femininity and masculinity; and its being the cornerstone of "African cultural identity"—need to be debated, dis-articulated, and reconstructed. Ilobolo is deemed to be "the most enduring part of African culture" (Mawere & Mawere, 2010, p. 5)—culture's quintessence. Contrary to this, Muptsoa (2014) argues that central to ilobolo is the way that "belonging and kinship are imagined and regulated" (p. 226).

We argue that rather than through ilobolo, which evidence shows has detrimental effects, continuity and affirmation of ethnic identities can be assured through cultural elements such as food, music, dance, dress, theatre, celebratory non-sexist birth and marriage rituals, and non-punitive, non-sexist cultural mourning practices. Developing critical consciousness through dialogue, rather than foreclosing debate on the grounds that "it's in our culture," may lead to critical action (Freire, 1970, 1973; Giroux, 1997; Gramsci, 1971). Awareness represents an important step in getting people to act in engaged and responsible ways to question, challenge, and confront the structural basis and social conventions of life, thus supporting the view that the Self must be the main site of politicization (Giroux, 1997; Sewpaul, 2014, 2015).

To attribute the negative aspects of ilobolo to colonialism and, at the same time, claim a timelessness and primordial essence for its practice is a paradox. It is incumbent on Africans (of all "races") to exercise agency, undo colonial legacies, and not remain slaves to colonial and imperialist impositions. One needs to question the logic of practices being reproduced simply because they have always been there, as these must be "decided by those who live today" (Sen, 1999, p. 32). One also needs to question whether holding onto an essentialist and fossilized ethnic identity might work against the goals of national unity and peace. We witness extreme forms of ethnic violence based on group identification in many parts of the world. Writing within the context of the Rwandan genocide, Adejumobi (2006) warned about the dangers of ethnic identification, asserting that "rights and citizenship have been largely defined and institutionalized as a group affair. . . . Citizenship . . . was not a 'universal' and common public good. . . . It was *exclusionary and bifurcated.*" (p. 255).

We are particularly concerned with the sociological evidence that points to the detrimental consequences of ilobolo for women, men, and children, which social workers deal with on a day-to-day basis. But we need to go beyond the remedial and merely picking up the pieces to work toward prevention, and the rebuilding of the fragmented fabrics of our societies. Social workers have roles to play in promoting social justice and human rights at micro and macro levels, and more especially at the intersections of these. Social work, as Sewpaul (2015) asserts, holds the potential to function in that "intermediary site where *life politics* meets Politics with a capital P, where private problems are translated as public issues and public solutions are sought, negotiated and agreed for private troubles" (Bauman, 2007, p. 24). Sociological evidence and practice experience must be used to influence social policy and legislation, and to engender attitudinal changes. Social workers have the requisite skills in empathy, active listening, facilitation, mediation, and interpersonal relationships to build bridges across cultures, to engage people in such a way that the harmful aspects of culture are confronted, while retaining those aspects that are positive, and that allow for intergenerational cultural continuity and human flourishing.

REFERENCES

Adejumobi, S. (2006). Citizenship, rights, and the problem of conflicts and civil wars in Africa. In C. Heyns & K. Stefiszyn (Eds.), *Human rights, peace and justice in Africa: A reader* (pp. 250–271). Pretoria, ZA: Pretoria University Law Press.

Althusser, L. (1971). Ideology and ideological state apparatuses (B. Brewster, Trans.). In *Lenin and philosophy, and other essays* (pp. 127–188). London, UK: New Left Books.

Ansell, N. (2011). "Because it's our culture!": (Re)negotiating the meaning of "lobola" in Southern African secondary schools." *Journal of Southern African Studies, 27*(4), 697–716.

Barnes, V. L., & Brody, J. (1995*). Aman: The story of a Somali girl.* New York, NY: Vintage Books.

Bauman, Z. (2007). 'Critique—Privatized and disarmed.' In A. Elliot (Ed.), *The contemporary Bauman* (pp. 19–26). London, UK: Routledge.

Chireshe, E., & Chireshe, R. (2010). Lobola: The perceptions of Great Zimbabwe University students. *Journal of Pan African Studies, 3*(9), 211–221.

Commission on Gender Equality (CGE). (2005). *National gender opinion survey.* Johannesburg, ZA: Author.

Fairclough, N. (1989). *Language and power.* London: Longmans.

Freire, P. (1970). *The pedagogy of the oppressed.* Harmondsworth, UK: Penguin

Freire, P. (1973). *Education for critical consciousness.* New York, NY: Seabury Press.

Gilbert, I., & Sewpaul. V. (2015). Challenging dominant discourses on abortion from a radical feminist perspective. *Affilia: Journal of Women and Social Work, 30*(1), 83–95.

Giroux, H. A. (1997). *Pedagogy and the politics of hope: Theory, culture and schooling.* Boulder, CO: Westview Press.

Gramsci, A. (1971). *Selections from the prison notebooks* (A. Hoare & G. N. Smith, Eds. & Trans.). London, UK: Lawrence & Wishart.

Hall, S. (1985). Signification, representation, ideology: Althusser and the post-structuralists debates. *Critical Studies in Mass Communication, 2,* 91–114.

Hunter, M. (2006). "Fathers without *amandla*: Zulu–speaking men and fatherhood." In L. Richter and R. Morrell (Eds.), *Baba: Men and fatherhood in South Africa* (pp. 99–107). Cape Town, ZA: HSRC Press.

Hunter, M. (2010). *Love in the time of AIDS.* Pietermaritzburg, ZA: University of KwaZulu–Natal Press.

Klot, J. F., & Nguyen, V. K. (2009). Introduction. In J. F. Klot & V. K. Nguyen (Eds.), *The fourth wave: Violence, gender, culture & HIV in the 21st century* (pp.15–26). New York, NY: UNESCO. Retrieved July 15, 2017 from http://www.unesco.org/new/fileadmin/MULTIMEDIA/HQ/BSP/GENDER/PDF/Fourth-Wave12.pdf

Kometsi, K. (2004). *(Un)Real—AIDS review 2004.* Pretoria, ZA: University of Pretoria.

Mawere, M., & Mawere, A. M. (2010). The changing philosophy of African marriage: The relevance of the Shona customary marriage practice of Kukumbira. *Journal of African Studies and Development, 2*(9), 224–233.

Mazrui, A. A. (1998). The Black woman and the problem of gender: An African perspective. In O. H. Kokole (Ed.), *The global African*. Asmara, ER: Africa World Press.

Morrell, R. (1998). "Of boys and men: Masculinity and gender in Southern African Studies." *Journal of Southern African Studies, 24*(4), 605–60.

Mupotsa, D. S. (2014). *White weddings* (Unpublished doctoral dissertation). University of the Witwatersrand, Johannesburg, ZA.

Murray, C. (1981). *Families divided: The impact of migrant labour in Lesotho*. Cambridge, UK: Cambridge University Press.

Mwamwenda, T. S., & Monyooe, L. A. (1997). Status of bridewealth in an African culture. *Journal of Social Psychology, 137*(2), 269–271.

Nkosi, S. (2011). *Lobola: Black students' perceptions of its role on gender power dynamics*. (Unpublished master's thesis). University of the Witwatersrand, Johannesburg, ZA.

Opoku, R. (2016). *Gendered violence: Patterns and causes of women-to-women violence in the Lake Zone regions of Tanzania, East Africa*. (Unpublished doctoral dissertation). University of Tampere, Tampere, FI:.

Posel, D., & Casale, D. (2013). The relationship between sex ratios and marriage rates in South Africa. *Applied Economics, 4*, 663–676.

Posel, D., Rudwick, S., & Casale, D. (2011). Is marriage a dying institution in South Africa? Exploring changes in marriage in the context of iobolo payments. *Agenda, 25(*1), 102–111

Richter, L. (2006). The importance of fathering for children. In L. Richter & R. Morrell (Eds.), *Baba: Men and fatherhood in South Africa* (pp. 53–69). Pretoria, ZA: HSRC.

Rudwick, S., & Posel, D. (2014). Ukukipita (cohabiting): Socio-cultural constraints in urban Zulu society. *Journal of Asian and African Studies, 49*, 282–97.

Said, E. W. (1993). *Culture and imperialism*. New York, NY: Vintage Books.

Sen, A. (1999). *Development as freedom*. Oxford, UK: Oxford University Press.

Sen, A. (2005). *The argumentative Indian: Writings on Indian culture, history and identity*. London, UK: Penguin.

Sewpaul, V. (2013). Inscribed in our blood: Confronting and challenging the ideology of sexism and racism. *Affilia: Journal of Women and Social Work, 28*(2), 116–125.

Sewpaul, V. (2014). Social work and human rights: An African perspective. In S. Hessle (Ed.), *Human rights and social equality: Challenges for social work* (pp. 13–27). Surrey, UK: Ashgate.

Sewpaul, V. (2015). Politics with soul: Social work and the legacy of Nelson Mandela. *International Social Work, 59*(6), 697–708. https://doi.org/10.1177/0020872815594226

Sewpaul, V. (2016). The West and the Rest divide: Human rights, culture and social work. *Journal of Human Rights & Social Work, 1,* 30–39. https://doi.org/10.1007/s41134-016-0003-2.

Sewpaul, V., & Jones, D. (2005). Global standards for the education and training of the social work profession. *International Journal of Social Welfare, 14*(3), 218–230.

Sewpaul, V., & Larsen, A. K. (2014). Community development: Towards an integrated emancipatory framework. In A. K. Larsen, V. Sewpaul, & G. Oline (Eds.), *Participation in community work: International perspectives* (pp. 230–246). London, UK: Routledge.

Shope, J. H. (2006) *"Lobola* is here to stay": Rural black women and the contradictory meanings of *lobolo* in post-apartheid South Africa. *Agenda 6,* 64–72.

Spaull, N. (2015). *Schooling in South Africa: How low quality of education becomes a poverty trap. South African Child Gauge, 12,* 34–41. Retrieved July 12, 2017 from http://ci.org.za/depts/ci/pubs/pdf/general/gauge2015/Child_Gauge_2015-Schooling.pdf

Statistics South Africa. (2017a). *Survey of activities of young people in South Africa.* Retrieved July 13, 2017 from http://www.statssa.gov.za/publications/P0212/P02122015.pdf

Statistics South Africa. (2017b). *Living conditions of households in South Africa: An analysis of household expenditure and income data using the LCS 2014/2015.* Retrieved July 14, 2017 from http://www.statssa.gov.za/publications/P0310/P03102014.pdf

Thorpe, S. A. (1991). *African traditional religions: An introduction.* Pretoria, ZA: University of South Africa.

Trading Economics. (2017). *South Africa's unemployment rate.* Retrieved July 6, 2017 from https://tradingeconomics.com/south-africa/unemployment-rate

Tsanga, A. S. (1999). *Taking law to the people: Gender, law reform and community legal education in Zimbabwe.* Harare, ZW: University of Zimbabwe, Women's Law Centre.

Wagner, N. (1999). Sexual violence against women: A key element of institutional patriarchy. *Southern African Feminist Review (SAFERE), 3*(2): 59–61.

Walker, C. (1995). Conceptualising motherhood in twentieth century South Africa. *Journal of Southern African Studies, 21*(3): 417–437.

Yarbrough, M. W. (2017). Very long engagements: The persistent authority of bridewealth in a post-apartheid South African Community. *Law & Social Inquiry, 43*(3),647–677. https://doi.org/10.1111/lsi.12275

Zeleza, P. T. (2006). The struggle for human rights in Africa. In C. Heyns & K. Stefiszyn (Eds.), *Human rights, peace and justice in Africa: A reader* (pp. 42–48). Pretoria, ZA: Pretoria University Law Press.

Nigerian Marital Cultural Practices and Implications for Human Rights

Augusta Yetunde Olaore, Julie Drolet, and Israel Bamidele Olaore

The universality of family is coloured in Africa by unique sets of values, principles, and practices that are significantly different from those of the Western world. The African world view is informed by a web of relationships between humans, animals, plants, natural forces, spirits, and landforms. Family systems and practices in the African setting are therefore heavily influenced by a cultural ontology of spirits or non-human persons who are believed to have the capacity for animating the world (Kirmayer, 2012). Sometimes these world views may be perceived as oppressive and harmful and sometimes they are helpful and enhance the well-being of people. "In Africa, tradition drives household relations, its possibilities and challenges" (Ayodele, 2016, p. 116). The chapter presents and examines underlying principles and values of marital cultural practices in Nigeria informed by a study funded by the Social Work in Nigeria Project (SWIN-P) and the Government of Canada. The marital cultural practices largely reflect the indigenous knowledge and beliefs of the local context. The chapter discusses three themes arising from the analysis of the study findings—(1) widowhood cultural practices, (2) inheritance and property rights, and (3) cultural responses to marital infidelity—along with their implications for human rights and social work practice.

The Nigerian Context

Marriage and family life is a celebrated aspect of the social system in Nigeria. Nigeria is one of the largest countries in Africa, with a population of 183 million in 2017 (National Population Commission, 2017). Africa in general and Nigeria in particular are culturally diverse, and there is no simplistic "African" culture per se. Cultural and ethnic diversity in Nigeria is represented by the Hausa-Fulani, the Yorubas, and the Igbos, who together make up about 70 percent of the population, and more than 300 smaller ethnic groups that account for the remainder of the population (Moscardino et al., 2006). The National Gender Policy formulated by Federal Ministry of Women Affairs and Social Development (2006) states that

> Nigeria is a highly patriarchal society, where men dominate all spheres of women's lives. Women are in a subordinate position (particularly at the community and household levels), and male children are preferred over the female. The influence of the mother and the father is particularly significant in shaping and perpetuating patriarchy. The mother provides the role model for daughters, while the father demonstrates to sons what it means to 'be a man'. (Section 1.2, p. 6)

Ntoimo and Isiugo-Abanihe (2014) found that most Nigerian communities are typically patriarchal, with beliefs that perpetuate unequal treatment of women, as so poignantly discussed by other authors in this volume, with Boateng and Sottie in chapter 5 also discussing issues related to widowhood rites in relation to Ghana. Makama (2013) states that patriarchy stratifies people based on gender and upholds male dominance. Para-Mallam (2010) posits that culture socializes males and females to internalize societal values, acquire a self-concept, and see themselves as members of their respective gender groups. In Nigeria, the pronatalist culture socializes citizens into the belief that the ultimate goal for any individual is to get married and have children. Childlessness has major psychological and social implications for affected persons, including a multitude of adverse consequences (Ibisomi & Mudege, 2013). Beyond the issue of having children is the preference for sons over daughters. Male child preference is also informed by the inheritance practices in marital culture. Male children not only inherit directly from their fathers, they are also the means by which their mothers may have access to their father's property when he dies (Alewo & Olong, 2012). Nigeria is extremely religious, with a majority of the population being either Muslim or Christian. According to Pew-Templeton Research Center (2016), 49.3 percent of Nigerians are Christians and 48.8 percent are Muslims. African traditional religion and others make up 1.9 percent. The African traditional religion is mainly practised in the southern regions of the country. All three religions strongly influence cultural marital practices. A customary marriage is one where the spouses are married in terms of customs as opposed to the laws of the country, usually referred to as a civil marriage registered with the government (Theron, 2017). The death of a wife of a customary marriage automatically brings the marriage to an end. However, the death of a husband does not end the marriage. The wife is inherited within the family and is expected to continue to perform matrimonial roles whether she likes it or not (Alewo & Olong, 2012).

The practice of widow transfer or "wife inheritance" is condemnable, for although it represents a traditional way of providing widows a little economic and social protection, their rights of choice are violated (Ayodele, 2016). Widowhood practices are performed among the Yoruba of South West Nigeria to protect the woman from being harmed by the spirit of the husband, for the woman to prove innocence of the death of her husband, and for the husband's family to ascertain if the woman was pregnant at the time the husband died so that they can claim responsibility and care for the woman among other reasons (Akinbi, 2015). Widowhood rituals are done to mourn the deceased husband and to ensure that the link between the dead and the living is intact (Durojaye, 2013). The grieving period involves a series of traditional activities and rituals that show respect for the dead. That period may range from seven days to a year across all religions (Oyeniyim & Ayodeji, 2010).

Widows undergo humiliating rituals following the death of their husbands, and are routinely subjected to painful, dehumanizing public treatment as a result of the continued application of discriminatory laws and practices in Nigeria (Ewelukwa, 2002). Widowhood burial rites include isolation, confinement, and hair shaving, among others. Such rites are modified for widows who are educated, have an active career life, or live in urban areas (Genyi, 2013). For such women, the rule for extended seclusion is adjusted to accommodate the need to return to work. However, the rules are strictly enforced for women who are uneducated or live in the rural areas where there are people who are predisposed to customary practices.

Another cultural element within the Nigerian marriage system involves inheritance practices. The brothers-in law of the deceased husband, under the widow inheritance practices, go on to assume personal relations with the wife, and her refusal may complicate her problems (Akinbi, 2015). The effects of inheritance hijacking practices in Nigeria on widows' well-being result in a culturally disapproved harmful practice that destabilizes the social and economic security of widows based on gender status (Ayodele, 2016). It has been described as unjust and cruel property grabbing by overzealous brothers-in-law who will drive widows out of their matrimonial homes and deprive them of their late husband's properties including furniture and bedding, thus completely disinheriting widows (Alewo & Olong, 2012; Cooper, 2010).

Given the cultural and religious diversity, and patriarchy, in Nigeria, this chapter presents norms and practices from a variety of tribal clusters included in the study.

Research Study

A qualitative research project was undertaken to better understand how indigenous social care practices contribute to child and family well-being in Nigeria. The study was funded by the Social Work in Nigeria Project (SWIN-P) and the Government of Canada. The overarching research question guiding the study was: "What indigenous knowledge, beliefs and cultural practices are valued with respect to care of children and the family in Nigeria?" The study had three objectives: (1) to document and analyze Nigerian indigenous cultural practices for children and families; (2) to integrate indigenous cultural practices for children and families into social work education, policy, and practice; and (3) to raise awareness of the value of Nigerian indigenous cultural practices for children and families, locally and internationally.

This study was conducted in five culturally diverse community sites in Nigeria: Aiyepe (West), Akure (South West), Enugu (East), Ibibio (South East), and Sokoto (North West). These sites represent the three major ethnic groups in Nigeria, which are the Igbos, Hausas, and Yorubas. Participants for the semi-structured interviews were selected through referrals from the community, while the focus group participants responded to general community announcements made at gatherings such as church services and town hall meetings. Some key community members such as health care workers and social workers were personally invited. Fifteen community leaders participated in semi-structured interviews, and 78 community members participated in focus group discussions in their communities. Consent forms were administered to all the participants before the interview and focus groups, and university research ethics approval was obtained at Thompson Rivers University in Canada in 2012, prior to data collection. Audio recordings of the interviews and focus groups were transcribed and translated verbatim for the purposes of data analysis.

The narratives were systematically analyzed by identifying emergent themes, patterns, interconnections, and consistency, for a full understanding of the meanings of the data (Olaore & Drolet, 2016). The oral traditions and storytelling narratives were analyzed within their cultural context, and recurrent themes or concepts relating to cultural practices were identified (Olaore & Drolet, 2016). Responses were analyzed using a grounded theory and thematic analysis approach. A grounded theory approach was used to guide analyses and interpretations using open coding and axial coding (Strauss & Corbin, 1998) for categories and themes (Glaser & Strauss, 1967). Verbatim quotations were used to illustrate the community responses on relevant themes. All data were coded by the authors and a graduate-level research assistant. In case of disagreement, original transcripts were re-examined and discussed until coding agreement was reached. Student research assistants were involved in data collection in Nigeria, as well as in the process of transcribing interviews and focus groups, and data analysis. The chapter will focus on cultural practices within the context of marriage, and implications for human rights and social work practice.

Widowhood Cultural Practices

There are marital cultural practices and beliefs that inform widowhood practices in Nigeria, and this section deals with widow transfer, widow burial rites, and inheritance and property rights discussed by participants in the study as well as secondary data from the literature.

Widow transfer

The care of widows is seen as the responsibility of the kin of the deceased husband. One of the study participants expressed the sentiments that in the Yoruba culture, the husband never dies.

> There is a tricky question to prospective groom's family. That is "Do husbands die in this family?" The intent is to find out if the family will continue to perform the role of the husband after the husband dies. (Interview participant, Community Leader from Ibadan)

The care usually takes the form of widow inheritance or widow transfer. In this practice, the younger brother of the deceased man marries the surviving widow and is expected to care for her.

> The family will not allow the woman to go because we believe that the brother to the deceased should be able take care of the late brother's family, if the woman chooses anyone in the family then he will be in charge of the woman and protect all what the brother has so no one intrudes and take[s] anything away from the woman. (Focus group participant, Ibibio Focus Group)

The widow is sometimes prohibited from remarrying outside the deceased husband's family, as discussed by an interview participant:

> If the woman stays in the family, she can either marry the younger brother of the man or remain single in the house. However, as a rule, a widow must not get pregnant from

another man outside the husband's family. (Interview participant, Aiyepe Traditional Ruler)

The intention of the widow transfer or inheritance is to provide social security and support for the wife and children of the deceased within the context of the husband's family of origin. This patrilocal system comes along with the assumption that once the bride price has been paid, the wife belongs to the husband's family for care, protection, and matrimonial duties.

The care of and sympathy for the widow are also dependent upon whether the husband's family sees her as being worthy of their care due to her good behaviour while her husband was alive or if the husband was in good standing in the community. Both the focus group and community leader in Akure attested to this finding in the study:

Decision as to whether she will be cared for will depend on the widow's behavior when the deceased was alive. She may be cared for depending on her behavior. (Interview participant, Akure Traditional Ruler)

Widow burial rites

After a husband dies, traditionally, the wife is expected to perform some rituals. The details of the expected activities vary between the different Nigerian tribes; however, there is a consensus that the family and community have expectations of what the widow is supposed to do.

Participants in the study conveyed several widow burial rites influenced by the sociocultural context in their community. One example is explained here:

If she is young she is to stay indoors for five months to see if she is pregnant so that she bears the child for the deceased. Her husband's people give her money to take care of herself and her children after fulfilling the death rite such as scraping her hair, staying indoors for four market days. [Approximately a month, as the market days may be every five to eight days.] (Interview participant, Head of market women in Aiyepe)

Inheritance and property rights

It is common knowledge in Nigeria that the native law and customs of some people prohibit a wife from inheriting her husband's properties. This practice cuts across all ethnic groups and religions. She is seen as a commodity to be inherited by her husband's kinsmen. However, the issue of children and the gender of the children puts a slant on property inheritance practices and beliefs.

> When a man dies his first son takes his main house called the *Obi* and the rest of the property is shared among other children including the first son. In the case of a man with many wives the remaining property apart from the *Obi* is shared according to the wives with male child. Male children are always given priority in Igbo Land. A woman without a male child has no share in the family but can stay in the family until she dies. (Focus group participant, Enugu)

According to one interview participant, inheritance of property differs in a childless marriage or where there is no male child:

> The brothers of the man will share everything the man has. His property will be shared among his children but if he had no male child, the brother of the man would also have some of the property. (Interview participant, Sokoto Community Leader)

While a woman is subjected to gruesome burial rites at the loss of her husband, she also must deal with the possible loss of shelter and property if all she can lay claim to is within the context of her marriage.

Cultural Responses to Marital infidelity

The data from the focus groups and interviews concerning marital infidelity found that men are accorded greater permissiveness than women with respect to engaging in extramarital affairs. It is the general belief that polygamy makes allowance for infidelity among men with no grievous sanction when compared to the consequences of infidelity by a married woman.

> Men being polygamous in nature have no law preventing them from being promiscuous. But women, in my own locality, she is prohibited from cooking for the husband if she is caught until she undergoes [a thorough] cleansing. Men are only frowned at if he goes out with another man's wife. Apart from that he's free to live his life as it pleases him, but women are forbidden from extramarital relationship. (Interview participant, Enugu Leader)

> "The punishment for a woman, if caught, will be more than if it was a man." (Interview participant, Akure Traditional Ruler)

According to participants in a focus group, polygamy may be justified for economic benefits:

> If I'm a farmer and I'm planting on a large portion of land, if I marry one wife she might produce three or four children but if I marry up to four or five wives they will bear a lot of children so that when the children enter the farm work will be fast. (Focus group participant, Ibibio)

In a focus group, participants expressed the belief that ancestral spirits punish the women but not the men:

> Culturally in Delta State until the present, when a woman goes out (has an extra-marital affair) the ancestors will

deal with the woman. Before you know what is happening her legs will start to swell or the face will begin to swell or in some cases the children will begin to die; later it will be discovered that the woman has gone out for extramarital affair, so the woman will confess and after that she will be asked to buy drinks and something's for sacrifice to stop the death of the children. But such a thing will not happen to a man. (Focus group participant, Aiyepe)

The community is also involved in infidelity cases:

According to our law such a person will be brought to the public, the person will be sent out of the community. Most of the time the punishment of the woman is more than that of the man. In our community if a woman is caught in another man's house, she will be sent out of the community. Some people are asked to swear and most time[s] that leads to death. (Focus group participant, Akure)

The act of swearing is intended to make the accused person say the absolute truth by invoking a curse upon oneself if there is a lie.

Focus group participants confirmed the horrific treatment of women in terms of marital infidelity:

"They will naked the woman at the market." (Focus group participant, Enugu)

The research data presented a gender bias when dealing with the issue of infidelity in marriage. All respondents, with a few exceptions, said that consequences of infidelity in marriage are more lenient for men than women. Since polygamy is an acceptable marital option practised in Nigeria, across both Christianity (while polygamy is frowned upon in Catholicism, it does not deter its practice) and Islam, a man having sexual partners outside of marriage is treated lightly. However, a woman having a sexual partner outside of marriage is prohibited with grievous sanctions, sometimes meted out by the gods.

In my family that is called "the spirit that takes care of a fornicator," this is how it works, if I have a wife and my wife fornicates with someone when she becomes pregnant that spirit will harm the woman and spirit will not allow the woman to deliver until she confesses; if she has slept with five men she must mention the names of the men that have slept with her. (Focus group participant, Ibibio)

Gender biases were also identified by interview participants in the study:

Families decide. A woman who is suspected of infidelity is made to swear [To the gods]. If found guilty, the woman will be inflicted with a disease. A man is free to marry many wives and can be bold in infidelity. (Interview participant, Aiyepe Ruler)

A participant mentioned that fellow women enforce disciplinary sanctions on a woman alleged of marital infidelity.

The women that are born and raised in that family [Umuada], some of them are married outside the community. The women will come to your house and bring out your luggage and bags for you and beat you up as the means of punishment. They say the woman want to bring shame to their family. . . . Wrappers [women's traditional attire] might be seized along with some other belongings. (Focus group participant, Enugu)

In summary, marital cultural practices in response to infidelity are shown to vary by gender and community context, and are mediated through perceived economic benefits of polygamy, ancestral spirits, and community involvement.

Human Rights Implications

The social work profession aims to advance human rights at the local, national, and international levels. Indigenous social care practices that affect the well-being of children and families can be considered using a human rights perspective, particularly for women.

Widowhood rites and property inheritance

Widowhood cultural practices infringe on women's rights to dignity, non-discrimination, equality, health, and life (Durojaye, 2010). They vary from tribe to tribe, but there are commonalities of culturally imposed self-abnegation: women being made to sleep with the dead body of their spouse or drink the corpse purification water, mandatory wailings, and uncomfortable living conditions during seclusions, to name a few. Some cultures accuse the wife as a suspect in the husband's death and are made to face a series of dehumanizing treatments from the in-laws in order to establish their innocence (Akinbi, 2015). These are demeaning and degrading practices that violate the human rights of women. The African Charter (Organization of African Unity, 1981, Article 5) also prohibits all forms of cruel, inhuman, and degrading treatment against any human being.

Men are not required to go through widower cultural rites, while women are expected to mourn their husbands in traditionally prescribed ways. Making a woman go through widow rites just because she is a woman disrespects her person and is a gross violation of women's fundamental rights and freedoms, which perpetuates gender inequality (Makama, 2013; Nyanzi, et al., 2009; Sossou, 2002).

The Protocol to the African Charter on Human and Peoples' Rights on the Rights of Women in Africa (African Commission on Human and Peoples' Rights [ACHPR], 2003, Article 21) provides that widows shall have the right to an equitable share in the inheritance of the property of their husbands. A widow shall have the right to continue to live in the matrimonial house. In case of remarriage, she shall retain this right if the house belongs to her or if she has inherited it. Cooper (2010) has suggested that property grabbing by patrilocal kinsmen is often the reason why statutory laws meant to protect women are ignored with impunity:

There is indeed growing evidence that traditions of widows being cared for amongst the kin of a deceased husband are being manipulated to justify the disinheritance of women. The families of men have been reported to manipulate the custom of taking care of a deceased brothers or son's wife, children and property by claiming the property by not upholding the accompanying responsibilities of caring for the deceased man's family. (Cooper, 2010, p. 12)

The bias in property inheritance practices is undergirded by the notion that the bride price makes a wife more or less part of the property of the husband. This perception was upheld in a court ruling in *Suberu v. Summonu* (1957) (as cited in Alewo & Olong, 2012), where it was stated that under the native law and custom of the Yoruba people, a wife could not inherit her husband's property since she is like a chattel, to be inherited by a relative of her husband.

Marital cultural responses to infidelity

Generally, marital infidelity has been found to be culturally unacceptable. However, responses from study participants do not indicate that due process is followed in investigations to substantiate an allegation of marital infidelity by women. The Universal Declaration of Human Rights (UN, 1948) states that "everyone is entitled in full equality to a fair and public hearing by an independent and impartial tribunal, in the determination of his rights and obligations and of any criminal charge against him" (Article 10) and that all are presumed innocent until proven guilty (Article 11). Sanctions against marital infidelity by a woman are determined by the collective wisdom of elders from the husband's kinsman and the entire village (Enwereji, 2008), which is not an impartial tribunal as stipulated in Article 10.

Smith (2010) observes that extramarital relations among southeastern Nigerian men are common and justified as an innate male predisposition for multiple sexual partners and condoned by the culturally acceptable polygamous marital option. Women, however, are subjected to demeaning punishments even at the point of suspicion. Women may not probe their husband's extramarital activity because if they do so they may be divorced after being stripped of resources, including custody of children (Enwereji, 2008).

The Protocol to the African Charter on Human and Peoples' Rights on the Rights of Women in Africa stipulates that "every woman shall have the right to dignity inherent in a human being and to the recognition and protection of her human and legal rights" (ACHPR, 2003, Article 3). "Every woman shall have the right to respect as a person and to the free development of her personality" (Article 3). Study participants confirmed that women accused of marital infidelity in their localities are punished by being deprived of their personal clothing, made to go naked publicly, and afflicted with diseases or even death. These cultural practices that rob women of dignity and respect are not written down as law yet have the force of law and are enforced by existing authorities and ruling bodies. These practices do not pass the repugnancy test of law and thus contravene known legal principles (Alewo & Olong, 2012). The repugnancy test requires that cultural practices enforceable by the court shall not be repugnant (offensive, distasteful, contrary) to natural justice, equity, and good conscience. The inequality of a man divorcing his wife at will and the wife not being able to do the same has been ruled as being repugnant in some Nigerian courts and may not be enforced by the customary courts (Attoh, 2016).

In conclusion, it is a violation of human rights and a discriminatory practice against women for them to be prohibited from questioning their husband on marital infidelity issues, or from taking the initiative to dissolve a marriage, or to be punished for marital infidelity without a fair hearing according to the Nigerian Constitution (Federal Republic of Nigeria, 1999), which states that, "every citizen shall have equality of rights, obligations and opportunities before the law" (Section 17[2]).

Recommendations

The following recommendations address the need to eliminate the discrimination and human rights infringements inherent in the marital cultural practices discussed in this chapter.

Upholding the repugnancy rule

Nigeria operates a pluralistic legal system where the customary courts and informal arbitration systems have the force of law. The repugnancy rule in law provides a guideline for denouncing the marital cultural practices that inherently discriminate against women, such as the exclusion of women in the bride price process, demeaning and inhumane burial rites, gender discrimination in spousal property inheritance, and heavily gendered responses to marital infidelity. These practices need to be consistently decried in all Nigerian courts because they are repugnant to natural justice, equity, and good conscience.

Cultural legitimization of human rights

There needs to be a harmonization of universal human rights and cultural rights. Also, there is a need for dialogue between the stakeholders and gatekeepers of culture in order for the cultural legitimization of human rights to be achieved. It is therefore proposed that social workers, whose profession is undergirded by principles of human rights, social justice, and cultural diversity competencies, take the lead at the national and the local levels (Juma, 2007).

Education and awareness

Social workers should collaborate with legal practitioners to provide psycho-educational services to women, informing them as to how to secure their property rights before the death of their husbands. Having proper documentation of the specific names of the wife and husband on the title deeds of real estate is helpful in securing and protecting the wife against property grabbing by the kinsmen of a deceased husband.

Community leaders need to be educated about the principles of the Universal Declaration of Human Rights and its derivatives such as Convention on the Elimination of All Forms of Discrimination against Women (CEDAW) (UN, 1979). Education and raising awareness of human rights provisions in the context of the community are vital for the eradication of cultural practices that infringe on human rights. It speaks to the world view of collective well-being in African communities that says "*Ubuntu,*" which means "I am because we are."

Support for women empowerment organizations

Organizations such as the International Federation of Women Lawyers, Nigeria (FIDA), Women's Consortium of Nigeria (WOCON), International Human Rights Law Group in Nigeria (IHRLG), and others advocating for enforcing human and women's rights laws are essential to the process of achieving success. Social workers are encouraged to become involved in the activities of these organizations to promote the visibility of women in politics, education, and economics. Having women in positions of authority fosters a reduction in discriminatory, disrespectful, and demeaning cultural practices.

General systemic overhauling of gender inequality in Nigeria

Issues of gender inequality need to be addressed holistically in the system. Para-Mallam (2010) highlighted the use of gender-neutral language such as chairperson, police officer, and others in daily discourse. Androgenic language should be discouraged in official publications and textbooks. We observed that the language of the human rights declarations and the Nigerian constitution are masculine, and indigenous communication tools should be designed to address folklores that perpetuate gender stereotypes. Nigerian female artists and playwrights are encouraged to produce plays and movies that reinforce gender equality.

Governmental responsibility

The Nigerian government should take decisive steps to address cultural practices that infringe on women's rights as urged by CEDAW. This includes customary laws and practices.

Conclusion

This chapter purposefully confronts the marital cultural practices of selected Nigerian communities that directly impinge on the human rights of women in society. Customary practices such as widow transfer and inheritance in many parts of Nigeria are oppressive to women, and the right to private ownership of property is denied the female gender. Some cultural practices against women are contrary to the doctrine of equity and the prevailing domestic and international laws. The marital cultural practices examined in this chapter included the communal nature of customary marriages, the practice of bride price (dowry), widowhood practices and cultural response to marital infidelity. The patriarchal continuities and contradictions from colonial to contemporary socio-cultural influences impact the marital cultural practices presented in this chapter. While culture is dynamic and yields to modernization, both the primary and reviewed literature of this study attest to the currency of the cultural practices considered. Modern realities, such as the education of women, only affect the degree of expectations. For example, an educated and corporately engaged widow is still required to perform the widow rituals, but the time for isolation is reduced. Ewelukwa (2002) states that "tensions exist between tradition and modernity; between individual autonomy and group solidarity; and between individual rights and duties" (p. 430). The positive aspects of these cultural practices manifest a deliberate desire and design for indigenous social care, yet the negative aspects marginalize women and subject them to inhumane situations that deprive them of their basic human rights.

The experiences of widows in particular reveal the painful position of women as both the defenders and the victims of culture, and their agency both in perpetuating practices dehumanizing to them and in overturning entrenched customary and religious practices (Ewelukwa, 2002). Extensive education and targeted advocacy aimed at altering the cultural landscape will begin to shift public opinion on these sensitive yet important subjects. In the struggle for social emancipation and women's rights, women's participation in higher education should empower them to be equal citizens with men rather than a subordinate group that enjoys paternal privilege only under certain conditions. The recommendations proposed in this chapter reflect the authors' belief that consistent and persistent resistance of these inhumane practices will lead to their collapse and eventual eradication from the societies in question. Customary laws and practices constructed largely by men in positions of power are resistant to change, and in their constructed form, continue to greatly oppress women. There is a need to amend discriminatory customary laws and practices related to widowhood cultural practices, inheritance, and property and marital infidelity, in accordance with international human rights standards on equality and non-discrimination.

REFERENCES

African Commission on Human and Peoples' Rights. (ACHPR). (2003). Protocol to the African Charter on Human and Peoples' Rights on the Rights of Women in Africa. https://www.un.org/en/africa/osaa/pdf/au/protocol_rights_women_africa_2003.pdf

Akinbi, J. O. (2015). Widowhood practices in some Nigerian societies: A retrospective examination. *International Journal of Humanities and Social Science, 5*(4), 67–74.

Alewo, A. J. M., & Olong, M. A. (2012). Cultural practices and traditional beliefs as impediments to the enjoyment of women's rights in Nigeria. *International Law Research, 1*(1), 134–143. https://doi.org/10.5539/ilr.v1n1p134

Attoh, N. R. (2016). *Repugnancy test of customary law.*

https://www.educationalresourceproviders.com/wp-content/uploads/2016/07/REPUGNANCY-TEST-OF-VALIDITY-OF-CUSTOMARY-LAW.pdf

Ayodele, J. O. (2016). Widows and inheritance hijacking practices in Ilara Mokin, Ondo State, Nigeria. *African Journal of Criminology & Justice Studies, 9*(1), 116–139.

Cooper, E. (2010). *Inheritance and the intergenerational transmission of poverty in Sub-Saharan Africa: Policy considerations* (Working Paper No. 159). Oxford, UK: Chronic Poverty Research Center, University of Oxford.

Durojaye, E. (2013). "Woman, but not human": Widowhood practices and human rights violations in Nigeria. *International Journal of Law, Policy and the Family, 27*(2), 176–196.

Enwereji, E. E. (2008). Indigenous marriage institutions and divorce in Nigeria: The case of Abia state of Nigeria. *European Journal of General Medicine, 5*(3), 165–169.

Ewelukwa, U. U. (2002). Post-colonialism, gender, customary injustice: Widows in African societies. *Human Rights Quarterly, 24*(2), 424–486.

Federal Ministry of Women Affairs and Social Development. (2006). *National genderpolicy.* http://www.aacoalition.org/national_policy_women.htm

Federal Republic of Nigeria. (1999). Constitution of the Federal Republic of Nigeria. http://publicofficialsfinancialdisclosure.worldbank.org/sites/fdl/files/assets/law-library-files/Nigeria_Constitution_1999_en.pdf

Genyi, G. A. (2013). Widowhood and Nigerian womanhood: Another context of gendered poverty in Nigeria. *Research on Humanities and Social Sciences, 3*(7), 68–73.

Glaser, B. G., & Strauss, A. L. (1967). *The discovery of grounded theory: Strategies for qualitative research.* Chicago, IL: Aldine.

Ibisomi, L., & Mudege, N. N. (2013). Childlessness in Nigeria: Perceptions and acceptability. *Culture, Health & Sexuality, 16*(1), 61–75.

Juma, L. (2007). From "repugnancy" to "bill of rights": African customary law and human rights in Lesotho and South Africa. *Speculum Juris, 1*, 88–112.

Kirmayer, L. J. (2012). Cultural competence and evidence-based practice in mental health: Epistemic communities and the politics of pluralism. *Social Science & Medicine, 75*(2), 249–256.

Makama, G. A. (2013). Patriarchy and gender inequality in Nigeria: The way forward. *European Scientific Journal, 9*(17), 115–144.

Moscardino, U., Nwobu, O., & Axia, G. (2006). Cultural beliefs and practices related to infant health and development among Nigerian immigrant mothers in Italy. *Journal of Reproductive and Infant Psychology, 24*(3), 241–255.

National Population Commission. (2017). *Nigeria's current estimated population.* http://population.gov.ng/

Ntoimo, L. F., & Isiugo-Abanihe, U. (2014). Patriarchy and singlehood among women in Lagos, Nigeria. *Journal of Family Issues, 35*(14), 1980–2008.

Nyanzi, S., Emodu-Walakira, M., & Serwaniko, W. (2009). The widow, the will, and widow-inheritance in Kampala: Revisiting victimisation arguments. *Canadian Journal of African Studies/La Revue canadienne des études africaines, 43*(1), 12–33.

Olaore, A., & Drolet, J. (2016). Indigenous knowledge, beliefs and cultural practices for children and families in Nigeria. *Journal of Ethnic & Cultural Diversity in Social Work, 26*(3), 254–270. https://doi.org/10.1080/15313204.2016.1241973

Organization of African Unity (OAU). (1981). African (Banjul) Charter on Human and Peoples' Rights. Addis Ababa, ET: Author

Oyeniyim, A. J., & Ayodeji, I. G. E. (2010). Widowhood practices among the Yorubas of south west Nigeria: Are there differences in what women experience due to their status? *Gender and Behaviour, 8*(2), 3152–3167.

Para-Mallam, F. J. (2010). Promoting gender equality in the context of Nigerian cultural and religious expression: Beyond increasing female access to education. *Compare, 40*(4), 459–477.

Pew-Templeton Research Center. (2016). Global Religious Futures Project. Retrieved March 2, 2020 from http://www.globalreligiousfutures.org/countries/nigeria#/?affiliations_religion_id=0&affiliations_year=2010&region_name=All%20Countries&restrictions_year=2016

Smith, D. J. (2010). Promiscuous girls, good wives, and cheating husbands: Gender inequality, transitions to marriage, and infidelity in southeastern Nigeria. *Anthropological Quarterly, 83*(1), 123–152.

Sossou, M. A. (2002). Widowhood practices in West Africa: The silent victims. *International Journal of Social Welfare, 11*(3), 201–209.

Strauss, A., & Corbin, J. (1998). *Basics of qualitative research: Techniques and procedures for developing grounded theory.* Thousand Oaks, CA: Sage.

Theron, S. (2017). *Customary marriage and divorce, how does it work and what is required?* http://www.bregmans.co.za/customary-marriage-divorce-work-required/

UN. (1948). Universal Declaration of Human Rights. Paris, FR: Author.

UN. (1979). Convention on the Elimination of All Forms of Discrimination against Women. Paris, FR: Author.

Socio-Cultural Constructions of Intensive Mothering and Othermothering: Domestic Workers' Experiences of Distance Parenting and their Conceptualization of Motherhood

Boitumelo Seepamore and Vishanthie Sewpaul

Child bearing is regarded as an expression of femininity, and motherhood and fertility are prized throughout the world (Akujobi, 2011; Sewpaul, 1995; 1999; Sudarkasa, 2004; Walker, 1995). Women's ability to create life and to reproduce evokes feelings of self-worth, celebration, and power. However, locating womanhood and femininity within child bearing is short-sighted as it focuses largely on the event of childbirth, while minimizing women's work in child rearing (Frizelle & Kell, 2010), and their role beyond the domestic sphere. In this chapter, we argue that the dominant intensive mothering construction is oppressive, and that it engenders guilt in women who cannot live up to this ideal, primarily on account of structural constraints. Social criteria such as gender, race (which is not real, but a socio-political and cultural construct used by some groups to subordinate others), and class intersect in significant ways to impact motherhood. Sewpaul (2013) argued that "while race and gender have lost their scientific credibility, they have not lost their ontological power" (p.

121), as these social criteria play powerful roles in determining access to power, status, and resources. While *othermothering* (Collins, 1994), as a social construct and cultural practice, is rarefied in the African context, the results of this study reflect that, while noble and a positive moral value, it is perhaps a practice born out of necessity. It is used by women who are forced, on account of economic circumstances, to parent from a distance, and it is not always in the best interests of their children.

Institutionalized, Intensive Mothering, and *Othermothering*

Mothering is multi-layered, with patriarchal, class, and racial undertones, and it is practised differently within diverse social and cultural contexts across the world. Ideas about what constitutes good mothering, while they appear innocuous and universal, are socio-culturally constructed. The intersections of race, gender, and class define mothering, and determine the conditions under which mothering is practised (Walker, 1995). The marginalization of women through the ideology of mothering is often overlooked, since mothering is considered normal, and something that all women should aspire to. Alldred (1996) highlighted the continuous contestation of mother identities and practices and argued that mothering is not necessarily normative. It is important to recognize the "diversity and multiplicity of women's self-identification and experiences as mothers" (Frizelle & Hayes, 1999, p. 18), and that mothering can be simultaneously resistant to and complicit with dominant norms (Walker, 1995).

Mothering often removes women from participation in the public sphere and places the burden of child care on women. The gendered nature of caregiving and breadwinning is institutionalized by the state, the economy, and dominant patriarchal cultural norms (Fraser, 1997). Mothering is unpaid and undervalued, and it is not recognized as work although it requires "complex, analytical, interpretive" skills similar to those of professionals (Hays, 1996, p. 159). The conceptualization of intensive motherhood as universal and naturally occurring in all women requires mothers to be constantly present, ever-giving and selfless (Hays, 1996). It assumes that all women live in middle-class, heterosexual nuclear families and devote themselves to full-time caregiving of children, while fathers act as providers and protectors. Others, for example young mothers (Macleod, 2001; Ntini & Sewpaul, 2017; Phoenix, 1991), mothers with disabilities (Malacrida, 2009), working mothers (Contreras & Griffith, 2012), single mothers (Ntini & Sewpaul, 2017), incarcerated mothers, and those in same sex relationships, tend to be "othered," as they mother outside the constructs of ideal motherhood. Women who choose not to be mothers (Kruger, 2003; Sewpaul, 1995) or postpone motherhood (Gillespie, 2003) are often pathologized. White, middle-class women are also under pressure to conform to intensive mothering. In their study of white, middle-class mothers in South Africa, Frizelle & Kell (2010) found that their participants, although they had access to resources that were not always available to other mothers, struggled with the expectations of intensive mothering.

In contrast to intensive mothering, other forms of mothering are deemed to be less intensive. Collins (1994) presented the history of mothering among African-Americans from the period of slavery when African-American women formed women-centred networks to raise children—a form of care evident to date in America and Africa. Mothering was shared by slave women who were often separated from their children. These women-centred networks contributed to cooperative childcare by biological and *othermothers*, whose role was important in the care and socialization of children (Collins, 1994), while child rearing remained, almost exclusively, the responsibility of women. In contemporary societies, women-centred networks centralize the care of children; it is mostly women who staff day-care centres and are involved in other childcare arrangements, such as being day and foster mothers.

Sudarkasa (2004) discussed the role of female kin in child care in African contexts. In extended families the division of labour is such that mothering is shared; child rearing is not the sole responsibility of the biological mother. *Othermothers* assist the biological mother with child care and support (Collins, 1994), and are huge assets. For example, in the Nguni groups, a mother's younger sister is *mamncane* (young mother), and the mother's older sister is referred to as *mamkhulu* (or older mother). Similarly, in the Sotho groups they are referred to as *mmangwane* and *mamogolo*, respectively—signifying their roles as *othermothers* in a child's life.

The absence of men from child rearing is glaring; the rigid status assigned to women in more patriarchal societies, in relation to reproduction and child rearing, keep gender roles firmly in place. While men are not entirely absent from day-to-day child rearing, they tend to have minimal child-rearing responsibilities. The emphasis is on their roles as providers, enforcers of discipline, and decision makers on behalf of the family, leaving the responsibility of child care squarely on the shoulders of women. But the results of this, and other studies (Gilbert & Sewpaul, 2015; Ntini & Sewpaul, 2017), reflect that men, for various reasons, often renege even on expected gendered roles.

In societies where other family forms operate, intensive mothering is not a norm (Sudarkasa, 2004). But its positioning as a dominant discourse places it at the centre and at the expense of those who "mother" differently, such as single-parent and working-class women. Their mothering skills are often questioned. The othering of mothers based on race is significant because Black mothers are often perceived as problematic and incompetent (Phoenix, 1996). Poor families with children are overwhelmingly Black, on welfare, and living in single-parent households (Phoenix, 1996). The implicit racism and classism in the interpretation of needs and the provision of welfare services marginalize women (Fraser, 1997), as bad mothering is equated with poverty and race. The labelling and pathologizing of Black mothers do not factor in structural issues, such as poverty and lack of resources, that affect caregiving (Gilbert & Sewpaul, 2015; Ntini & Sewpaul, 2017).

One group of othered mothers are domestic workers, whose employment occupies low status, is low paying, and is seen to be demeaning. Women in such positions, who do not have the luxury of exclusively looking after their children, are othered and marginalized. Intensive mothering "maintain[s] the privileged positions of those who are native-born, those who are white, and those who are members of the middle and upper classes" (Hays, 1996, p. 163). It is maintained and reproduced by normative standards, constructed by professionals in middle-class and privileged positions in society. Intensive mothering is perpetuated through dominant psychological theories that are used as a yardstick against which ideal motherhood is measured. They determine circumstances under which mothering should be practised and how mothers should interact with their children (Phoenix & Woollett, 1991; Schwartz, 1994). These normative ideas have been heavily influenced by males, for instance Winnicott (1953), Bowlby (1969), and Spock (1946), studying able-bodied, middle-class, white women in heterosexual, nuclear families.

Mothering is continuously shaped by others—often males—who have come to be regarded as "experts" in the practice of mothering (Phoenix & Woollett, 1991). An emphasis on mothers as sole caregivers, whose intensive mothering practices will manifest in psychologically healthy and well-rounded children, tends to be reductionist, deterministic, linear, and mother-blaming. These theories attribute much of adult mental illness to mothers. They do not take into consideration intersecting structural influences, and different childrearing practices and beliefs. Mother-blaming in psychiatry reached its extreme with Fromm-Reichmann coining the concept "schizophrenogenic mother" in 1948.

Of particular relevance to the social work profession is that women who mother differently might be put under surveillance. Professional "support" might mask the control, instruction, and supervision of "unfit" and "incompetent" mothers, who are treated in punitive and judgmental ways. The expectation that all women will conform to intensive mothering expectations justifies the criticism, scrutiny, and blaming of mothers. The judgment of mothers against white middle-class norms, ethnocentrism, and the processes of othering are all evident in the following (see Ylvisaker et al., 2015), which is an actual recording of a social worker:

> In the boy's home the family sits on the floor when they eat, and the apartment is hardly furnished. The visiting-home is a beautiful home according to Norwegian standards. The Norwegian family is engaged in aesthetics and cultural values. In the boy's home, food is just a necessity, whereas in the visiting-home meals are shared, planned and enjoyed. In the boy's home they do not speak Norwegian, whereas in the visiting-home they are all very social and love having conversations. The boy is occupied with after-school activities but is not guided by his mother. . . . In his home there are lots of different people that come and go—aunts, uncles and others. In the visiting-home they are engaged in life as a

nuclear family, but they meet with other families at planned activities (p. 227).

In the case above, it was a single, divorced mother of Indian descent who called social services to ask for help, saying that she was having difficulties and not coping. The social worker arranged for the boy to spend time in a Norwegian visiting-home that was "positive" and "resourceful" (Ylvisaker et al., 2015).

It is against this background of the dominant discourse on intensive mothering, and the alternative discourse on *othermothering*, that this study was conceptualized to understand distance parenting among domestic workers.

Methodology

This qualitative study, informed by the lens of intersectionality, which "enables us to examine the social divisions and power relations that affect people's lives" (Sewpaul, 2013, p. 118), was designed to understand the experiences of domestic workers who parent from a distance, and the meanings that participants attached to motherhood. The study was undertaken in the eThekwini Metropolitan Municipality. Data were collected via conversational type, in-depth interviews, and two focus group discussions with the aid of interview guides, with 33 women, whose children were left in rural areas with female kin—and in rare cases, their fathers.

Incidental and snowball sampling were used to access the participants. The duration of the interviews ranged from one hour to two and a half hours, with either telephone or face-to-face follow-up interviews, when necessary. Participants were fully informed about the purpose and nature of the study, and all ethical requirements were adhered to. Pseudonyms are used to ensure the anonymity of the participants. Permission to conduct the study was obtained from the University of KwaZulu-Natal Research Ethics Committee. All interviews were conducted in isiZulu or seSotho and were tape recorded, with permission of the participants, and were transcribed and translated into English. Thematic analysis was complemented with Critical Discourse Analysis (CDA), which sees language as a social practice, where discourse is understood as socially constitutive and socially conditioned. CDA analyzes written texts and spoken words to unveil sources of power, dominance, resistance, and inequality, and how these are maintained within socio-cultural, economic, and political contexts. It accepts the central premise that language is not neutral; language not only reflects the world but actively constructs and reproduces the world that we live in, and it speaks to the complex relationship between structure and agency (Fairclough, 2009; Wodak & Meyer, 2009). The results focus on the participants' experiences, and their constructions of motherhood.

Results and Discussion

The participants' ages ranged between 24 to 42 years. The women had an average of two children each. A majority (22) of the participants were not married; 11 of the 33 mothers were married, and 17 had their first child at or before 19 years of age. Two of the participants had seven children each; one had her first child at 14 and the other at 18 years. Another participant who had five children gave birth to her first child at 19 years. While poverty, and its concomitants, are important precursors to, and consequences of, teenage pregnancies (Ntini & Sewpaul, 2017), motherhood is often a way of gaining social status, recognition, and respect, symbolizing a passage to adulthood, despite single mothers being stigmatized and often having to carry the responsibility of child rearing alone (Macleod, 2001; Ntini & Sewpaul, 2017). Four participants had four children each, with their ages ranging from 16 to 21 years, and none of them was married when they had their first child. Almost a third of them were live-in domestic workers; others rented accommodation near their work and returned home to the rural areas periodically.

The results are discussed under four interrelated themes: (1) The legitimacy and the legitimating role of children; (2) Caregiving by *othermothers*; (3) The desire for, and the impossibility of, intensive mothering; and (4) Self-blaming in absent mothers.

The Legitimacy and the Legitimating Role of Children

For their children to gain legitimacy, customary law, as set forth in the Recognition of Customary Marriages Act (Government of South Africa,1998), requires that damages (*inhlawulo*) be paid in instances where men impregnate women out of wedlock. Ten of the unmarried participants in this study never had damages paid by the fathers, which is tantamount to denial of paternity and of legitimacy of the children. The men abandoned their partners either during pregnancy or soon after the birth of the children, a finding that resonates with that of other studies (Gilbert & Sewpaul, 2015; Ntini & Sewpaul, 2017). In almost all the cases, the participants wanted acknowledgment from the fathers, even if the fathers were no longer interested in them or their children. Puseletso's despair was clear:

> They don't have one father. . . . Katleho's father . . . I last saw him when I was 3 months pregnant . . . with Bareng. . . . His father is alive, he knows him very well . . . but he does nothing. Nothing for the child." Similarly, Bavumile, who had seven children, none of whom had damages paid for, said: "They stayed with my mother from the beginning. . . . Their father was never there, I have two children with him.

The centrality of motherhood, and the legitimating role that children played in their lives, is noted in most of them having introduced themselves as "mother of . . ." For instance, one participant said, "They call me maItumeleng" (mother of Itumeleng) instead of using her birth name. The other participants, particularly from Lesotho, used their married names in introducing themselves, such as MaTebello, maTshepo, maPalesa. It is customary within the Basotho group to refer to women with their children's names—or names they were given when they got married. Those who are not married would not have these naming ceremonies for children born out of wedlock. Being given a married name not only prepares one for motherhood, but also puts pressure on women to procreate. The name of the child may also be gender-specific, which further pressures one to produce children of a specific gender, usually male. Their identity changed with marriage and motherhood, and their children gained legitimacy with marriage.

Caregiving by *Othermothers*

Of the 33 participants, five of the mothers identified as being the primary caregivers of their children even though their fathers stayed at home with the children. In almost a third of the participants (21), grandmothers were the primary caregivers, four were cared for by the participants' eldest daughters, and the rest by maternal aunts and uncles, neighbours, or paid caregivers. Caregiving is disproportionately feminized, and those who stepped in were women, often female relatives such as *mamkhulus, mmangwanes*, and grannies. Caregiving by relatives was taken for granted. When asked if they had negotiated caregiving, many of the participants said that they did not have to ask; it was a given that the female relatives would take over this role. Khanyo was cohabiting with her partner and left her children with her mother, and she did not see the need to take her children to live with her at any point. She said:

> I will never turn my back on them. He [partner] understands my situation, so I will have to continue working so that I can support my children. . . . They will stay with my mother and I will continue staying with him.

The literature tends to rarefy the popular cultural adage "it takes a village to raise a child"—the importance of the collective in child rearing in African contexts. But villages in South Africa are in crisis. Systems of care have been eroded as families struggle under the weight of HIV/ AIDS, poverty, and the onslaught of free-market capitalist ideology. *Othermothers,* especially grandmothers, do play a critical role, and often offer their services as a labour of love in unpaid service. But there are other realities too, as reflected in the experiences of some of the women, who spoke about relatives prioritizing their own children above theirs; harsh punishment being meted out to their children compared with those of the relatives' children; and of food, clothes, school uniforms, and toiletries that they sent, intended for their children's use, being used by relatives. In their study of Zimbabwean mothers living in the UK, Madziva and Zontini (2011) found that the competition for remittances contributed to relatives fighting for the children, and some of the mothers were reluctant to leave their children with relatives, preferring paid caregivers to family members. While the experiences of the women were by no means homogeneous, they expressed a deeply held desire for intensive mothering, a privilege—perhaps more a right—that they were denied.

The Desire for, and the Impossibility of, Intensive Mothering

By virtue of domestic employment, the participants either lived on their employers' property or rented a room nearby. None of them lived with their children, although they visited them periodically, generally once every one to three months. The participants from Lesotho, and those outside of KwaZulu-Natal, visited their children less frequently—about once every nine months or once per year, on account of distance and the costs of travel. While they were separated from their children, the women subscribed to the idea of intensive mothering, and saw good mothers as those who are involved in the everyday lives of their children.

The women had to constantly negotiate the tensions between two parallel, competing discourses—the universal discourse of intense mothering, on the one hand, and the contextual, normalized discourse of distant mothering, on the other. Feelings of "double belonging" (Boccagni, 2012, p. 266) were evident. Despite physical distance, their thoughts were with their children. The general wish was to co-reside with their children and raise them themselves, not through substitute caregivers. The centrality of their children in their lives was clear. MaTshepo, whose baby was 18 months old when she left home, said quite poignantly, "Some of us . . . our children even forget who we are." Although it was impossible to mother intensively, the mothers tried to approximate intensive mothering as closely as they could.

In order to reduce spatial distance, and to maintain co-presence across geographical distances, the participants used technology. Contreras and Griffith (2012) found that Mexican mothers working in the US often called their children numerous times a week to enquire about their well-being, school, and health, and even assisted with homework. Unlike other studies where the mothers had an array of means of keeping in touch (Merla, 2012), mothers in this study depended on the mobile telephone. They used WhatsApp because it was free to download, and enabled audio messaging and video calling. They could speak to their children, hear their voices, and see their faces even when they were hundreds of kilometres away. Rethabile said, "If not [visit] then I will have to continue speaking with them over the phone . . . and try to ensure that they remember why I am not able to stay with them. . . . They have to understand the reasons for my absence." For Rathabile, her children making meaning of her absence was important. As reflected in the voices of some of the other women, the children needed to know that they were "working for them"; that they were, indeed, the self-sacrificing mothers that institutionalized, intensive mothering valorizes.

Other transnational mothers made an effort to speak to their children more than once a day, despite the high costs of airtime and data. Noma, who depended on the phone to supervise her son, explained:

> I have to use the phone to wake him up [at 5 a.m.] because they sleep. They do, even when you are there. Yes, so I must have airtime to wake him up . . . and if I don't, he is late for school. . . . But then my boy does try . . . "today I was late at school and the teacher made me pick up all the papers" and I tell him . . . "my baby just hang in there. . . . It will get better one day." There is nothing else I can do [softly], it is very hard.

Similarly, Puseletso phoned her children every night before she went to bed. This arrangement meant that her children and caregiver had to stay up very late so that she could speak to them after retiring at 10 p.m. when she returned to her room. These attempts to make up for a lack of face-to-face interaction were often expensive and time consuming, but they provided some semblance of normalcy and enabled daily contact, including real-time decision making and support. However, it did not make up for maternal absence.

Self-Blaming in Absent Mothers

Mothers who parent from a distance often face negative consequences when their children do not behave (Macleod, 2001). Apart from societal condemnation, the women themselves had internalized the dominant constructions of intensive mothering and they felt embarrassed, guilty and responsible for things that went wrong with their children. Thandaza said:

> Drinking, that's it. . . . I think that perhaps he [son] saw it as the right thing to do so he also did it, he started drinking very, very young. I mean if he is in high school now, then what does that say to you?

Although her husband stayed with the children, she blamed herself for not being around to guide them. She believed that her son would not have started drinking if she had been present.

The safety of children was a constant concern, and the participants yearned to protect their children from harm even across distances. Madziva and Zontini (2011) argued that the availability of suitable caregivers facilitated migration to places of employment, but that the unavailability of good caregivers placed children at risk. Rethabile was overwhelmed by grief after her child, whose sister served as the *othermother*, was raped. She said:

> And I was very upset, I have never ever felt so hurt in my life. My child raped by my brother-in-law. . . . I really miss them, they miss me too. . . . I get worried because they get unhappy. They think about me all the time.

Rethabile blamed herself for her inability to protect her children and regretted leaving her children in the care of her sister. Her desire and that of her children was to live together. Although Frizelle's and Kell's (2010) study was with a different sample of middle-class, white women, the results of this study cohere with their conclusion that by "personifying the ideal against which marginalised mothers . . . are defined . . . they become particularly vulnerable to self-regulatory mothering discourses and practices" (p. 42).

The concerns expressed by the women, and their desire for intensive mothering, are understandable, given that children living in households with a migrant parent are more likely to experience abuse, frequent illnesses, chronic illness, and emotional and behavioural problems than children living in households where the parent is present (Heymann et al., 2009). Parreñas (2001) and Millman (2013) discussed the detrimental consequences of separating parents from their children for extended periods of time, in relation to emotional distance, erosion of family relationships, indiscipline, disruption of family roles and household routines, and insecurity and confusion on the part of children. Children may have feelings of abandonment, anger, and loss even in instances where the decision to migrate was discussed with the children beforehand (Bennett et al., 2014; Boccagni, 2012).

Conclusions and Recommendations

Despite the criticism of intensive mothering being "racist, colonialist, masculinist" (Alldred, 1996, p. 127), and its leaning toward white, middle-class, nuclear, able-bodied families, its centrality, as an ideal form of mothering, is not diminished. The women in this study yearned for togetherness with their children and for intensive mothering. Intensive mothering places a disproportionate burden of responsibility on women, and reinforces mother-blaming, as children's difficulties and adult mental health problems are often located in mothering practices. Social workers have always played a central role in working with families, and more particularly in child protection, and they need to ensure that they do not collude with ideologies and practices that continue to marginalize women by deliberately or inadvertently maintaining the status quo. While social workers are bound by law and ethical imperatives to protect children and ensure their best interests, they must guard against being enforcers of punitive, abusive, and ethnocentric practices that other and disadvantage women.

The gendered nature of the discourse is such that there is no such thrust toward intensive fathering. Yet the importance of warm, loving, supportive, authoritative parenting (Baumrind, 1991; Querido et al., 2002) in ensuring the best interests of children must not be underestimated. Disarticulated from its negative connotations and consequences, which are elucidated in this chapter, intensive parenting—where parents are validating of children, and are engaged and responsive to their needs—does work in the interests of children. But parenting does not occur in a vacuum; it is influenced by broader socio-economic and cultural contexts, and it is critical that mezzo- and macro-level policies and programs be put in place to support parenting by both men and women. Normative gender roles must be challenged and changed, with an emphasis on alternative masculinities so that men begin to appreciate and adopt their roles as fathers (Morrell & Jewkes, 2014). The women in this study lamented the fact that they had little or no support from the fathers of their children. Maharaj and Sewpaul (2016) asserted that "greater efforts must be made towards gender equality, and the inclusion of men in parenting practices, if we are to minimize the burdens of care that women carry" (p. 57). But we need to work beyond gender equality; structural interventions to reduce poverty and inequality across race must be prioritized.

The women in this study attempted to approximate, as closely as possible, the ideals of intensive mothering. As in Frizelle's and Kell's (2010) study, the women's struggle with mothering, and their unquestioning acceptance of their responsibility as primary caregivers, led to their internalization of the dominant discourse around institutionalized, intensive motherhood. Yet there was a simultaneous normalization of their distant parenting and reliance on *othermothers*, as "everybody does it [leaves their children to go to work]," thus supporting the notion that women can both resist and be complicit with dominant norms at the same time (Walker, 1995). The normalization might be reflective of the women's resilience, in coping with adverse and difficult life circumstances over which they had little or no control. In the face of competing discourses, intensive mothering gained pre-eminence. Rationalizing that they were "working for the children" so that the children "have something to eat," providing for the children's material needs and maintaining remote contact affirmed their mothering identities.

While the literature tends to rarefy *othermothering* and communal caring (Akujobi, 2011; Collins, 1994; Sudarkasa, 2004), which are positive moral values linked to the principle of *Ubuntu*, the practice allows for exploitation of poor women who often provide unpaid labour. Furthermore, research results detail the negative consequences of separation of children from their parents, and the narratives of the women in this study reflect their concerns about their children living with *othermothers*. It would seem that the exalting of *othermothering* reflects a need to make a virtue out of necessity. The women loved their children, missed them, and wanted to be with them, but were forced to leave their children in the care of others. Rather than construct socio-economic deprivations and their consequences as cultural issues (IASSW, 2018), state and non-state actors in South Africa must challenge structural injustices, agitate for structural changes, and support, for example, the goals of the White Paper on Families in relation to the promotion, strengthening, and preservation of families (Department of Social Development, 2012).

The structural constraints of the intersection of race, class, and gender can be seen in the fact that less than a third (29 percent) of Black children lived with both their parents, while the majority of Indian (84 percent) and white children (77 percent) lived with both biological parents in South Africa in 2013 (Meintjes et al., 2015). Single-parent families are primarily female-headed. It is estimated that nine million children were growing up with fathers that were living, but absent from their lives, while 42 percent of Black children lived with their mothers but not their fathers (Mathews et al., 2014). These demographics are accompanied by huge disparities in the ownership of wealth along racial lines, where the life opportunities of Black children are compromised compared with those of their white and Indian counterparts. The women witnessed, on a daily basis, other women—usually their "madams" and their children—living with the advantages of intensive mothering, so whether "racist, colonialist, masculinist" (Alldred, 1996) or not, and perhaps precisely *because* intensive mothering is associated with "members of the middle and upper classes" (Hays, 1996, p. 163), the women desired this! They were Black women, struggling in low-wage labour, but they loved their children no less. To expect that they would want anything less than that deemed fit for women in middle and upper classes would be to maintain double standards; it is a violation of their dignity and a negation of their humanity, which are contrary to the core values of Afrocentricity, as discussed in the introduction and conclusion of this book. The discourse needs to shift from the *privilege* of intensive mothering to the *right* to intensive parenting for all people in South Africa, irrespective of race, class, gender, sexual orientation, family structure, or family type.

REFERENCES

Akujobi, R. (2011). Motherhood in African literature and culture. *CLCWeb: Comparative Literature and Culture, 13*(1), 2.

Alldred, P. (1996). Whose expertise? Conceptualising resistance to advice about childrearing. In E. Burman, G. Aitken, P. Alldred, R. Allwood, T. Billington, B. Goldberg, A. J. Gordo Lopez, C. Heenan, D. Maks, & S. Warner (Eds.), *Psychology discourse practice: From regulation to resistance* (pp. 133–151). London, UK: Taylor & Francis.

Baumrind, D. (1991). The influence of parenting style on adolescent competence and substance use. *Journal of Early Adolescence, 11*(1), 56–95. https://doi.org/10.1177/0272431691111004

Bennett, R., Hosegood, V., Newell, M-L., & McGarth, N. (2014). Understanding family migration in rural South Africa: Exploring children's inclusion in the destination household of migrant parents. *Population, Space and Place, 21*(4), 310–321.

Boccagni, P. (2012). Practising motherhood at a distance: Retention and loss in Ecuadorian transnational families. *Journal of Ethnic and Migration Studies, 38*(2), 261–277.

Bowlby, J. (1969). *Attachment and loss*. New York, NY: Basic Books.

Collins, P. H. (1994). Shifting the centre: Race, class and feminist theorizing about motherhood. In E. N. Glenn, G. Chang, & L. R. Forcey (Eds.), *Mothering: Ideology, experience and agency* (pp. 45–65). New York, NY: Routledge.

Contreras, R., & Griffith, D. (2012). Managing migration, managing motherhood: The moral economy of gendered migration. *International Migration, 50*(4), 51–66.

Department of Social Development. (2012). *White paper on families in South Africa*. Pretoria: Republic of South Africa. Retrieved August 2018 from http://www.dsd.gov.za/index.php?option=com_docman&task=cat_view&gid=33&Itemid=3

Fairclough, N. (2009). A dialectical-relational approach to critical discourse analysis in social research. In R. Wodak & M. Meyer (Eds.), *Methods of critical discourse analysis* (pp. 162–186). London, UK: Sage.

Fraser, N. (1997). *Justice interruptus: Critical reflections on the "postsocialist" condition*. New York, NY: Routledge.

Frizelle, K., & Hayes, G. (1999). Experiences of motherhood: Challenging ideas. *Psychology in Society (PINS), 25*, 17–36.

Frizelle, K., & Kell, G. (2010). A contextual account of motherhood. *Psychology in Society (PINS), 39*, 26–44.

Fromm-Reichmann, F. (1948). Notes on the development of treatment of schizophrenics by psychoanalysis and psychotherapy. *Psychiatry, 11*, 263–273.

Gilbert, I., & Sewpaul, V. (2015). Challenging dominant discourses on abortion from a radical feminist standpoint. *Affilia: Journal of Women and Social Work, 30*(1), 83–95.

Gillespie, R. (2003). Childfree and feminine: Understanding the gender identity of voluntary childless women. *Gender and Society, 17*, 122–136.

Government of South Africa. (1998). Recognition of Customary Marriages Act, 1998 (Act 120 of 1998) and Regulations. Pretoria, ZA: Government Gazette 6909, 1 November 2000.

Hays, S. (1996). *The cultural contradictions of motherhood*. New Haven, CT: Yale University Press.

Heymann, J., Flores-Macias, F., Hayes, J. A., Kennedy, M., Lahaie, C., & Earle, A. (2009). The impact of migration on the well-being of transnational families: New data from sending communities in Mexico. *Community, Work & Family, 12*(1): 91–103.

IASSW. (2018). *Global social work statement of ethical principles*. Retrieved April 2018 from https://www.iassw-aiets.org/wp-content/uploads/2018/04/Global-Social-Work-Statement-of-Ethical-Principles-IASSW-27-April-2018.pdf

Kruger, L-M. (2003). Narrating motherhood: The transformative potential of individual stories. *South African Journal of Psychology, 33*(4), 198–204.

Macleod, C. (2001). Teenage motherhood and the regulation of mothering in the scientific literature: The South African example. *Feminism & Psychology, 11*(4), 493–510.

Madziva, R., & Zontini, E. (2011). Transnational mothering and forced migration: Understanding the experiences of Zimbabwean mothers in the UK. *European Journal of Women's Studies, 19*(4), 428–443.

Maharaj, S., & Sewpaul, V. (2016). Accidental burns in children under five years of age: The gendered burden of care and socio-economic deprivation. *Child and Youth Services Review, 68*, 51–58.

Malacrida, C. (2009). Performing motherhood in a disablist world: Dilemmas of motherhood, femininity and disability. *International Journal of Qualitative Studies in Education, 22*(1), 99–117.

Mathews, S., Jamieson, L., Lake, L., & Smith, C. (2014). *South African Child Gauge 2014*. Cape Town, ZA: Children's Institute, University of Cape Town.

Meintjes, H., Hall, K., & Sambu, W. (2015). Demography of South Africa's children. In A. De Lannoy, S. Swartz, L. Lake, & C. Smith (Eds.), *South African Child Gauge 2015*. Cape Town, ZA: Children's Institute, University of Cape Town.

Merla, L. (2012). Salvadoran migrants in Australia: An analysis of transnational families' capability to care across borders. *International Migration, 53*(6): 153–165. https://doi.org/10.1111/imig.12024.

Millman, H. L. (2013). Mothering from afar: Conceptualizing transnational motherhood. *Totem: The University of Western Ontario Journal of Anthropology, 21*, 72–82.

Morrell, R., & Jewkes, R. (2014). "I am a male, although I am a little bit soft": Men, gender, and care work in South Africa. In V. Reddy, S. Meyer, T. Shefer, & T. Meyiwa (Eds.), *Care in context: Transnational gender perspectives* (pp. 326–341). Cape Town, ZA: HSRC Press.

Ntini, T., & Sewpaul, V. (2017). School-going teenage mothers and fathers: Gender, challenges and the negotiation of learner-parent roles. *Child and Youth Services Review, 76* (Issue C), 250–257.

Parreñas, R. S. (2001). Mothering from a distance: Emotions, gender, and intergenerational relations in Filipino transnational families. *Feminist Studies, 27*(2), 361–390.

Phoenix, A. (1991). Mothers under twenty: Outsider and insider views. In A. Phoenix, A. Wollett, & E. Lloyd (Eds.), *Motherhood: Meanings, practices and ideologies* (pp. 86–102). London, UK: Sage.

Phoenix, A. (1996). Social constructions of lone motherhood: A case of competing discourses. In E. B. Silva (Ed.), *Good enough mothering? Feminist perspectives on lone motherhood* (pp. 175–190). London, UK: Routledge.

Phoenix, A., & Woollett, A. (1991). Introduction. In A. Phoenix, A. Wollett, & E Lloyd (Eds.), *Motherhood: Meanings, practices and ideologies* (pp. 1–12). London, UK: Sage.

Querido, J. G., Warner, T., & Eyberg, S. (2002). Parenting styles and child behavior in African American families of preschool children. *Journal of Clinical Child Psychology, 31*, 272–277.

Schwartz, A. (1994). Taking the nature out of motherhood. In D. Bassin, M. Honey, & M. M. Kaplan (Eds.), *Representations of motherhood*. New York, NY: Yale University Press.

Sewpaul, V. (1995). *Confronting the pain of infertility: Feminist, ethical and religious aspects of infertility and the new reproductive technologies* (Unpublished doctoral dissertation). University of Natal, Durban, ZA.

Sewpaul, V. (1999). Culture, religion and infertility: A South African perspective. *British Journal of Social Work, 29*, 741–754.

Sewpaul, V. (2013). Inscribed in our blood: Confronting and challenging the ideology of sexism and racism. *Affilia: Journal of Women and Social Work, 28*(2), 116–125.

Spock, B. (1946). *The common sense book of baby and child care*. New York: Pocket Books.

Sudarkasa, N. (2004). Conceptions of motherhood in nuclear and extended families, with special reference to comparative studies involving African societies. *JENdA: A Journal of Culture and African Women Studies, 5*, 1–27.

Walker, C. (1995). Conceptualising motherhood in twentieth century South Africa. *Journal of Southern African Studies, 21*(3), 417–437.

Winnicott, D. (1953). Transitional objects and transitional phenomena. *International Journal of Psychoanalysis, 34*, 89–97.

Wodak, R., & Meyer, M. (2009). Critical discourse analysis: History, agenda, theory and methodology. In R. Wodak & M. Meyer (Eds.), *Methods of critical discourse analysis* (pp. 1–33). London, UK: Sage.

Ylvisaker, S., Rugkasa, M., & Eide, K. (2015). Silenced stories of social work with minority ethnic families in Norway. *Critical and Radical Social Work, 3*(2): 221–236.

Misrecognition of the Rights of People with Epilepsy in Zimbabwe: A Social Justice Perspective

Jacob Rugare Mugumbate and Mel Gray

Epilepsy affects 4 to 14 people per 1,000, that is, an estimated 50 million people worldwide, making it the most common global neurological condition (Shorvon, 2009; WHO, 2016). It is more prevalent in the Global South, where 80 percent of people with epilepsy reside, due to "poorer perinatal care and standards of nutrition and public hygiene, and the greater risk of brain injury, cerebral infection, or other acquired cerebral conditions" (Shorvon, 2009, p. 3). In Africa alone, epilepsy directly affects about 10 million people (WHO, 2015). Indigenous cultural and religious misunderstanding affects the management of this neurological condition in many parts of the world, especially in Africa. This has led to misrecognition of the rights of people living with epilepsy, which leaves them socially isolated and makes it difficult for them to develop social networks and to access treatment, education and training, and employment. This chapter explores the misrecognition and misrepresentation of people with epilepsy, and associated injustices relating to dominant indigenous cultural and religious perspectives on epilepsy in Africa and consequent human rights omissions found in a study of persons with epilepsy in Harare, Zimbabwe. It provides an overview of perspectives on epilepsy in Africa and the injustices stemming from the continued exclusion of people with epilepsy in Zimbabwe. It suggests that Nancy Fraser's (2000, 2001, 2008,

2010) theory of social justice offers a framework for understanding the injustices ensuing from the misrecognition of people with epilepsy and ends by suggesting an integrated rights-based model for epilepsy management in Zimbabwe and other African countries.

Dominant Historical Indigenous Cultural and Religious Perspectives

In Africa, as in other parts of the world, non-medical interpretations of epilepsy abound. Indigenous cultural and religious perspectives view epilepsy as a contagious spiritual condition caused by supernatural forces treatable through cultural and/or religious practices. These are sometimes termed complementary or alternative therapies (CAMs), and traditional healers use them instead of, or in combination with, conventional biomedical interventions (Baker, 2002, Ferguson, 2012; Green, 2000; Mushi et al., 2011). Though understandings of epilepsy vary from society to society in Africa, historically they are rooted in indigenous, cultural, and Christian and Islamic religious beliefs.

Indigenous cultural perspectives

Traditional healers advocate various methods of healing given their belief in epilepsy's supernatural origins. In Zimbabwe, for example, a popular indigenous healing ritual involves locating the witch responsible for supernatural interference and destroying her medicines or goblins to render her powerless (Chavunduka, 1986). Ceremonial offerings as diverse as alcohol and animals are made to appease an angry god or ancestors, while the person with epilepsy, or family elders, pray for healing, deliverance, and forgiveness (Epilepsy Support Foundation [ESF], 1992; Mutanana & Mutara, 2015). People swallow, inhale, or insert herbs into the bloodstream through small cuts on the skin (ESF, 1992). Prescriptions include drinking, or bathing in, animal fat, blood, or urine or rubbing it on the skin or the wearing of red cloths and beads, or refraining from certain foods (Chavunduka, 1986). Healers often run shrines where people with epilepsy receive treatment. Researchers found indigenous healing methods similar to those in Zimbabwe in Uganda, Tanzania, Malawi, Morocco, South Africa, and Zambia (Baskind & Birbeck, 2005a; Duggan, 2013; Ferguson,

2012; Keikelame & Swartz, 2015; Mushi et al., 2011; Watts, 1989; Winkler et al., 2009). In most of these countries, people link epilepsy to witchcraft curable only by traditional healers. In Malawi and South Africa, traditional healers claim to treat the spiritual cause of epilepsy but agree that its physical manifestations require medical treatment (Keikelame & Swartz, 2015; Watts, 1989). These culturally embedded explanations often misrecognize epilepsy. This leads to violations of people's rights to medical treatment, education, employment, marriage, and inheritance. Misconceptions about epilepsy reinforce the stigma and marginalization faced by people with epilepsy and their families (Baskind & Birbeck, 2005a).

Religious perspectives

Some African Christians believe that Satan, demons, and evil spirits cause epilepsy. In the Bible, Jesus healed a demon-possessed boy: "Lord, have mercy on my son. . . . He has seizures and is suffering greatly. He often falls into the fire or into the water. I brought him to your disciples, but they could not heal him" (Matthew 17:14–16, New International Version). Another example from the Bible says, "She had suffered a great deal under the care of many doctors and had spent all she had, yet instead of getting better she grew worse" (Mark 5:26, New International Version). These verses strengthen religious interpretations of epilepsy, although, in this case, Jesus healed the woman of chronic bleeding, which she had endured for 12 years. The Bible says Jesus healed her when she touched his robe and he said, "Daughter, your faith has healed you. Go in peace and be freed from your suffering" (Mark, 5:34, New International Version). Most churches in Africa advise adherents to have faith in God, read the Bible, fast, pray, and seek help from prophets, who use anointing oils, water, stones, and touch for healing. Some churches entreat patients to wear bracelets with Bible verses or a waistcloth.

Adherents of the Islamic religion believe illness comes from Allah or God, as a test of faith in Allah, or an atonement for past sins (Mughees, 2006). They believe Allah created, and is responsible for healing, every disease: "And when I am ill, it is He who cures me" (Quran, 26:80). Sickness is a wake-up call for enhanced spiritual connection with God through prayer, charity, meditation, forgiveness, or remembrance of Allah and reading the Quran (Lawrence & Rozmus, 2001). In Morocco, for example, people view epilepsy as a religious, supernatural, and cultural condition caused by evil spirits or demons called *jinn* (Ferguson, 2012). A *fquih* or an imam, a religious scholar well-versed in the Quran, uses his supernatural powers to speak with, and expel, the *jinn,* while touching the patient. If this fails, the *fquih* recites passages from the Quran or treats the "possessed person" with smoke and scents. Sick people often wear charms and amulets with Quran verses on them to stave off evil. If none of these rituals work, this means the *jinn* has married the patient, parented children, and is unwilling to leave. To prevent evil possession, people must have faith in Allah and the Prophet Mohamed, pray and perform daily rituals and ablutions, and avoid haunted places, such as dark spaces and abandoned buildings (Ferguson, 2012).

These indigenous cultural and religious models persist in the absence of evidence of their effectiveness in treating seizures and managing epilepsy, and many argue we should not dismiss them without further evaluation (Baskind & Birbeck, 2005a; Green, 2000; Watts, 1989, 1992). There are some similarities between traditional and modern medical approaches. Both involve assembling a thorough historical background to reach a diagnosis, agree on epilepsy's genetic aetiology, and suggest dietary practices, such as abstention from alcohol (Baskind & Birbeck, 2005b; Magazi, 2017). One might equate the psychosocial support ensuing from cultural and religious consultations, rituals, and ceremonies to the benefits of counselling and group therapy in Western psychology. Furthermore, indigenous methods are often more socio-culturally acceptable and accessible than biomedical treatment

Contemporary Perspectives on Epilepsy

Biomedical perspective

From a biomedical perspective, epilepsy is a chronic, non-communicable neurological condition characterized by recurrent seizures and long-term social stigma (Baskind & Birbeck, 2005a; Shorvon, 2009; WHO, 2016). Medically, seizures emanate from neurons in the brain, the nerve cells responsible for communication between the brain and the body, through the transmission of electrical impulses. A disturbance in this transmission process may result in an excessive discharge of "messages," with body parts failing to respond. This may lead to lapses in attention, loss of sensation, jerking movements, falling, or muscle stiffening. Such disturbances are largely the result of brain damage, either before or after birth (WHO, 2005, 2016). There are numerous causes of brain damage, including a lack of oxygen to the brain, head trauma at birth, or accidents, drug or alcohol abuse, brain tumours, genetic syndromes, and infections, such as meningitis. Most of these causes are preventable or treatable through lifelong daily doses of anti-epileptic medication or, in some cases, brain surgery. The discovery of potassium bromide in 1857 strengthened the biomedical model (Scott, 1992) and positioned people with epilepsy as patients in need of health care. Supported by scientific research, medical treatment became the most effective method of seizure control in Africa, as elsewhere. Other treatment approaches include a ketogenic diet and vagus nerve and deep-brain or trigeminal nerve stimulation (International Bureau for Epilepsy [IBE], 2014).

Non-Western treatments for epilepsy, often termed complementary, alternative, or non-conventional, include religious and cultural practices, herbal remedies, homeopathy, aromatherapy, acupuncture, and Chinese medicine. Uncontrolled epilepsy temporarily or permanently limits daily activities, such as speech, mobility, memory, sensation, and social interaction (Birbeck & Kalichi, 2003). Control of epileptic seizures has improved as advances in medicine have significantly increased the number of people living seizure-free, productive lives. Despite affordable medical treatment for epilepsy, clinicians do not properly diagnose or treat most people with the condition in resource-poor settings (Baskind & Birbeck, 2005a; Shorvon, 2009). Poverty creates a medical treatment gap ranging from 25 to100 percent in some communities (Newton & Garcia, 2012).

Biopsychosocial perspective

The biopsychosocial perspective views epilepsy as a biological (physical), psychological, and social issue requiring multipronged interventions (Baker, 2002; de Boer, 2010; Dekker, 2002; Elger & Schmidt, 2008; Mugumbate et al., 2017). The first pillar is physical, as discussed under the biomedical perspective. The second is psychological and includes depression, anxiety, stigma, and low self-esteem (Baker, 2002; Dekker, 2002). The important addition of the tripartite biopsychosocial was the recognition of its social impacts and the need for social policy, social services, social care, and social support for people with epilepsy. Most importantly, it recognizes the structural factors that result in stigma and discrimination, and the marginalization and exclusion of people with epilepsy (Dekker, 2002; Mugumbate et al., 2017). It seeks to address the socio-cultural, economic, and political barriers to their participation in society, including unfriendly workplace policies and practices and ignorance about epilepsy. It highlights the importance of public education and awareness to reduce the stigma, which is sometimes more difficult to overcome than the seizures (Dekker, 2002; Elger & Schmidt, 2008; Mugumbate et al., 2017). The International League Against Epilepsy (ILAE) and International Bureau for Epilepsy (IBE) have promoted the biopsychosocial model and, with the WHO, embarked on a Global Campaign Against Epilepsy. The campaign sought to advance the rights of people with epilepsy contained in the WHO Resolution by urging member states to strengthen access to health and social care for people with epilepsy (WHO, 2015).

Disability perspective

There is debate on whether epilepsy is a disability (Calvert, 2011; Epilepsy South Africa [ESA], 2014) because it is a medically treatable condition. Once treated, it leads to normal social functioning for most people with epilepsy. However, epilepsy is a disabling condition for many people in Africa due to prevailing socio-cultural attitudes that lead to social stigma, discrimination, and exclusion and a lack of appropriate social and health care resources (Baker, 2002). Without appropriate biomedical treatment, it leads to impaired cognitive functioning, intellectual capacity, and physical ability and has psychological impacts, such as depression and anxiety (WHO, 2016). The WHO's (2001) definition of epilepsy aligns with the social model of disability that promotes holistic biopsychosocial intervention for people with epilepsy. Calvert (2011) pointed to the complex interrelationship between epilepsy and disability, while the ESA (2014) argued that epilepsy fits the definition of disability in the Employment Equity Act (Government of South Africa, 1998) and the International Classification of Functioning, Disability and Health (ICF) (WHO, 2001) in terms of impairment and barriers to equal participation. The ESF in

Zimbabwe is registered as a disability organization, and some people with epilepsy, disabled by the condition, qualify for (though few receive) government disability payments. Most epilepsy associations in Africa form part of the region's disability movement, even though many people with epilepsy are able bodied, since seizure control enables them to live full and satisfying lives.

Economic perspective

An economic perspective evaluates epilepsy in terms of its socio-economic impacts, such as low economic and employment participation and high health care and social care costs. It suggests interventions for economic empowerment such as those offered by Epilepsy South Africa (ESA, 2014). They include sheltered workshops in Cape Town employing people with epilepsy in a factory supplying furniture to local and foreign markets and another producing mats and baskets. ESA (2014) administers a program named the Epilepsy Disability Employment Support Services (eDESS) to provide employment preparation, workplace adjustment, legal compliance, skills development, and mentoring. The Employment Equity Act (Government of South Africa, 1998) promotes affirmative action, education and vocational training, and sensitization of employers to foster positive attitudes toward people with epilepsy. The IBE (2014) supports self-help projects in Cameroon, Kenya, Uganda, Zambia, and Zimbabwe.

Human rights perspective

With the WHO Resolution and Global Campaign Against Epilepsy, the focus shifted to a rights-based social justice approach. This approach focuses on legal entitlements and guarantees and calls for international and national government action to address economic, socio-cultural, and political inequities and reduce disadvantages for people with epilepsy. Like the social model of disability, it extends individualistic medical and bio-psychosocial interventions to address structural and political barriers to justice and identify injustices resulting from misrecognition of the rights of people with epilepsy. The WHO Resolution best reflects the human rights perspective that informed the Zimbabwean study described below.

Misrecognition of the Rights of People with Epilepsy: Findings from a Zimbabwean Study

Background to the study

A qualitative study was conducted using semi-structured, in-depth interviews with 16 unemployed and 14 employed people with epilepsy (n=30), who were members of the Epilepsy Support Foundation (ESF) in Harare, Zimbabwe's capital. The study sought to identify social injustices arising from misrecognition of the rights of participants through lack of access to educational and vocational support, health services, public social welfare and disability support, employment services, and recourse to justice. The participants comprised 13 females and 17 males with a mean age of 33 years. To deepen understanding of the interview findings, the perspectives of ESF service providers (n=7) were sought through a focus group discussion. They included two nurses, three social service workers, and two advocacy workers. The two datasets were analyzed separately using NVivo, a computer-assisted, qualitative data-analysis package. The findings of this study include: (1) lack of educational and vocational support services; (2) lack of medical health services; (3) lack of public social welfare and disability services; (4) lack of employment opportunities; and (5) lack of recourse to justice in the workplace.

Lack of educational and vocational support services

Consistent with the literature, participants reported a lack of educational and vocational services (Elger & Schmidt, 2008; Mushi et al., 2011) even though the Education Act (Government of Zimbabwe, 2001) mandated the government to provide accessible subsidized education for all, including free education for people with disabilities, such as epilepsy. However, due mainly to misinformation and stigma, the participants experienced barriers to education, in an education system once considered one of the best in Africa (UN Development Programme [UNDP], 2013). Participants with childhood-onset epilepsy reported limited access to primary and secondary school education. Some had attended sporadically, while others had dropped out of school. Some teachers had not known about medical treatment or had not supported it, encouraging students with epilepsy to seek traditional healing. Services to support vocational training were equally lacking. None of the participants had benefited from the government-run vocational training and human-resource development schemes, apprenticeships, cadetships, and scholarships. Service providers were critical of government rehabilitation services, such as Ruwa Rehabilitation Centre near Harare, which offered medical rehabilitation and job-skills training, as its capacity was low, it was highly selective, and it favoured people with physical disabilities.

Lack of medical health services

Health services were of poor quality and expensive and beyond reach for most study participants. Consistent with findings from studies in Malawi and many other African countries, people with epilepsy in Zimbabwe delayed treatment by several years (Baskind & Birbeck, 2005a; Watts, 1989, 1992; WHO, 2016). Vital medicines and medical services were often not available and, when they were, were expensive. The Health Services Act (Government of Zimbabwe, 2004) promised the availability of health services, yet most people with epilepsy in this study could not afford hospital bills and essential medicines. Though public health services were available in urban areas, their quality was erratic. Hospitals were overcrowded and under-resourced, while the community health workforce lacked the capacity to complement hospital-based treatment or to educate communities about epilepsy and the ease with which they could treat it if they properly understood it as a neurological condition. Another factor that compromised health services related to health personnel, notably the fact that there was no neurologist available in Zimbabwe at the time of the research. Service providers reported that nurses, not trained to manage epilepsy, had most often attended to them. Long waiting lists for doctors to diagnose and treat them increased delays to medical treatment. Previous studies in Zimbabwe and other African countries have reported issues of poor health services and inadequately trained nurses (Baskind & Birbeck, 2005a; Duggan, 2013; Mushi et al., 2011).

Lack of public social welfare and disability services

There were no welfare and disability services, and the families of most participants, who were poor, had trouble accessing public services. They could not meet their basic needs for health, education, and food without government assistance, let alone gain employment skills or startup capital for informal enterprises, as confirmed by service providers in this study. None of the participants was receiving government social assistance even though the Social Welfare Assistance Act (Government of Zimbabwe, 1988) and the Disabled Persons Act (Government of Zimbabwe, 1992) provided for minimal monthly means-tested disability grants of US$20. Since these depended on the type and severity of the disability, people with epilepsy, who did not have recognizable impairments, were often excluded.

Lack of employment opportunities

There were no social interventions or dedicated government disability employment services for most participants in this study even though Zimbabwe's National Employment Services department was supposed to enhance people's employment prospects. The ESF and other non-government organizations did not offer dedicated employment services. Studies have shown that economic problems were paramount for people with epilepsy (Mugumbate & Nyanguru, 2013), yet none of the participants received income support services.

Lack of recourse to justice in the workplace

Participants were unable to challenge unfair dismissals related to seizures in the workplace or other discriminatory employment practices in court. Existing legal channels, such as they were, were expensive, as lawyers who could help them navigate the complex legal system charged exorbitant fees. While the Labour Court of Zimbabwe was a sound institution, without legal assistance they could not withstand the counter-challenge of their employers. Further, it took a long time before judges heard cases or delivered judgments. There was little chance of success in a policy environment characterized by negative social attitudes toward people with epilepsy. Although the Disabled Persons Act (Government of Zimbabwe, 1992) had anti-discrimination clauses, no one had brought a case to court. Thus, those facing discrimination suffered in silence, as did the participants in this study who effectively had no recourse to justice.

Nancy Fraser's Theory of Social Justice

Feminist political philosopher and critical theorist Nancy Fraser offers a theoretical explanation for why injustices such as the misrecognition of rights found in the Zimbabwean study described above, and other African studies, persists. She proposes a three-dimensional theory of social justice encompassing the economic, cultural/legal, and political domains (Fraser et al., 2004). She views social injustices as emanating from structural inequalities arising from maldistribution, misrecognition, and misrepresentation in the economic, cultural/legal, and political domains respectively. Her framework is particularly pertinent to the multifaceted issues facing people with disabilities in Zimbabwe, who endure economic disadvantage and social stigma, and lack a political voice. Even though her work does not address disability directly, it analyzes social harms generally (Danermark & Coniavitis, 2004). In her early theorizing, Fraser was interested in the intersection between "economic inequalities and culture and discourse" (Fraser et al., 2004, p. 375). She initially drew an analytic distinction between two conceptions of injustice, which she saw as closely interwoven in practice: "socioeconomic injustice . . . rooted in the political-economic structure of society [and] cultural or symbolic [injustice which is] . . . rooted in social patterns of representation, interpretation, and communication" (Fraser, 1995, p. 70). She saw all forms of injustice as "rooted in processes and practices that systematically disadvantage some groups of people vis-à-vis others" (Fraser, 1995, p. 71). Such groups included women; racial, ethnic, religious, and sexual minorities; some nationalities; unemployed and poor people; and people with disabilities. Economic and cultural forms of injustice were pervasive in society and in need of remedying (Fraser, 1995). As Fraser explained in an interview with Dahl, Stoltz, and Willig in 2004, in the 1980s, she found herself drawing on Karl Marx and Max Weber. She argued for "an account of modern society as comprising two analytically distinct orders of stratification, an economic order of distributive relations that generated inequalities of class and a cultural order of recognition relations that generated inequalities of status" (Fraser et al., 2004, p. 377).

Later, she argued for a third form of injustice, political subordination (Fraser, 2008, 2010). Neither redistribution nor recognition was adequate for this kind of injustice, resulting in a third remedy, representation, or democratic participation. Fraser's final argument was that these three remedies could potentially address injustice if disadvantaged people could participate in society as peers. Hence, parity of participation was pivotal to Fraser's theory of social justice. She argued that, to remedy injustice, marginalized groups had to participate as peers economically, culturally and legally, and politically. Hence, parity of participation was a core dimension of Fraser's theory that cut across all three forms of injustice and their remedies, all of which were central to the claims of people with disability.

Fraser (2001) argued that social justice did not require group identity recognition but rather recognition of the status of individuals making up a group or of the group itself relative to other groups. Taken in the context of disability, this meant recognizing not only individuals as unique actors who were being denied the opportunity to participate as equals in society, but also groups of people being stigmatized because of their differences. Fraser (2001) argued for "parity of participation" to allow "all (adult) members of society to interact with one another as peers" (p. 6). This meant participation in economic (redistribution), cultural and legal (recognition), and political (representation) forums. Redistribution involved dealing with welfare dependence, inequality, deprivation, exploitation, and other factors that denied people opportunities to interact with their equals as peers (Fraser, 2008, 2010). Parity of participation required acceptance of differences, respect for diverse identities, and equal treatment. Justice required fair interaction in society, so all could participate as peers to dismantle "patterns of advantage and disadvantage that systematically prevent some people from participating on terms of parity" (Fraser et al., 2004, p. 378). Fraser argued that injustice pertained "by definition to social institutions and social structures" (Fraser et al., 2004, p. 378) and the barriers that prevented marginalized individuals and groups from participating as peers (Danermark & Coniavitis, 2004). Consistent with Fraser's theory of social justice, this chapter argues that the barriers faced by people with epilepsy result in injustices, most notably misrecognition due to pervasive indigenous and cultural beliefs about epilepsy and the resultant social stigma and reduced access to resources and opportunities attendant upon this. We now examine the potential of a rights-based approach to foster recognition for people with epilepsy.

Rights-Based Approach to Foster Recognition for People with Epilepsy

A rights-based approach to foster recognition for people with epilepsy would include the following measures: (1) public education and awareness programs; (2) research on indigenous cultural and religious approaches; (3) an improved policy environment; (4) adequate resourcing and funding; and (5) enhanced representation.

Public education and awareness programs

Persistent indigenous and cultural misunderstandings of epilepsy in Africa lead to unfounded misrecognition. Public education about epilepsy and attendant outmoded cultural practices would overcome the ignorance, stigma, and discrimination arising from negative social attitudes toward people with epilepsy. As described by participants in this study, we could learn from the successful HIV and AIDS campaign model that enjoyed widespread political support and attracted adequate funding to curtail AIDS-related stigma. The behaviour change campaign for HIV was aligned with effective free treatments and community-based health offered by village health workers. An epilepsy awareness campaign should target traditional healers, schools, communities, and service providers, including government agencies.

Research on indigenous cultural and religious approaches

Traditional methods remain popular and compete with medical treatment in Africa. Recognition of traditional healing acknowledges cultural diversity though it overlooks questions of efficacy and the lack of evidence to justify its continued use. This violates rights to effective medical treatment and reduces opportunities for achieving a better quality of life for people with epilepsy. Without common ground, the medical treatment gap in Africa would be difficult to close. A research program on the effectiveness of traditional treatments might assist in highlighting the complementarity between traditional and medical interventions. This type of research might also highlight potential harm of both traditional and Western medicines and develop strategies to address them.

Improved policy environment

Zimbabwe needs a comprehensive and inclusive National Epilepsy Policy to give effect to the WHO Resolution and provide for coordinated government and non-government service provision, including accessible and affordable medical treatment; social, educational, and employment support; and improved case management. A special board and epilepsy fund would support the implementation of the epilepsy policy in schools and training institutions, providing inclusive guidelines for children and adults with epilepsy to achieve an equitable free education. It should provide standards to regulate traditional cultural and religious healing. It should include employer-friendly work policies for people with epilepsy and access to legal support in cases of unfair dismissals or exclusionary employment practices.

Adequate resourcing and funding

The National Epilepsy Policy – through the special board and epilepsy fund – should ensure adequate resources, including free first- and second-line medical treatment and supportive health services with well-stocked primary health care clinics to ensure early seizure control and ongoing seizure management following the HIV and AIDS model. It should ensure the availability and affordability of third-line specialist services and medications, where appropriate. A dedicated training budget should ensure training for schoolteachers, primary health care nurses, and employers to ensure an inclusive educational, health care, and work environment for people with epilepsy. Parent education programs should ensure that parents, too, receive education and support, along with assistance with school and medical costs. Finally, community education and awareness programs would ensure responsive, inclusive, and informed community members.

Enhanced representation

Disabled People's Organizations (DPOs) need to enhance representation for, and build their capacity to ensure, the rights of people with epilepsy, especially since, in Zimbabwe, the government has failed to expand public services or support non-government services for people with epilepsy. They should advocate for increased financial and technical support for

DPOs, including grants for staff salaries and research, and air time on public broadcasting media, including radio, television, and newspapers.

Conclusion and Recommendations

The misrecognition of people with epilepsy arises from structural factors that lead to social injustice and the denial of opportunities to participate as peers in society. These structural barriers arise from avoidable misinformation and stigma. There is an urgent need for economic and socio-cultural measures, including reduction of poverty, and public education and awareness to ensure recognition of people with epilepsy. This chapter drew on Nancy Fraser's (2000, 2001, 2008, 2010) theory of social justice, which essentially accords with the recommendations based on Afrocentricity and *Ubuntu* discussed in the Conclusion chapter, to inform a National Epilepsy Policy and an integrated epilepsy-management model aimed at the recognition of, and representation for, people with epilepsy, and to achieve parity of participation for them.

Prior epilepsy-management models, such as Watts (1989) and the Global Campaign Against Epilepsy (2012), focused on medical treatment and overlooked social and economic impacts for people with epilepsy and their families. The resultant individualistic approach neglected systemic and structural factors that disadvantaged people with epilepsy, such as poverty, lack of representation, culture, and barriers to education and employment. An integrated model of epilepsy management would focus on the diverse economic, cultural/legal, and political factors that affect the well-being of people with epilepsy and include economic redistribution, cultural and legal recognition, and political representation respectively as follows:

1. Economic redistribution

    a. Adequate supply of free anti-epileptic drugs and epilepsy-management services.

    b. Health education and promotion through accurate information about the nature of epilepsy and the availability of effective medical treatment.

    c. Policies to ensure income transfers, social welfare support, and adequate funding of essential services.

    d. Accessible education and training and employment services and opportunities.

2.   Cultural/legal recognition

    a. Training for educators, employers, service providers, parents, and community members to provide accurate information about epilepsy and its treatment and recognition of disabling stigma that disadvantages people with epilepsy and their families.

    b. Standards for, and regulation of, traditional treatment methods.

    c. Targeted national epilepsy legislation and management plans to implement the WHO Resolution.

3.   Political representation

    a. Support for DPOs to give voice to people with epilepsy to break down structural barriers to education and employment and ensure adequate health care and service provision.

    b. Access to the legal system to challenge injustices against people with epilepsy in schools, workplaces, and other social institutions.

An integrated model would support health and social service providers in ensuring recognition of the rights of people with epilepsy. Within Fraser's model, these injustices result from the maldistribution of resources and opportunities, misrecognition through stigma and discrimination, and misrepresentation due to their lack of voice in ensuring rights-based justice. Legal measures are essential to ensure the fulfillment of the rights of people with epilepsy to education, employment, and recourse to justice (Fraser, 2000). Misrecognition subjects people with epilepsy to stigma and prevents them from participating as peers in society. An integrated epilepsy-management model would focus on removing the barriers that prevent parity of participation for people with epilepsy (Fraser, 2008).

REFERENCES

Baker, G. A. (2002). The psychosocial burden of epilepsy. *Epilepsia, 43,* 26–30. https://doi.org/10.1046/j.1528-1157.43.s.6.12.x

Baskind, R., & Birbeck, G. L. (2005a). Epilepsy care in Zambia: A study of traditional healers. *Epilepsia, 46*(7), 1121–1126. https://doi.org/10.1111/j.1528-1167.2005.03505.x

Baskind, R., & Birbeck, G. L. (2005b). Epilepsy-associated stigma in sub-Saharan Africa: The social landscape of a disease. *Epilepsy & Behavior, 7*(1), 68–73. http://dx.doi.org/10.1016/j.yebeh.2005.04.009

Birbeck, G. L., & Kalichi, E. M. N. (2003). The functional status of people with epilepsy in rural sub-Saharan Africa. *Journal of the Neurological Sciences, 209*(1–2), 65–68. https://doi.org/10.1016/S0022-510X(02)00467-7

Calvert, S. (2011). *Epilepsy and disability: National Centre for Young People with Epilepsy.* Retrieved May 31, 2017 from http://www.epilepsy.org.au/sites/default/files/Epilepsy%20and%20Disability%20-%20Sophie%20Calvert.pdf

Chavunduka, G. L. (1986). *Realities of witchcraft.* Harare, ZW: University of Zimbabwe.

Danermark, B., & Coniavitis, L. G. (2004). Social justice: Redistribution and recognition—A non-reductionist perspective on disability. *Disability and Society, 19*(4), 339–353.

de Boer, H. M. (2010). Epilepsy stigma: Moving from a global problem to global solutions. *Seizure, 19*(10), 630–636. http://dx.doi.org/10.1016/j.seizure.2010.10.017

Dekker, P. A. (2002). *Epilepsy: A manual for medical and clinical officers in Africa* (Rev. ed.). Geneva, CH: WHO.

Duggan, M. B. (2013). Epilepsy and its effects on children and families in rural Uganda. *African Health Sciences, 13*(3), 613–623. http://dx.doi.org/10.4314/ahs.v13i3.14

Elger, C. E., & Schmidt, D. (2008). Modern management of epilepsy: A practical approach. *Epilepsy & Behavior, 12*(4), 501–539. http://dx.doi.org/10.1016/j.yebeh.2008.01.003

Epilepsy South Africa (ESA). (2014). *eDESS (Epilepsy Disability Employment Support Services).* Retrieved July 15, 2017 from http://epilepsysa-westerncape.co.za/edess.html

Epilepsy Support Foundation (ESF). (1992). *Pfari muZimbabwe/Epilepsy in Zimbabwe.* Documentary. Harare, ZW.

Ferguson, C. (2012). Perceptions of epilepsy in Morocco seen by an American neuroscientist. *North African and Middle East Epilepsy Journal, 1*(4), 4–7.

Fraser, N. (1995). From redistribution to recognition? Dilemmas of justice in a "post-socialist" age. *New Left Review, 212,* 68–93.

Fraser, N. (2000). Rethinking recognition. *New Left Review, 3*(May–June), 107–120.

Fraser, N. (2001). *Social justice in the knowledge society: Redistribution, recognition and participation.* Berlin, DE: Heinrich Boll Stiftung.

Fraser, N. (2008). *Scales of justice: Reimaging political space in a globalizing world.* Cambridge, UK: Polity Press.

Fraser, N. (2010). *Scales of justice: Reimagining political space in a globalizing world.* New York, NY: Columbia University Press.

Fraser, N., Dahl, H. M., Stoltz, P., & Willig, R. (2004). Recognition, redistribution and representation in capitalist global society: An interview. *Acta Sociologica, 47*(4), 374–382.

Global Campaign against Epilepsy. (2012). Addressing the hidden, neglected but global problems of people with epilepsy. Retrieved September 8, 2018 from http://www.globalcampaignagainstepilepsy.org/

Government of South Africa. (1998). Employment Equity Act. Cape Town, ZA. Retrieved November 19, 2020 from https://www.labourguide.co.za/download-top/135-eepdf/file

Government of Zimbabwe. (1988). Social Welfare Assistance Act. Harare, ZW. Retrieved November 19, 2020 from http://www.veritaszim.net/node/1850

Government of Zimbabwe. (1992). Disabled Persons Act. Harare, ZW. Retrieved November 19, 2020 from https://www.justice.gov/sites/default/files/eoir/legacy/2013/11/08/disabled_persons_act.pdf

Government of Zimbabwe. (2001). Education Act. Harare, ZW. Retrieved November 19, 2020 from https://zimlii.org/zw/legislation/act/1987/5

Government of Zimbabwe. (2004). Health Services Act. Harare, ZW. Retrieved November 19, 2020 from https://ntjwg.uwazi.io/en/document/c5btkr60e1m?page=3

Green, C. E. (2000). *Indigenous theory of contagious disease.* Lanham, CA: Altamira.

International Bureau for Epilepsy (IBE). (2014). *What is epilepsy?* Retrieved December 12, 2016 from http://www.ibe-epilepsy.org/what-is-epilepsy-2/

International League Against Epilepsy (ILAE), WHO, & International Bureau for Epilepsy (IBE). (2000). *African Declaration on Epilepsy.* Retrieved July 12, 2015 from http://www.who.int/mental_health/neurology/epilepsy/african_declaration_2000.pdf

Keikelame, M. J., & Swartz, L. (2015). "A thing full of stories": Traditional healers' explanations of epilepsy and perspectives on collaboration with biomedical health care in Cape Town. *Transcultural Psychiatry, 52*(5), 659–680. https://doi.org/10.1177/1363461515571626

Lawrence, P., & Rozmus, C. (2001). Culturally sensitive care of the Muslim patient. *Journal of Transcultural Nursing, 12*(3), 228–233.

Magazi, D. (2017, May 5–7). *The role of traditional healers in the ongoing management of epilepsy.* Paper presented at the 3rd African Epilepsy Congress, Dakar, Senegal.

Mughees, A. (2006). Better caring for Muslim patients. *World of Irish Nursing and Midwifery, 14*(7), 24–15.

Mugumbate, J., & Nyanguru, A. (2013). Measuring the challenges of people with epilepsy in Harare, Zimbabwe. *Neurology Asia, 18*(1), 29–33.

Mugumbate, J., Riphagenn, H., & Gathara, R. (2017). The role of social workers in the social management of epilepsy in Africa. In M. Gray (Ed.), *The handbook of social work and social development in Africa* (pp. 168–180). London, UK: Routledge.

Mushi, D., Hunter, E., Mtuya, C., Mshana, G., Aris, E., & Walker, R. (2011). Social-cultural aspects of epilepsy in Kilimanjaro Region, Tanzania: Knowledge and experience among patients and carers. *Epilepsy and Behaviour, 20*, 338–343.

Mutanana, N., & Mutara, G. (2015). Health seeking behaviours of people with epilepsy in a rural community of Zimbabwe. *International Journal of Research in Humanities and Social Studies, 2*(2), 87–96.

Newton, C. R., & Garcia, H. H. (2012). Epilepsy in poor regions of the world. *Lancet, 380*(9848), 1193–1201. https://doi.org/10.1016/s0140-6736(12)61381-6

Scott, D. F. (1992). The discovery of anti-epileptic drugs. *Journal of the History of the Neurosciences, 1*(2), 111–118. https://doi.org/10.1080/09647049209525522

Shorvon, S. (2009). *Epilepsy.* Oxford, UK: Oxford University Press.

UN Development Programme (UNDP). (2013). *Human development report.* New York, NY: Oxford University Press.

Watts, A. E. (1989). A model for managing epilepsy in a rural community in Africa. *British Medical Journal, 298*, 235–268. https://doi.org/10.1136/bmj.298.6676.805

Watts, A. E. (1992). The natural history of untreated epilepsy in a rural community in Africa. *Epilepsia, 33*(3), 464–468.

Winkler, A. S., Mayer, M., Ombay, M., Mathias, B., Schmutzhard, E., & Jilek-Aall, L. (2009). Attitudes towards African traditional medicine and Christian spiritual healing regarding treatment of epilepsy in a rural community of northern Tanzania. *African Journal of Traditional, Complementary and Alternative Medicines, 7*(2), 162–170.

WHO. (2001). *International Classification of Functioning, Disability and Health (ICF).* Retrieved April 10, 2016 from http://www.who.int/classifications/icf/en/

WHO. (2005). *Atlas: Epilepsy care in the world.* Geneva, CH: WHO.

WHO. (2015). *Sixty-eighth World Health Assembly adopts resolution on epilepsy.* Retrieved December 13, 2016 from http://www.who.int/mental_health/neurology/epilepsy/resolution_68_20/en/ on

WHO. (2016). *Epilepsy.* Retrieved October 16, 2016 from http://www.who.int/mediacentre/factsheets/fs999/en/

Harmful Cultural Practices against Women and Girls in Ghana: Implications for Human Rights and Social Work

Alice Boateng and Cynthia A. Sottie

Ghana, located on the west coast of Africa, and the first African country to gain independence from British colonial rule, boasts a rich and diverse cultural heritage. Ghana has a population of about 27.8 million, with 45 percent being rural and 51.2 percent female (National Population Council, 2017). Ghana has been experiencing an economic growth rate of 7 percent per year since 2010, although wide disparities continue to exist (Cooke et al., 2016). Ghana, which has been a democratic nation since 1992, has enjoyed relative peace and is often a haven for people from countries experiencing instability in the region.

Ghana is home to about 100 linguistic and cultural groups categorized under the Niger-Congo language family. Ethnic groups across the world have specific cultural or traditional practices, which reflect beliefs held by members for periods often covering generations. In this volume, Olaore, Drolet, and Olaore, in chapter 2, discuss harmful cultural practices related to widowhood, inheritance, and property, and cultural responses to infidelity in the Nigerian context, while in chapter 8 Muchacha, Matsika, and Nhapi discuss the phenomenon of child marriages among the Apostolic sect of Zimbabwe. Some of these beliefs are beneficial to members, while others are controversial, and harmful to specific groups, such as women or girls. Harmful traditional practices are practices that are justified on grounds of religion or culture but violate international human rights norms. These practices, under international law, fall under contemporary forms of slavery (Ame, 2011; UN Office of the High Commission for Human Rights [UNOHCHR], 2013). Countries across the world have signed and ratified laws to protect women/girls and children; though there has been some progress in implementation of these laws, it has been very slow, particularly for the most marginalized, with serious gaps and violations across the world, including Ghana (UNICEF, 2011).

This chapter is intended to generate discussions on these negative practices, with reference to Ghana, to create some awareness of the topic's importance, in line with the struggle for gender equality and women's human rights. The chapter provides the definition, reasons, and the effects of each of these practices. It further discusses some efforts made to address them and examines the effectiveness of these efforts. Finally, the implications of these practices and the way forward are deliberated. The harmful cultural/traditional/religious practices discussed in this chapter are: widowhood rites, widow inheritance, female genital mutilation/cutting (FGM/C), female ritual bondage (trokosi), and early marriage.

Widowhood Rites

Widowhood rites are cultural practices/rituals that a bereaved spouse goes through upon becoming a widow. The death of a husband can be very devastating, stressful, and traumatic for a wife, since it involves a physical, emotional, and psychological break in their union. This should be a period to sympathize with and care for the widow, but unfortunately, it is often not the case. Instead, in many African countries, culture demands that a widow go through certain traditional mourning practices, before and after the burial of her husband. Although it is prescribed for both widows and widowers, the latter goes through less harsh rituals than the former. Widowhood rites are found in every community in Africa, and the harsh treatment meted out to widows emanates from the husband's family, tradition, and the society as a whole (Dolphyne, 2005; Limann, 2003). The nature and duration of the rites differ from one traditional society to another, due to the specific common beliefs of each group, cause of death, and the age and number of children of the widow at the time of her husband's death (Sossou, 2002). However, the common theme that runs through widowhood rites is that widows in all cultures suffer isolation, marginalization, and discrimination.

Widowhood rites are practised across the different ethnic groups in Ghana, including the Akan, Ewe, Ga, and in some communities in the northern regions, though there might be some differences in the form the rituals take. Among these groups, custom requires that the widow go through certain extensive endurance rituals in the process of mourning her husband. These rituals sometimes include seclusion, prescribed dress code, walking barefoot, fasting for a period, and, in more extreme cases, enduring the application of pepper to her eyes, sleeping in the same room where the corpse is laid, and bathing with water used to wash the corpse (UN Development Programme [UNDP], 2007; Korang-Okrah & Haight, 2014; Sossou, 2002). Some reasons put forth for observation of widowhood rites include bidding farewell to the dead, proving the widow's innocence of husband's death, showing that a widow really loved her husband, receiving blessings from the husband's spirit rather than incur bad luck for failure to go through the rites, and purifying oneself, since a widow is seen as impure and contaminated (Edemikpong, 2005; Sossou, 2002). That there are, however, no extensive widower rites for men clearly shows the inequality between men and women.

A common characteristic of these practices is that they are linked to women's sexuality and are often enforced as a way to keep women in subordinate roles. In African culture, women have always taken a subordinate role to men (Dolphyne, 2005). Through the socialization process, males view themselves as breadwinners and heads of households while females are socialized to be obedient and submissive. This conditioning diminishes the ability of women to challenge societal norms, customs, and practices, rooted in religion and culture, that are perpetuated by the patriarchal value system.

Widow Inheritance

Widow inheritance is a customary practice whereby a widow is compelled to marry her deceased husband's brother or the agnatic heir of the deceased. The decision as to who marries the widow may be made without her consent. This practice is to ensure that a widow and her children continue to be supported by the deceased man's estate and family. A widow who refuses to marry her brother-in-law may forfeit her late husband's land and other properties and may have to return her bride price (Dolphyne, 2005; International Fund for Agricultural Development [IFAD], 1998; Korang-Okrah & Haight, 2014; Perry et al., 2014;). According to the authors just cited, some of the harsh treatments meted out to widows in Ghana are gradually disappearing. However, in certain areas such as in the northern regions, and within some Akan rural communities, widow inheritance is still a common practice.

The fact that widows can be inherited presupposes that women are considered property inheritable, which undoubtedly is an insult to their dignity. Problems that may emerge in widow inheritance include rivalry, especially if the new husband already has a wife, and the likelihood that little attention may be given to the deceased's wife and children, since he may love and pay more attention to his own nuclear family. The widow may contract infections, including HIV/AIDS, because of the new husband having multiple partners (Oluoch & Nyongesa, 2013; Perry et al., 2014). In Ghana, widowhood rites have been criticized for the severity of the rituals and their effect on widows. This has led to the introduction of a provision in the criminal law that makes it an offence for a person to compel a bereaved spouse to undergo any custom or practice that is harmful or cruel in nature (Government of Ghana [1960], Section 278A).

Female Genital Mutilation/Cutting (FGM/C)

Female genital mutilation, also known as female genital cutting, or female circumcision, is a traditional practice that involves the cutting and removal of part of the female sexual organ. There are three main types of FGM/C, namely clitoridectomy—the removal of the clitoral prepuce or tip of the clitoris; excision—the removal of the clitoris and the inner lips of the female external genitalia or labia minora; and infibulation—the removal of the clitoris, labia minora, and parts of the labia majora (WHO, 2008). An additional type is classified under other mutilations that affect the female genitalia. According to the WHO's estimation, 100 to 130 million girls/women have gone through FGM/C in Africa, Asia, and the Middle East. In Ghana FGM/C is practised among a few ethnic groups in the three northern regions, namely, the Frafras, Kusasis, Nankanis, Wallas, Busangas, Sisalas, Builsas, and Dagarbas. It also exists in some southern areas of Ghana where migrants from neighbouring countries reside and have transported their customs with them (UNICEF, 2011). Many superstitions and beliefs add to the supposed reasons for the existence of FGM/C. These include preservation of tradition, preservation of virginity before marriage, ensuring fidelity during marriage, initiation of girls into womanhood, fulfillment of religious requirements, enhancement of fertility, preventing promiscuity of women/girls, enhancing male sexual pleasure, and keeping the female clean, beautiful, and hygienic. FGM/C is thus considered an essential part of raising a girl, and a way to initiate her into adulthood and marriage (UNOHCHR, 2015; WHO, 2008, 2018).

The negative consequences associated with FGM/C revolve around the health risks of this practice. It exposes women/girls to severe medical risk, which violates their right to health. Considered as a health risk, FGM/C is now regarded as an act of violence against women (UNOHCHR, 2013; WHO, 2018), sometimes with fatal consequences, including death (UNOHCHR, 2015). The practice is recognized as discriminatory because it treats women and girls differently from men and boys (UNPD, 2007). Its short-term complications may include infection, severe pain, injury to surrounding genital tissue, and urinary problems. Infections (e.g., tetanus), wound healing problems, hemorrhage, or shock from blood loss can lead to psychological damage and, potentially, death. The possible long-term effects may include difficulty with urination and menstruation, painful sexual intercourse, obstructed labour, and contracting HIV as the same unsanitary tools (such as unclean shards of glass, razor blades, etc.) are used to perform the surgery on many different women without being sanitized between procedures. Other effects include psychological problems (anxiety, depression, post-traumatic stress disorder, low self-esteem)

(UNICEF, 2011; WHO, 2008). In Ghana, the Criminal Code Amendment Act 484 was passed in 1994 to criminalize FGM/C.

Female Ritual Bondage—The Troxovi System

Female ritual bondage is one of the cultural practices in Ghana that human rights activists and the Ghana government have fought for years to eradicate. In 1998, Ghana passed a law against ritual or customary servitude that carried a three-year prison sentence for those caught in the practice (Government of Ghana, 1998, Section 13.1). However, no one has been imprisoned and the practice continues, an indication that in Ghana compulsion is ineffective in ending cultural and religious practices that are deemed harmful. Ghanaian researchers have carried out studies on the practice (see Ababio, 2000, Akpabli-Honu, 2014; Ameh, 2001, Asomah, 2015; Bilyeu 1999; Dovlo & Adzoye, 1995; Nukunya & Kwafo, 1998). The practice is prevalent among the Ewe and Dangbe and the Fon of Benin, as well as in South West Nigeria and Togo. Among the important questions to be answered are: What is the origin of this practice? What motivates it? Why does the law not serve as deterrence?

Female ritual bondage is known in the local language as *troxovi* (pronounced trohorvi). This term literally means "the deity or god who receives a child" (Akpabli-Honu, 2014, p. 1). The practice, which according to Robson (2006) commenced somewhere in the 16th century in Nigeria, requires female virgins to be given to a deity for services rendered and in atonement for crimes committed by a family member to prevent the anger of the deity from destroying the family through sickness, death, and other calamities (Ameh, 2001; Dovlo & Adzoye, 1995; Kufogbe & Dovlo, 1998; Nukunya, 2003). The young maiden may not know the perpetrator of the crime personally, but affiliation through family ties is enough for her to be used as atonement. The female virgin is referred to as a *Trokosi* (pronounced trokoshi). This means wife or slave of a deity. Among some ethnic groups, she is referred to as *Fiasidi*, which literally means wife of a chief, where the chief in this case is the deity (Akpabli-Honu & Agbanu, 2014). In Ghana, this practice is found in the southern parts of the country, among the Ewe and the Ga ethnic groups. The authors will, however, focus on the Ewe in the southern Volta region. The terms used to describe the practice are therefore in the Ewe language.

The origin of the practice has been documented by Akpabli-Honu (2014), Glover (1992), and Nukunya (2003). The caution here is that there are several versions of its origin because these accounts are based on oral tradition that relies on memory and hence some details may be inaccurate. Robson (2006) noted that it started in Nigeria but spread through migration of the Ewe people from the Niger Delta. As narrated by oral tradition, historically, education of children was carried out at the clan level. Every clan was linked to a deity and education took place through shrines. This education covered a wide range of fields from psychology to morality and ethics, vocational skills, and child care (Glover, 1992). The original intention of the *troxovi* system as documented by these authors was to train young girls to become responsible members of society and transfer the knowledge they had acquired to their children.

Some researchers have placed blame for the adulteration of the practice on Western education. Western education took over traditional education and, to ensure cultic schools (schools grounded in a system of religious worship, characterized by rites and ceremonies) did not lose out, men who seduced any of the girls were made to atone with a female virgin from their family. Furthermore, offences and requests for services from the shrines (e.g., fertility, prosperity, and cure for diseases) were paid for by committing female virgins to shrines (Glover 1992). The latter was originally paid for with animals, but this was later replaced with virgin girls. A girl is sent to the shrine without her consent. If she runs away or dies, she must be replaced by another girl from the family because so long as she remains in the shrine the anger of the gods is diverted from the rest of the family. Some girls in ritual servitude are the third or fourth girl in their family atoning for the same offence. Some of these girls are as young as eight years old (Ameh, 2001; Bilyeu, 1999; Dovlo & Adzoye, 1995).

According to Akpabli-Honu (2014), there is psychological compulsion behind this practice, as families are made aware that refusal to send a female virgin to the shrine when requested is equivalent to challenging the gods. This could have serious consequences for the family and generations not yet born. The girls are considered married to the god of the shrine, who is represented by the traditional priest. The priest engages in sexual relations with the girls and they have children for him. The girls work on farms owned by the shrine to take care of their basic needs.

Child Marriage

The ages of marriage and consent to sex in Ghana are 18 years and 16 years respectively. A child under 18 is considered incapable of making decisions regarding marriage. In Ghana, child marriage is illegal and punishable by law. Sections 14 and 15 of the Children's Act (Government of Ghana, 1998) spell out the minimum age, caution against forcing children to marry or to be betrothed, and indicate a penalty of one year in prison and/or a fine.

Ghana's 2011 Multiple Indicator Cluster Survey (MICS) report summarizes the reasons for child marriage as "poverty, protection of girls, family honour and the provision of stability during unstable social periods" (Ghana Statistical Service, 2012, p. 216). Marriage is viewed in the Ghanaian culture as prestigious; it brings respect to a family and safeguards a girl from immoral behaviour and pregnancy outside marriage. For very poor families, marriage provides a way out of poverty. Families are involved in actively searching for an appropriate partner. Furthermore, traditionally, the main contribution of women to society is viewed in terms of being wives, mothers, and homemakers. For communities that do not particularly place much value on female education, in order not to risk pregnancy outside marriage (which is highly stigmatized, lowers the "value" of the girl, and often renders her "unmarriageable" and a liability to parents), she is married off early to a suitor who is willing to pay the marriage price. Marriage price sometimes includes cattle, which in some communities measures the wealth of a family.

These marriages are often contracted without the consent of the child, and sometimes betrothal happens during infancy. Marriage to a rich spouse indicates the girl's family of origin can meet their basic needs. Since marriage in Ghana is contracted between the families and not two individuals, the welfare of a spouse's parents and sometimes siblings becomes one's responsibility.

Statistics from the 2011 MCIS indicate that approximately 6 percent of girls in Ghana married before the age of 15 and about 18 percent before age 18 (Ghana Statistical Service, 2012). Some of these girls are found in polygynous marriages. Early marriage is gendered because compared to the above figures for women, only about 5 percent of men married before age 18. Child marriage is mostly prevalent in the northern parts of Ghana (with the highest being in the Upper East Region—50 percent) but can be found in all the 10 regions (Women in Law and Development in Africa [WiLDAF], 2012), with rural communities having a higher prevalence rate (36 percent) than urban communities (19 percent). Child marriage is most prevalent among poor families. About 41.2 percent of females from poor families married before age 18 as compared to 11.5 percent of those above the poverty line.

Some questions have arisen about the two-year discrepancy between age of consent to sex (16 years) and age of marriage (18 years). If a child of 16 years is not able to take on the responsibilities that come with marriage, is the law implying that this same child is able to take on those responsibilities that come with having sex outside marriage? Some would insist that a child at age 16 is better "protected" in a marriage recognized by both families. The law against defilement (sex with a child under the age of consent) and child marriage appears to imply that marrying a child is less of a crime than defiling a minor. While marrying a child attracts a prison sentence of one year, defilement attracts between 7 and 25 years (Government of Ghana, 1960, Section 101). This may send a wrong message to potential violators of the law. There was a 2009 case in which the principal of a school impregnated a 16-year-old girl and married her (Oye Lithur, 2009). He was charged under Section 15 of the Children's Act (Government of Ghana, 1998) instead of Section 101 of the Criminal Code (Government of Ghana, 1960), and the case was later discharged.

Human Rights versus Harmful Traditional Practices: A Look at Related Instruments

The human rights of women and girls are an inalienable, integral, and indivisible part of universal human rights. The harmful cultural/traditional/religious practices are mainly carried out without the consent of the woman/girl involved, and as such constitute violation of human rights, as stipulated in the Universal Declaration of Human Rights (UN, 1948). These practices have been widely condemned by human rights groups, while proponents of the practices disagree that it is a violation (Ame, 2011; Sarpong, 2012). In Ghana, conventions and laws to enhance the protection of women and the girl child include: the UN Convention on the Rights of the Child (UN, 1989), the Convention on the Elimination of All Forms of Discrimination against Women (CEDAW) (UN, 1979), the African Charter (OAU, 1981), the Constitution of the Republic of Ghana (Government of Ghana, 1992), and the Children's Act of Ghana (Government of Ghana, 1998).

International legal and policy frameworks mandate legislative action to address harmful practices. The Universal Declaration prohibits all forms of discrimination based on sex and ensures the right to life, liberty, and security of persons, recognizes equal protection, and equality before the law, and calls for the elimination of laws, and practices/prejudices that affect women's well-being. Article 5 of the CEDAW (UN, 1979), for instance, charges state parties to take all appropriate measures to modify the social and cultural patterns of conduct of men and women, with a view to achieving the elimination of prejudices that make one sex inferior and the other superior. Article 16(2) also states that the betrothal and the marriage of a child shall have no legal effect, and stipulates that all necessary action, including legislation, be taken to specify a minimum age for marriage and to make the registration of marriages in an official registry compulsory. The Beijing Declaration and Platform for Action (UN, 1995) specifies steps to fully implement all human rights instruments, especially CEDAW, to ensure equality and non-discrimination under the law and in practice, and to promote legal literacy. Nearly 22 years on, these promises have been fulfilled only partially, because they are deeply rooted in traditional (cultural and religious) beliefs, and hence difficult to change.

Besides national efforts, Ghana is noted to be the first country to ratify the 1989 UN Convention on the Rights of the Child (CRC) in 1990 (Twum-Danso, 2011). According to Twum-Danso (2011), Article 24 of the CRC charges state parties to take all effective and appropriate measures to abolish traditional practices prejudicial to the health of children. Article 34 charges state parties to protect the child from all forms of sexual exploitation, contrary to the practice of trokosi, where the deities take the girls as wives. Other rights are the right of the child to education (Article 28, Section1); and protection from torture and cruel treatment (Article 37).

Regional and national instruments also mandate legislative action to address harmful practices: The Protocol to the African Charter on Human and Peoples' Rights on the Rights of Women in Africa (African Commission on Human and People's Rights [ACHPR], 2003) charges state parties to take all legislative and other measures to eliminate all forms of harmful practices that negatively affect human rights of women, including all forms of female genital mutilation. Article 2(5) also stipulates that state parties shall commit themselves to modify the social and cultural conduct of women and men through public education, with a view to achieving the elimination of harmful cultural and traditional practices. As outlined by the 1992 Constitution of the Republic of Ghana (Government of Ghana, 1992), children are not to be subjected to torture, or cruel, inhuman, or degrading treatment or punishment. The Children's Act of Ghana (Government of Ghana, 1998) also addresses non-discrimination (Section 3); the right to grow up with parents (Section 5); the right to education and well-being (Section 8, paras. 1 & 2); and the right to refuse betrothal and marriage (Section 14). The Criminal Code Amendment Act (Government of Ghana, 2003) makes all forms of FGM/C illegal. This code was amended in 2007 to include not only the performers of the operation, but also persons who request or promote FGM/C, as offenders who must face imprisonment or fines.

Harmful traditional practices have also attracted the attention of the United Nations for many years. UN efforts include seminars and conferences on traditional practices affecting the health of women and children held at Ouagadougou, Burkina Faso, in 1991, and at Colombo, Sri Lanka, in 1994; and the World Conference on Human Rights, held in Vienna in 1993. An expert group meeting was held in 1999 on good practices in legislation to address harmful practices against women in Addis Ababa, Ethiopia, where the UN developed a model framework for legislation on violence against women in 2008 (UNOHCHR, 2015). Together with UNICEF and the United Nations Population Fund (UNFPA), the WHO has issued joint statements against the practice of FGM/C, for instance, to support advocacy for its elimination. There has also been a series of strategies/guidelines/resolutions to stop the practice. Some progress has been achieved in combating FGM/C through research, community work, and changes in public policy (UNICEF, 2016).

In Ghana, government, NGOs, and other human rights organizations have made efforts to stop these harmful traditional practices. For instance, on December 10, 2014, the Ministry of Gender, Children and Social Protection, together with the Ministry of Chieftaincy and Traditional Affairs, Action Aid Ghana, and others, held a conference in Accra, on witchcraft accusations, and other human rights violations against women. In northern Ghana, a harmful traditional practice, which is a type of human rights abuse, manifests itself in the form of witchcraft allegations, with the victims (women) confined to witch camps that serve as a refuge for accused/alleged witches. This conference served as a road map for the closure of some of the witch camps in the northern regions of Ghana, and reintegration of the alleged witches into the community, after a comprehensive report of the camps had been submitted to the government in 2012. However, not everyone in the community agrees to the closure of the camps, partly because of the risk of violence against the alleged witches in their original communities. The camps are still in operation, as witchcraft accusations, and death threats, continue to drive women in the northern regions away from their homes (*The Africa Report*, 2014).

Another effort is by the Ghana Baptist Convention, in collaboration with the First Baptist Church of Midland, Michigan, USA. These faith-based organizations established the Baptist Vocational Training Centre at Frankadua in the Asuogyaman District of the Eastern Region of Ghana, where redeemed troxovi girls undertake a three-year course in dressmaking, catering, kente weaving, batik printing, beads making, and hairdressing, among other skills. The centre, established in 1998, graduates more than 20 students a year. The goal of the program is to help the girls/women recover from their traumatic experience, learn to be independent, and adapt to a normal life. Upon completion of their training, and with their specialized skills, they are provided funding to start their own businesses as entrepreneurs. One major concern is that for each girl that is redeemed from the troxovi shrine, her family is obliged to replace her with another girl. As such, there seems to be no end in sight for the troxovi practice.

Despite the support that the human rights conventions enjoy from human rights organizations, and from states who have signed, ratified, and are obliged to respect and obey the laws, many discriminatory, degrading, inhuman treatments, including harmful traditional practices that negatively affect the well-being of women and girls, continue in many parts of the world. It is, however, encouraging that the activities of human rights activists, governments, NGOs, and the UN have resulted in some progress. Harmful traditional practices have been recognized as an issue affecting the human rights of female children and women, and Ghana can do more to eradicate these practices. The upside is that Ghana's ratifying of treaties and putting legislation in place indicates her acceptance of the obligation to ensure these rights.

Implications and the Way Forward

In Ghana, as in other parts of Africa, cultural and societal norms often put groups (children, girls, and women) in difficult circumstances and infringe on their human rights. For instance, there seems to be conflict between the desire to eliminate harmful practices on the one hand and the desire to preserve traditional values on the other. Values are centred on concepts such as obedience, responsibility from an early age, and reciprocity, which conflict with the idea of inalienable rights for individuals and groups (Twum-Danso, 2011). Additionally, in a society that gives power to adults, some see the idea of children's rights as giving too much power to children. The need to accommodate and respect culture, and at the same time adhere to internationally recognized rights of individuals, is challenging (Twum-Danso, 2011, p. 161).

Practices that are founded on religion and culture are difficult to eliminate as indigenes of those communities have much more trepidation about chastisement by the gods for contraventions than punishments by the law of the land, which is human-made and involves only the person who committed the crime. Punishment by a deity is believed to run through generations and to be very severe (abject poverty, incurable diseases, infertility, etc.). The ineffectiveness of the Ghanaian laws in eradicating troxovi and other cultural practices considered harmful such as child marriage and FGM/C, after about two decades since legislation has come into force, attest to how tightly people hold onto such beliefs as well as the fear they have for the supernatural. Knowledge of this fear of the supernatural is also used as a tool by certain individuals and groups to exploit the vulnerable. The troxovi system supplies young virgins to custodians of shrines, who are most often men. Child marriage and FGM/C serve as a source of income for the unemployed.

As one ponders cultural practices and human rights, some of the questions that emerge are: Where do cultural and religious freedoms end, and human rights begin? Given that international human rights conventions and state laws have so far not been as effective as expected, is it time to brainstorm alternatives that are acceptable to all involved? From a social work perspective, is it prudent to make people give up their religious and cultural beliefs and practices without first researching the significance it holds for them? The time has come to adopt a less punitive stance and to engage with custodians of traditional and religious practices to gain a deeper understanding of the beliefs behind these practices and together brainstorm ways in which such beliefs can be expressed without having any harmful effects on the vulnerable. The attitude of "we" are more enlightened than "them" does not encourage dialogue. In Ghana, poverty and unemployment also fuel certain harmful practices. If the local *Wansam* (person who performs FGM/C) is gainfully employed, for instance, cutting girls will no longer be appealing, since it is against the law.

As Sarpong (2012) opined, though these practices are generally held to be harsh, cruel, senseless, and archaic, they cannot just be abandoned, and perpetrators condemned. Rather, the alternative approach is to understand the genesis of the practices, the meanings the groups attach to those practices, and the reasons these practices have been so resilient. In other words, we do not have to use our own methods of change; instead we should adopt explanation, persuasion, and conviction methods. Sarpong (2012), for instance, prefers the term labiadectomy or clitoridectomy, and rejects the term female genital mutilation, to make the reader aware that for those who practice it, it has got nothing to do with mutilation; it is the female version of the male circumcision, meant to usher the initiate into adulthood. Thus, sitting as partners and allowing indigenes of such cultures to educate us signals that we respect them, and this could make them more open to engaging in conversations to modify such practices.

Additionally, there needs to be a liberal approach to the practice of these outmoded/barbaric customs. Social workers can spearhead a social change campaign, to stand against such outmoded and dehumanizing practices. They can advocate for victims' support, for instance, resources for redeemed trokosi girls and widows. The survival of the excluded, especially when they face such hardships, is threatened when they lack support, material resources, and do not enjoy protection from an inclusive group (UNDP, 2007). Oftentimes, among the challenges that face an excluded group is reintegration into a society that is unwelcoming. The alleged witches in the northern regions of Ghana, for instance, refuse to return to their homes and communities, due to the fear of rejection by their own people. Therefore, a meaningful reintegration of such victims includes showing empathy, love, care, and support.

Efforts to change harmful practices or traditions are more effective when they emerge within the culture/community that practises them. The social worker as a mobilizer can adopt the Community Conversation Framework to foster stronger partnership among stakeholders (government, civil society, traditional and religious leaders, gender advocates, the media, the international community, victims, and perpetrators of the practices). This is a tool to promote community discussion and active dialogue and interaction without fear and discrimination, to assist community members in understanding the harmful impact of the traditional practices, and to decide what action to take to abandon these practices (Banda & Atansah, 2016). At this forum, the social worker and other human rights activists can use the media to raise awareness about the negative effects of the practices, explore alternatives, and create public declarations to foster wider public pressure and commitment to support the elimination of the practices. The social worker can also mobilize community members, including students, churches, and assembly members, to declare in public gatherings the need to abandon these practices, and devise their own solutions. Such conversations may not only dramatically decrease the support for the harmful traditional practices but may also direct the government to act on enforcing human rights laws.

It is crucial for social workers to advocate for empowerment of women and girls. Most women/girls in developing countries are not aware of their basic human rights. It is this state of ignorance that fosters the acceptance and, consequently, the perpetuation of harmful traditional practices affecting their well-being and that of their children. Even when women acquire higher education and exercise some awareness, they often feel powerless to bring about the change necessary to eliminate gender inequality (Banda & Atansah, 2006). Empowering women is vital to any process of change and to the elimination of these harmful traditional practices. Social workers should target political empowerment by creating real opportunities for women, girls, and vulnerable people to be active and be heard by people in authority. For instance, why should a girl be silent when she is going to be used at the troxovi shrine as atonement for the sins of her parents or even unknown relatives? Why should marriage be contracted without the consent of the girl child (bride)? In many parts of Africa, long before the girl child attends school, she is disadvantaged by these traditional practices that minimize her potential for educational achievement and self-actualization. This mindset is one that emerges from the day a girl is born and manifests strongly in socialization in the home, eventually justifying harmful rituals and low investment in the girl child (Banda & Atansah, 2016).

There needs to be a shift in the cultural mindsets and behaviours that discriminate against and devalue girls. Social workers should also target the economic empowerment of women and girls, for instance, finding resources to assist them through formal education and vocational skills training, so they have opportunities to gain better livelihoods and, ultimately, a voice in decision-making processes that affect their lives.

Social workers also have a responsibility to promote social justice, in relation to their clients and society in general. This means challenging discriminatory practices, including harmful traditional or cultural practices. The social worker can take the initiative by acquiring knowledge in understanding the negative practices, as well as knowledge on the human rights laws discussed in this chapter. Social workers, in partnership with teachers and other stakeholders, can create educational awareness in schools, lobbying government to cover the traditional practices in the secondary school curriculum. In Burkina Faso, for example, the government assisted in incorporating the risks of FGM/C into their science curriculum and provided anti-FGM/C trainings for teachers, and a Gambian organization, GAMCOTRAP, lobbied the government of Gambia to incorporate the risks of FGM/C into their public-school curriculum (WHO, 2008).

Additionally, social workers can help generate public pressure during public activities and events, such as Independence Day celebrations, festivals, and conferences. These gatherings, where large groups come together, can be used to garner support, and to take a collective stand against these negative practices. People may, for instance, show their support by appending their signatures on a document that would be sent to key stakeholders, such as traditional/religious leaders, government, and both national and international human rights NGOs. Thus, lobbying individuals, organizations, and communities is critical in efforts to eradicate these practices. Also, the lack of scholarly research and the scarcity of contemporary data on these negative practices call for research to understand how the realities women/girls experience as victims affect their lives, since lack of research and accurate demographic data contribute to misconceptions about prevalence and effects of these practices. We suggest that social workers do research on these practices, present their findings to policy makers and at conferences, and publish their work, to add to knowledge on the topic.

Conclusion

Women and girls disproportionately bear the brunt of the harmful cultural practices in society. They are the target of outmoded customs/beliefs/practices intended to control women's behaviour. Ghana is seen as a leader in human rights on the continent, but the country has its share of negative traditional practices. These practices are discriminatory because they treat women and girls differently from men/boys, and are associated with rites that are harmful, degrading, and injurious to the health and welfare of women/girls. Though these practices have received global attention because of their negative impact on females, they persist, and thus reflect society's inhumanity to women, and signify gaps in laws and their enforcement. Though womens' and girls' human rights are more widely understood and championed today, it needs to be the reality for every woman and every girl, including those undergoing harmful traditional/cultural practices. This calls for a concerted effort to increase education about the existence of these laws, enforcing the laws to deal with violations, improving rights awareness in communities, modernizing customary/traditional practices, and partnering with all stakeholders.

REFERENCES

Ababio, A. M. H. (2000). *Trokosi, woryokwe, cultural and individual rights: A case study of women's empowerment and community rights in Ghana.* (Unpublished master's thesis). St. Mary's University, Halifax, NS.

African Commission on Human and People's Rights. (ACHPR). (2003). Protocol to the African Charter on Human and People's Rights on the Rights of Women in Africa. Banjul, GM. https://www.un.org/en/africa/osaa/pdf/au/protocol_rights_women_africa_2003.pdf

Akpabli-Honu, K. (2014). *Female ritual bondage: A study of Troxovi System among the Ewes of Ghana.* Accra, GH: Woeli.

Akpabli-Honu, K., & Agbanu, H. K. (2014). Types and statuses of children of Troxovi shrines. *International Journal of Humanities and Social Studies, 2*(12), 308–317.

Ame, R. K. (2011). *Children's rights, controversial traditional practices, and the Trokosi system: A critical socio-legal perspective.* New York, NY: Lexington Press.

Ameh, R. K. (2001). *Child ritual bondage in Ghana: A contextual policy analysis of Trokosi* (Unpublished doctoral dissertation). Simon Fraser University, Vancouver, BC.

Asomah, J. Y. (2015). Cultural rights versus human rights: A critical analysis of the trokosi practice in Ghana and the role of civil society. *African Human Rights Law Journal, 15,* 129–149.

Banda, J., & Atansah, P. (2016). *An agenda for harmful cultural practices and girls' empowerment.* Center for Global Development. https://www.cgdev.org/publication/agenda-harmful-cultural-practices-and-girls-empowerment

Bilyeu, A. S. (1999). Trokosi—The practice of sexual slavery in Ghana: Religious and cultural freedom vs. human rights. *Indiana International Comparative Law Review, 9*(2), 457–504.

Cooke, E., Hague, S., & McKay, A. (2016). *The Ghana poverty and inequality report.* UNICEF. https://www.unicef.org/ghana/Ghana_Poverty_and_Inequality_Analysis_FINAL_Match_2016(1).pdf

Dolphyne, F. A. (2005). *The emancipation of women: An African perspective,* Accra, GH: Ghana University Press.

Dovlo, E., & Adzoye, K. A. (1995). *Report on the Trokosi institution.* Accra, GH: Department of the Study of Religions, University of Ghana Report Commissioned by International Needs Ghana.

Edemikpong, H. (2005). Widowhood rites: Nigerian women's collective fights a dehumanizing tradition, *Off Our Backs, 35*(3/4), 34–35.

Ghana Statistical Service. (2012). *Ghana multiple indicator cluster survey 2011 final report.* Accra, GH. https://www.dhsprogram.com/pubs/pdf/FR262/FR262.pdf

Glover, Y. (1992). *Vestal virgins* (Unpublished doctoral dissertation). University of Ghana, Accra, GH.

Government of Ghana. (1960). The Criminal Code (Act 29). http://www.wipo.int/edocs/lexdocs/laws/en/gh/gh010en.pdf

Government of Ghana. (1992). Constitution of the Republic of Ghana. http://www.ghana.gov.gh/images/documents/constitution_ghana.pdf

Government of Ghana. (1998). The Children's Act (Act 560). http://www.ilo.org/dyn/natlex/docs/WEBTEXT/56216/65194/E98GHA01.htm

International Fund for Agricultural Development (IFAD). (1998). *Ghana: Mid-Term evaluation of LACOSREP I.* Rome, IT: IFAD Office of Evaluation and Studies.

Korang-Okrah, R., & Haight, W. (2014). Ghanaian (Akan) women's experiences of widowhood and property rights violations: An ethnographic inquiry. *Qualitative Social Work, 14*(2), 224–241.

Kufogbe, S. K., & Dovlo, E. (1998). The geographical spread of Trokosi in Ghana. *Bulletin of the Ghana Geographical Association, 21,* 143–156.

Limann, L. H. (2003). *Widowhood rites and the rights of women in Africa: The Ugandan experience* (Unpublished master's thesis). Makerere University, Kampala, UG.

National Population Council. (2017). *Population of Ghana: Population and the economy factsheet no. 8.* Accra, GH: Government of Ghana.

Nukunya, G. K. (2003). *Tradition and change in Ghana.* Accra, GH: Ghana Universities Press

Nukunya, G. K., & Kwafo, S. K. (1998). *Report on de-criminalizing trokosi: A research into the nature and operations of ritual enslavement in south eastern Ghana.* Accra, GH: National Population Council.

Oluoch, E. A., & Nyongesa, W. J. (2013). Perception of the rural Luo community on widow inheritance and HIV/AIDs in Kenya: Towards developing risk communication messages. *International Journal of Business and Social Science, 4*(1), 213–219.

Organization of African Unity (OAU). (1981). African Charter on Human and People's Rights. https://au.int/en/treaties/african-charter-human-and-peoples-rights

Oye Lithur, N. (2009). *Lamptey-Mills case—Matters arising. Modern Ghana.* https://www.modernghana.com/blogs/246549/lamptey-mills-case-matters-arising.html

Perry, B., Oluoch L., Agot, K., Taylor, J., Onyango, J., Ouma, L., Otieno, C., Wong, C., & Corneli, A. (2014). Widow cleansing and inheritance among the Luo in Kenya: The need for additional women-centred HIV prevention options. *Journal of International AIDS Society, 17*(1), 1–7.

Robson, A. (2006, Oct. 26). Slavery in the name of God. *The Independent,* London. 1–3.

Sarpong, P. K. (2012). *Odd customs, stereotypes and prejudices.* Accra, GH: Sub-Saharan Publishers.

Sossou, M. A. (2002). Widowhood practices in West Africa: The silent victim. *International Journal of Social Welfare, 2*(2), 201–209.

The Africa Report. (2014). *Ghana shuts down witches' camp.* http://www.theafricareport.com/Society-and-Culture/ghana-shuts-down-witches-camp.html

Twum-Danso, A. (2011). Assessing the progress of the 1998 Children's Act of Ghana: Achievements, opportunities, and challenges of the first ten years. In R. K. Ame, D. L. Agbenyiga, & N. A. Apt (Eds.), *Children's rights in Ghana: Reality or rhetoric?* (pp. 151–168). New York, NY: Lexington Books.

UN. (1948). Universal Declaration of Human Rights. http://www.jus.uio.no/lm/un.universal.declaration.of.human.rights.1948/portrait.a4.pdf

UN. (1979). Convention on the Elimination of All Forms of Discrimination against Women (CEDAW). http://www.ohchr.org/Documents/ProfessionalInterest/cedaw.pdf

UN. (1989). Convention on the Rights of the Child (CRC). https://www.unicef.org/crc/

UN. (1995). Beijing Declaration and Platform for Action. Adopted at the Fourth World Conference on Women (Beijing Conference). UN Women, the United Nations Entity for Gender Equality and the Empowerment of Women. https://www.un.org/en/events/pastevents/pdfs/Beijing_Declaration_and_Platform_for_Action.pdf

UN Development Programme (UNDP). (2007). *Ghana human development report: Ghana: Towards an inclusive society*. UNDP, Ghana Office.http://hdr.undp.org/sites/default/files/nhdr_2007_ghana.pdf

UNICEF. (2011). *Ghana's multiple indicator cluster survey report*. https://www.unicef.org/ghana/Ghana_MICS_Final.pdf

UNICEF. (2016). *Female genital mutilation/cutting: A global concern*. http://www.unicef.org/media/files/FGMC_2016_brochure_final_UNICEF_SPREAD.pdf

UN Office of the High Commission for Human Rights (OHCHR). (2013)., *Harmful traditional practices affecting the health of women and children* (Fact sheet No. 23). http://www.ohchr.org/Documents/Publications/FactSheet23en.pdf.

UN Office of the High Commission for Human Rights (OHCHR). (2015). *An assessment of human rights issues emanating from traditional practices in Liberia*. http://www.ohchr.org/Documents/Countries/LR/Harmful_traditional_practices18Dec.2015.pdf.

Women in Law and Development in Africa (WiLDAF). (2012). *Early and Forced marriage and gender based violence*. Accra, GH: WiLDAF.

WHO. (2008). *Eliminating female genital mutilation: An interagency statement*. Geneva, CH: WHO.

WHO. (2018). *Female genital mutilation fact sheet*. http://www.who.int/mediacentre/factsheets/fs241/en/

6

The Intersection of Culture, Religion (Islam), and Women's Human Rights in Ethiopia: Private Lives in Focus

Yania Seid-Mekiye and Linda Kreitzer

Ethiopia is a diversified nation in different aspects such as religion and ethnic background. In 2007, the estimation of the Ethiopian population was 73.9 million (Federal Democratic Republic of Ethiopia [FDRE], 2007). Ethiopia has more than 80 ethnic groups and religions. Among religious groups, the Orthodox Christian are estimated to be 43.5 percent, the Muslim population is 33.9 percent, protestant Christians are 12.6 percent, traditional religious groups are 2.6 percent, Catholic Christians are 0.7 percent, and others 0.6 percent (FDRE, 2007). In Ethiopia, women constitute half of the population (Knoema, n.d.); however, our observation indicates their status in the society is lower than that of the male population.

As a measure for the disadvantaged status of women and for protection of women's human rights, Ethiopia has signed international legal instruments such as the Declaration on the Elimination of Violence Against Women (DEVAW) (UN, 1993) and the Convention on the Elimination of All Forms of Discrimination Against Women (CEDAW) (UN, 1979). National laws such as the Constitution of Ethiopia (Government of Ethiopia, 1995, e.g., Article 35) were formulated to complement the Universal Declaration of Human Rights (UDHR) (UN, 1948) as well as

6

the National Policy on Women (Government of Ethiopia, 1993), which have emphasized the protection of women's human rights.

Despite the presence of international and national legal frameworks, Ethiopian society, like other societies as described in the various chapters of this book, is mainly characterized by patriarchy where men hold more socio-economic and political power than women and exercise authority over women, both in the home and in the public sphere. Ethiopia is also a country where perceptions of religion and culture have a powerful influence over people's lives. Thus, the intersection of culture and religious texts and the translation and interpretation of these texts provide a set of social rules, which play a major role in shaping gender roles that contribute to the perpetuation of gender inequality and violation of women's rights.

Cultural and Religious Texts

Different female Muslim authors have dealt with the male-centred interpretation of Islamic scriptures (Jawad, 1998; Keddie, 2012). As Jawad (1998) discussed, Muslim religious scripture is influenced by culture as well as by the viewpoints of religious scholars, who are usually males. It is not only culture. Time and place also influence the interpretation of the Quran. For instance, Keddie (2012) explains:

> As in other religions, the meaning of scripture has been rendered differently in different times and places. Over the centuries the words of the *Quran* and *hadiths* have been interpreted in ways that are in accord with the beliefs and mores of the time of interpretation. (p. 4)

Keddie (2012) further points out that in past centuries, the Quran was interpreted as being far more male supremacist than its text implies, in a way that emphasized gender-biased traditions; this gender biased interpretation is still dominant among many conservative Muslims. Today, however, new interpretations of the Quran are more accepted as an important means to further gender-egalitarian laws and programs, and Muslims who believe in gender equality often interpret the Quran as supporting such equality. Despite the current egalitarian interpretations, Muslim women's human rights are not fully respected due to male-centred interpretations that are the result of societal norms, values, and related practices.

Regarding male-dominated relationships in Muslim communities, Wadud (2006) argues that the idea of men being superior to women violates the principle of Islam that upholds the superiority/greatness of God/Allah. According to Wadud (2006), if Allah is the greatest and is unique, then there can be no other relationship between any two persons except the one of horizontal reciprocity. The horizontal plane is mutually cooperative because the role of the one can be exchanged with the role of the other with no loss of integrity. However, in the patriarchal framework, man is superior to woman, which is a relationship on a vertical plane, which in turn goes against Islam and establishes a basis for violations of women's human rights.

This study deals with the idea that interpretations of women's rights under Islam and the possible implications for women's human rights generally are profoundly affected by various socio-cultural patterns and economic factors (Barlas, 2002; Mir-Hosseini, 2006; Roald, 2001). Based on this assumption, this chapter discusses the intersection of Islam and culture in relation to three specific areas of Muslim women's human rights: (1) marital relationships; (2) polygamy; and (3) property/inheritance rights.

As social constructivists, the authors believe that Muslim women develop subjective meanings of their experiences as Muslim women. These subjective meanings are varied and multiple and are formed by interaction with others through religious and cultural norms that operate in individuals' lives. This chapter presents research that looked at the intersection of culture, religion, and women's human rights in Ethiopia. The findings reflect the human rights of Muslim women in their families, which are influenced by gender stereotypes, religious interpretations, and culture.

Methodology

For this study, a qualitative research design and descriptive phenomenology was employed. Phenomenology is a research design in which the researcher describes the essence of the experiences for individuals who have all experienced the phenomenon (Creswell, 2014). It helps the researcher to attain a deeper understanding of the nature and meaning of everyday experiences related to the topic of the study. The research questions were: (1) How does the intersection of cultural practices with Islam within the marital relationship affect women's human rights? (2) How do practices of polygamy in Muslim families violate women's human rights? and (3) How do women's rights to work and property inheritance rights intersect with discrimination practised in the name of Islam? To answer these questions, a purposive sampling technique was used to select study participants who have experience and perception of the direct or indirect intersection of religious interpretation, culture, gender relations, and human rights violations. As Patton (2002) indicates, "the purpose of a small purposeful random sample is credibility of the data, not representativeness" (p. 241). Semi-structured interviews were used to collect data from five interviewees, who were selected based on the following criteria: (1) a willingness to share life experiences; (2) experience of one of the three issues such as polygamous relations, marital relationship, and property inheritance concerns; and (3) a claim to knowledge of women's status in Islam. The first author also used her own experience of inheritance-related issues in the family and as a member of the Muslim community in Ethiopia to inform this study.

Findings Regarding Culture, Islam and Women's Human Rights in Ethiopia

This section presents three major themes: (1) the intersection of culture and Islam in the sphere of marital relationships; (2) polygamy practices and women's human rights; and (3) property and inheritance rights. The substantive argument is that Islam is understood and applied in a way that favours men and limits women's human rights in family relationships.

The intersection of culture and Islam in the sphere of marital relationships

In marital relationships discourse among Muslims, the most frequently quoted verse in the Quran is 4:34,[1] which discusses the roles of the husband and wife. The verse is translated in the sense of the husband being the head of the family/wife; some translate it in terms of the husband being the maintainer and protector and the wife as obedient to him. The overall intention of Islam is supposed to be maintaining justice, mercy, and compassion between spouses, but the culture of patriarchy undermines the intentions of Islam.

Patriarchy and the Quran

In practice, in Ethiopia, the teaching of Islam is integrated with patriarchy and used to perpetuate gender inequality, which the study participants consider not to be the intention of Islam. One of the interviewees, Amira (pseudonym) explains:

> Muslims are not living Islam [in the socio-economic aspect] and more is expected from women with the fact that we [Muslims] have a culture in which women are expected to live an Islamic life whereas the men are expected to live as they want. . . . We see the men live as they want whether they could live according to Islamic framework or not.

The above statement indicates that when only women are expected to follow the Islamic rules and regulations, the result is suppression, whereas both parties equally fulfilling their responsibilities would result in a just and fair relationship. The interviewee further indicates that legitimizing these skewed relations begins when the marriage is established. When couples live together, Islam is mostly forgotten but emerges again whenever necessary to legitimize men's power and rights, and women's responsibility. If the marriage is terminated, there is also the tendency to go back to Islamic principles and use them in a way that favours men. Similarly, another participant indicated that some Muslim husbands' act like "small gods," thus creating an unequal marital partnership of superior and inferior beings. This serves as an instrument for the violation of women's human rights in the name of Islam. Similarly, Muslim women scholars such as Al-Hibri (2000), Barlas (2002), and Wadud (1999) have different points of view on the verse and its implications in relation to human rights. These authors argue that the Quran itself has no intention of endorsing such unfair behaviour in marital relationships. The core problem is the way its teachings are adopted by most of the traditional interpreters of certain verses, which tend to be male biased.

Religious preaching programs

Supporting the views of the Muslim women scholars mentioned above, four of the study participants, Amira, Nefisa, Zainab, and Naeema (pseudonyms), indicated that in their religious preaching program, Muslim preachers (most of whom are men) treat scriptures in a way that perpetuates a teaching of superiority among men and makes them unaccountable for how they treat their wives. Often this leads to the violation of women's human rights. For instance, Nefisa explained:

> The *daees* [preachers] tell you the types of Hadith [sayings of the prophet, which are stated by the respective men of the time] that perpetuate the superiority of men without considering the other side of the Hadith. They just tell you the Hadith supports their superiority; however, there are several Hadith that help people to be morally kind. Since they are the ones who are preachers, they tell you what is good for them. Of course, they are superior in the culture too, since we [women] grew up with the expectation of going to the kitchen while they are expected to enjoy and work. And the *daawa* [The act of preaching in the Muslim religion] program tells you to [only] be obedient and explains the right of man [husband], but your [women's] rights are not told to you.

The idea that men automatically gain the right to be the leader of the family, as commonly accepted and practised among Muslims, reflects inequality and represents a violation of women's rights (Al-Hibri, 2000; Barlas, 2002 & Wadud, 1999). Furthermore, Barlas (2002) argues that even though the Quran charges the husband with being the breadwinner, it does not designate him head of the household. This interpretation is strongly motivated to sustain the patriarchal system that is very dominant among Muslims (Adnan, 2004).

Women, obedience, and human rights

It is not only culture and men's understanding of Islam that have an impact on women's human rights protection and violations. Some women understand Islam as protecting their rights, whereas others interpret some women-related issues in the Quran literally, word-for-word, instead of considering the context. As a result, they disregard the justice aspect of Islam, thus keeping themselves within the abusive relationship. For instance, one participant, Zainab (pseudonym) justified her husband's right over her as follows:

> I believe that the husband is *'ameer'* (leader), so that he must be respected, accepted, be loved and [I must] always be truthful to him. As a Muslim woman this is what is expected from me, so I must apply it. The problem is that what if my husband could not be a respected Muslim husband? Should I obey or what? I do not want to be obedient in the issue which is not important to me and to the family.

Similarly, another participant, Naeema, explained that though there is the idea of obedience in Islam, husbands who do not value women's rights need to be stopped.

> I do not accept boosting their ego with telling them that "Allah ordered women to be obedient," as we must be capable to stop our husbands using that [Islamic expectation of women's obedience] to their advantage. It is not always so since there is the place to be obedient and disobedient. You must consider whether the person is worthy enough to obey him or not. I am trying to be obedient when he deserves and when I do not believe, I just "pretend," which he considers positively; since as any traditional person, they want us [women] to say OK [in any kind of interaction]. When their [husband's] action is beyond the limit and touching our [women's] dignity, then we must stop them.

Contrary to the above quotations, Amira offered another understanding of obedience:

It is Allah, who ordered me to be obedient, not he. Even if he is a bad man, I must be obedient considering that I will get a return [reward] from Allah. I believe that Allah ordered me to do so and even if the man is bad, Allah will make him good to me.

Similarly, another participant explained:

In Islam, there is no formula of I do not care. Whether he becomes obedient or disobedient to me, Allah says for me to "be obedient" so that I must be obedient, but we are in competition with each other. Therefore, we are not living as Islam.

Thus, women's understanding of obedience in the Quran are different depending on their own cultural and religious socialization.

Male role as protector

Al-Hibri (2000) states that men can be *qawwamuna* (responsible/ protector/maintainer) when they fulfill two conditions: (1) being the financial maintainer of the woman; and (2) possessing the qualities needed to advise the woman in reaching a decision when she needs his help to do so. Like Barlas (2002) and Wadud (1999), Al-Hibri (2000) also argues that without these two qualifications, which may change from time to time and from one situation to another, men may not even assume to provide advice, let alone to be a responsible protector/maintainer. It is also further argued that the exegesis that establishes the husband as a ruler over his wife or, at the very least, as the head of the household, ignores the fact that the Quran appoints women and men as each other's mutual protectors. In verse 9:71–72, it states that "the believing men and women are allies of one another. They enjoy what is right and forbid what is wrong. . . . Allah has promised the believing men, the believing women gardens beneath which rivers flow . . . (translated by Saheeh International, 2004), which it could not do if men were superior to women (Barlas, 2002; Wadud, 1999).

The way religion makes a difference in marital life depends on many factors, including the importance of religion to the individual and the extent of devoted practices, as well as specific beliefs and the rewards expected from faith (Hatch & Schumm, 2003). Meanwhile, the Quran says, "Be persistently standing firm in justice, witnesses for Allah, even if it be against yourselves or parents and relatives. . . . So follow not [personal] inclination, lest you not be just. . . ." (Quran, 4:135, translated by Saheeh International, 2004). Therefore, unless Muslim women come to terms with justice within Islam and become empowered, it will be difficult to deal with Muslim women's rights violations in the name of religion and culture. This means that a continuous effort of educating Muslim women is necessary to help them become aware of the patriarchal culture within Islam that is used as pretext against Muslim women's human rights.

Polygamy Practices and Women's Human Rights

Polygamy is one of the most controversial topics in relation to Islam and women's rights. This is caused by differences in the interpretation of the Quran verses 4:3,[2] and 4:129,[3] which talk about men's alternative choices for multiple marriages to two, three, or four women, meanwhile warning men of their responsibility of maintaining justice among wives.

The Quran and polygamy

The verses having to do with fairness in the Quran can be understood in two ways, in material terms and in terms of love/compassion. The quotes state that "you will never be able to be equal [in feeling between wives], even if you should strive [to do so]." In this case, the inability to be fair, particularly in terms of love and compassion, is recognized. In the meantime, the Quran also states, in verse 4:3, that if you cannot give justice to all wives then marry only one (translated by Saheeh International, 2004).

Hassen (2006) indicates that though polygamy was permitted by the Quran and it was only used in the context of safeguarding the property or rights of orphans, it has been widely misused in Muslim families (Hassan, 2006; Jawad, 1998). In addition, Islam regulated polygamy by limiting the number of wives and presented it as the then solution for the social crisis that happened because of the increasing number of widows and orphaned children, which was the result of the war between the followers of Islam and those against it (Barlas, 2002; Hassan, 2006; Jawad, 1998). In addition, in the Ethiopian context, having more than one wife can be a social choice and solution. For instance, when the first wife gets tired and unable to satisfy her husband sexually, and if the husband's sexual desire is strong, they have to agree on one of the following alternatives: (1) he has to abstain and live without satisfaction; (2) he has to divorce her and marry another woman; (3) he has to establish an extramarital relationship; or 4) she has to agree that he will have a second marriage. With these alternatives, either both partners compromise in each other's interests or they quit their marriage based on consent. However, the reality is different. In Ethiopia, most polygamous marriages among Muslims happen regardless of the first wife's agreement. Men marry as they wish, whether the first wife agrees or not. In this case, the first wife's status as partner is meaningless; instead the woman's status in that family is as the sexual property of the husband.

Polygamy and women's status and health

Among the knowledgeable members of the Muslim community, polygamy may be attributed to lack of understanding of women's status in Islam, chauvinistic attitudes, or to men ignoring the first wife and marrying as they wish. The case of one study participant is presented as follows:

> Munira (pseudonym) separated (not divorced) from her husband and had six children and lived for 20 years with her husband. When she gave birth to her 6th child, her husband left her for another woman and married this woman secretly. This second wife of the family was widowed and had two children. After two months of his second marriage, he told Munira about this second marriage. She said there were two reasons for his marriage: 1) "the woman [his second woman] is alone and needs a supporting person near to her"; and 2) his right to a second marriage. Her argument was that "if he wanted to marry another woman, he has to let me know before that marriage, and at that time, I may allow him. But what he did was to undermine me with the perception that I cannot do anything." When Munira heard about the marriage of her husband, she left her husband's home with her three younger kids to go to her mother's home. When she was requested to return to him, Munira provided two

alternatives: 1) divorce; and 2) leave his second marriage. The man refused to divorce either woman as he wanted to be married to both. Munira was requesting . . . a divorce until the data collection for this research but the man continued to refuse. She has also requested to have some of his property for her children and again the man refused to respond. At the time of this study, she was living with her six children as a single mother in her brother's house. After her separation, she was criticized not only by him, but also by the rest of the men from her ethnic community due to her rejection of his second marriage. Right after his marriage, she had experienced psychological and emotional violence that was observed on her face as well as weight loss (which she also mentioned as an impact of her condition).

When polygamy is practised in disregard of the will of wives, it affects women's social status, economic position, and health, and consequently, it violates women's human rights such as the right to dignity and security. According to Abd Al 'Ati (1995), the role of the husband in the Quran states that it is his solemn duty to God to treat his wife with kindness, honour, and patience, to keep her honourably or free her from the marital bond honourably, and to cause her no harm or grief. Therefore, this participant's case is contrary to Islam and the Ethiopian Constitution's rights to liberty and freedom.

Polygamy hurts first wives, as well as second or later wives, emotionally and psychologically. As there are many negative factors that could arise in a polygamous marriage, one might question why a young woman would enter a polygamous marriage with an older man, or at least a married man. Is marrying a married man the right of women or not? As mentioned earlier, the marital relationship in patriarchal society does not involve only those who are in the relationships; there is also the societal institution itself that mainly depends on the society's cultural traditions. When women get divorced, are widowed, or are relatively older, their chances to marry single men are limited.

Therefore, women in such societies are obliged to marry, if possible, a single man; otherwise, they will join the already established family as the second, third, or fourth wife. For instance, one of the first author's cousins, who is in a polygamous relationship, mentioned to her that "no one wants to be the second wife unless it is with the intention of having children." There is also one of the first author's sisters, who stayed in Saudi Arabia for a decade, and when she came back to Ethiopia, she was much older. Therefore, she was obliged to marry as the second wife. This is because Ethiopian society does not allow women to stay single, and she is forced to have children. Thus, to submit to the society's expectations, women also do not want to stay single or remain childless. In the meantime, it is prohibited to give birth outside of marriage. Therefore, in this case, it is the societal culture that forces women to engage in the polygamous marriage. However, women involved in polygamous relationships see it as in their interest to get married. To summarize, women's engagement in a polygamous marital relationship holds a hidden power of gender inequality that perpetuates itself, which in turn makes violations of women's human rights (such as the right to freedom) a normal part of daily life.

The right to work, and inheritance of property

The Quran generally supports women's rights to acquire, hold, use, administer, and organize property and inherit family property, though there are certain differences in the understanding of the Quran's prescription of family inheritance. However, property inheritance as a right of women in Islam was hijacked by the oppressive socio-economic context of the then pre-Islamic Arabia, and the socio-cultural context of the society in which Muslim women lived and the expected role or function of a male or female within it (Barlas, 2002; Jawad, 1998; Syed, 2004).

The right to work and own property

In relation to work and property rights, throughout the first author's experience as a member of the Muslim society, Muslim women in general can work and own property, which is also supported by the Quran.[4] However, there are two special cases in which women are denied work and property rights: (1) level of understanding of Islam; and (2) the socialization of women to be dependent on family males. First, in some Muslim families, women are denied the right to work because of the assumption that it is the husband who is supposed to be the breadwinner. Although the Qur'an charges the husband with the duty of being the breadwinner in the verse 4:34, this does not mean women cannot or should not provide for themselves. It simply means that the Qur'an does not expect women to be the breadwinners (Barlas, 2002; Wadud, 1999). For example, husbands who are unable to provide for their wives' make them economically needy throughout their life. Second, in most families, women grow up and are socialized to be dependent on the men of their family, and therefore they do not challenge the status quo. Despite these facts, if male family members agree (which also depends on the wife's ability to claim their rights), or she is determined to work and become independent, the wife can work and control her own property. However, the problem is that Islam is used to prohibit women's right to work instead of emphasizing men's responsibilities. For instance, Zainab explained:

> Most Ethiopian married Muslim status is really confusing in many aspects. This is because, firstly, there is no system that protects women in terms of Sharia. Theoretically, the Sharia system protects women. In the place where there is the application of Islam, women and children must not get hungry. Before the beginning, when women are created, fathers are responsible to fulfil at least their basic needs. . . . If there is no father, the uncle is responsible to protect her. But, in our case, which uncle thinks and feels responsible to protect women and children? If there is no uncle, then a brother is responsible, [and] here again, there might not be a brother, and even if there is, they are busy. When she gets married, the husband is responsible. And, even if it is a must for her to work and protect herself, she does not have access, with the fact that Muslim men understand that women must stay at home. Therefore, women are denied access to education, and then job and then to protect herself. When she is denied access to work, then she is also denied access to power.

The above quote indicates that women's right to work is affected directly and indirectly. In some Ethiopian Muslim families, men claim that it is their right to control their wives, and in the name of sharia they refuse to allow their wives to go out to work. There are also cases where, when female students go to high school, it is assumed they are ready for marriage, and that this is a priority for Muslim girls. After marriage, they mostly depend on their husbands' income and the level of his awareness and devotion in supporting them. Therefore, in the case of women's right to work, the nature of rights abuse is directly and indirectly influenced by the culture of the society and level of understanding of Islam.

Family property and inheritance right

Among most Ethiopian Muslims, including the first author's own family, the problem of inheritance and property ownership lies in the nature of the woman's right to own family property and inheritance rights. From Islamic point of view, the existing rule for sharing family inheritance is that women are entitled to half of that of the male family members, which is stated in Quran verses 4:11, 4:12, and 4:176. These verses indicate that a daughter gets half of what a son gets, a brother receives double shares compared to his sister, and the share of the surviving wife is half of what a surviving husband would receive from the deceased family member. The purpose of the differential rule of inheritance is that the male is expected to fulfill all family responsibilities, whereas the female invests her share for personal purposes unless she wants to share with family. However, these female family members' inheritance rules are used to discriminate against women (Jawad, 1998; Syed, 2004).

As stated above, verses of the Quran such as 4:34[5] and 65:6–7[6] stipulate that all financial family responsibility belongs to male family members. But in most families in Ethiopian Muslim society, it is the opposite when it comes to taking care of their families. Many women in general, and Muslim women in particular, become the heads of their households and play a major part in providing for their families. What is the solution where Muslim men fail to fulfill their family maintenance responsibility and Muslim women become the sole responsible persons in the family maintenance, domestic, and reproductive roles as well? In this case, first, women must consider verses such as 4:32[7] and 4:40[8] from the Quran to protect their rights, which may be violated through the misogynistic interpretation of verse 4:34 of the Quran.

Secondly, the right to get a *mahr* (dowry/obligatory marriage gift) from their husbands, stated by 4:4[9] of the Quran, would give women financial security in their marital lives. Therefore married women have to maintain such rights to address the problems they experience when the issue of inheritance and property rights becomes contested. Thirdly, in cases where the woman of the family cannot get married, or the male family member, whether he is father, brother, or son, does not fulfill his responsibility, it would be necessary to examine the provisions of the Quran in 2:180[10] and 2:181[11] that deal with bequests which provide additional rights to the property of the deceased, apart from the Quranic shares stated earlier.

Despite different problems related to the interpretations of the Quran and the presence of Quran-based solutions, the woman's contribution, and her family responsibilities, the gender-differentiated Islamic inheritance rules have mostly endured. Also, most Muslim women abstain from challenging the apparent discrimination practised in the name of Islam due to their low level of knowledge about their status in Islam, lack of awareness of how to deal with their rights as Muslims, and their belief that submitting to the male family members is the duty of women.

In addition, in the context of property and inheritance rights for women, culture seems to have prevailed. This means that in Muslim society and community, customary norms through family and ethnic community structures seem to have overshadowed Islamic principles of justice by making property and inheritance rights often merely theoretical, or even used to disadvantage women. For instance, one interviewee, Zainab, stated that the "real intention of the *Sharia* [Muslim-based law from the Quran, Hadith, and consensus of Muslim religious scholars] and its safety and protection mechanism[s] for women and maintenance of justice are forgotten. Instead they are used as a pretext to deny women their socio-economic rights." The customary understanding of sharia is also in terms of restricting women rather than benefiting/protecting their rights and maintaining justice. Sharia does not oppose humanity, so the denial of women's rights and protection is opposite to sharia; however, sharia is used as a pretext to deny women's basic rights.

When it comes to culture, particularly in rural Ethiopia, families often fear that it is inappropriate for a girl to be given property because she will eventually marry and leave her natal family to become part of her husband's family. Thus, if she takes any property with her, she essentially removes it from her family to a new family. In this way, women only receive a half-share of the property from the natal family in inheritance form as well as of her own property from her husbands' family. Therefore, women experience double restrictions of property and inheritance rights. Recently, the Ethiopian government ordered wives' names to be registered in the land ownership registration at *Kebele/district* level. The registration was done but mostly remains in name only; the right to use and control the land and related products remains in the hands of men. Thus, access to property is theoretically there in most parts of rural Ethiopia in the land rights registration card, but control and benefit of the land is minimal. In this regard, it is not the country's official law governing women's rights to property but rather culture and gender that are governing the women's economic rights. In most Muslim communities this is associated with Islam, which silences women from claiming any kind of property rights.

Discussion

The Quran[12] addresses the priority of justice in human relationships, which is also the basis for women's human rights in Muslim society. However, in Muslim families or communities women's human rights are violated in the name of Islam by interpreting some verses from the Quran and the prophetic Hadith that permit differential treatment of women and men based on their functional roles. This interpretation stems from a lack of understanding of the context of the ' verses, which were originally revealed as a solution for specific problems. If women's human rights are to be protected, the religious sources must be interpreted in the context of the period in which they were written and the spirit of the message—especially equity—must be applied to our times (Barlas, 2002; Jawad; 1998; Wadud, 1999). Organizing Muslim women in different associations and dealing with their rights as women has paramount importance in this regard. Some Muslim male scholars can also help when women try to make a difference. Moreover, with the current political condition of the country,

Ethiopia has a great opportunity to use Islamic rules and regulation in the way that is more favourable to women in the context of the time. This is because currently Ethiopia is undergoing dramatic political change that has affected the civil rights of citizens and equal representation of women in ministerial positions. This political change is also impacting Muslims' participation in party politics, which the authors believe will encourage interpretation of the religious sources that is more compatible with equity and protection of human rights of women in socio-economic and political aspects of the country.

In addition to consideration of the verses of the Quran in the context of their original revelation, holistic understanding of the Quran would be part of a healing solution for gender justice within Muslim communities. Usually individual verses are taken out of context, distorting the intended meaning and purposes. Therefore, to enable better understanding of the Quran as a basis for the Muslim women's human rights protection, all verses related to the same subject should be taken into consideration when finding an appropriate interpretation. Wadud (1999) states:

> The way to believe in 'the whole of the book' (3:119) is to recognize that 'spirit' of the book and accept its worldview, vision, and ultimate intent. In examining the Qur'an, we need 'to accurately determine the rationales behind its statements, comments and injunctions'. (p. 81)

The above quote from a Muslim female scholar, Amina Wadud, indicates that unless Muslim scripture (Quran) is understood and interpreted holistically, it is be easy for it to be co-opted by specific societal cultures and gender relations within Muslim families that in turn legitimize violations of women's human rights in the name of Islam.

When dealing with Ethiopian Muslim women's human rights, focusing on the woman's rights as an individual rather than as part of the extended family, and basing them on international laws and disregarding religious precept, does not address the challenges of the majority of Muslim women. Individualistic advocacy, based on a secularist view of women's human rights, may be important for a few educated Muslim women who are not dependent on the economic support of their families. But a relativist view, rather than a universalist claim of human rights, is important for the protection of the' human rights of the majority of women in the current context of gender relations among the Ethiopian Muslim population. This is because advocating for the rights of women as individuals, while they live in the Muslim family, will not help women to achieve their intended rights; rather it may result in annihilation of individual women or resistance of the Muslims in general, or disintegration of families. Therefore, working for the protection of each woman's human rights for the benefit of all with whom she lives is of paramount importance to the empowerment of women and protection of their rights. Besides, some restrictions made on the rights and responsibilities of Muslims that emanate from the Quran also need to be considered from the relativist perspective of human rights. Therefore, advancement of Ethiopian women's human rights can better be addressed through a relativist perspective of human rights.

Implications for Social Work Practice

Social work practice related to women's human rights advocacy must separate religion from culture by engaging in textual analysis to uncover the Islamic perspective of women's human rights. To maintain Muslim women's human rights protection, there needs to be a Muslim-based system that teaches about justice and fairness in the family. Social workers need to advocate for just relationships and work with Muslims who can understand them. Social workers need to advocate for the establishment of a system to abolish or reinterpret the unjust readings and interpretations of Islam's scriptures and help Muslims who hold extreme patriarchal views and understanding to move toward balanced, fair, and just relationships.

To protect their human rights, Muslim women must help their men to assume their own responsibilities as indicated in the Quran, rather than accepting the burden themselves. Muslim women must express their concerns in a manner that helps their voices to be heard in the family rather than keeping silent. This is because Islam does not order any person to be oppressed; rather it calls everybody toward justice (Quran, 4:135). Muslim women must take this into account in their discussion of their human rights protection. Advocacy should be the major role of social workers in promoting women's human rights. Empowerment sessions directed toward, for example, training women and establishing stronger associations of Muslim women that specifically promote women's understanding of their rights in Islamic scriptures, are of paramount importance. The focus must be on the way Islam and culture intersect to negatively affect the human rights of Muslim women in Ethiopia.

Conclusion

The intersection of patriarchal culture with Islamic understanding of women's rights among Muslim society normalizes violations of women's human rights. Unless Muslim women come to terms with justice within Islam and become empowered, it will be difficult to deal with Muslim women's rights violations in the name of religion and culture. Therefore, a continuous effort of education, training, and advocacy is vital in helping Muslim women become aware of these intersections, which are used as pretexts to violate their 'rights.

NOTES

1 Men are in charge of women by [right of] what Allah has given one over the other and what they spend [for maintenance] from their wealth. So righteous women are devoutly obedient, guarding in absence what Allah would have them guard. But those from whom you fear arrogance—first, advise them; [then if they persist] forsake them in bed; and finally, strike them (translated by Saheeh International, 2004).

2 And if you fear that you will not deal justly with the orphan girls, then marry those that please you of [other] women, two or three, or four. But, if you fear that you will not be just, then [marry only] one. . . . (4:3, Saheeh International, 2004)

3 And, you will never be able to be equal [in feeling] between wives, even if you should strive [to do so]. So, do not incline completely [toward one] and leave another hanging (4:129, Saheeh International, 2004)

4 " . . . to men is allotted what they earn, and to women what they earn" (Quran 4:32, Saheeh International, 2004).

5 Men are in charge of women by [rights of] what Allah has given one over the other and what they spend [for maintenance] from their wealth. . . .

6 65:6. Lodge them [in a section] of where you dwell out of your means and do not harm them in order to oppress them. and if they should be pregnant, then spend on them until they give birth. And if they breastfeed for you, then give them their payment and confer among yourselves in the acceptable way. . . . 65:7. Let a man of wealth spend from

his wealth, and he whose provision is restricted, let him spend from what Allah has given him. Allah does not charge a soul except [according to] what He has given it.

7   And do not wish for that by which Allah has made some of you exceed others. for men is a share of what they have earned, and for women is a share of what they have earned.

8   Indeed, Allah does not do injustice, [even] as much as an atom's weight; while if there is a good deed, He multiplies it and gives from Himself a great reward.

9   And give the women [upon marriage] their [bridal] gifts [obligatory] graciously. But if they give up willingly to you anything of it, then take it in satisfaction and ease.

10 Prescribed for you when death approaches [any] one of you if he leaves wealth [is that he should make] a bequest for the parents and near relatives according to what is acceptable—a duty upon the righteous.

11 Then whoever alters it [i.e., the bequest] after he has heard it—the sin is only upon those who have altered it.

12 O you, who have believed, be persistently standing firm in justice, witnesses for Allah, even if it be against yourselves or parents and relatives. Whether one is rich or poor, Allah is more worthy of both. So, follow not [personal] inclination, lest you not be just. And if you distort [your testimony] or refuse [to give it], then indeed Allah is ever, with what you do, Acquainted (Quran, 4:135, translated by Saheeh International, 2004).

REFERENCES

Abd al 'Atī, H. (1995). *The family structure in Islam* (4th ed.). Baltimore, MD: American Foundation Publications.

Adnan, G. (2004). *Women and the glorious Qur'an: An analytical study of women related verses of sura An-Nisa'a.* Göttingen, DE: Universitäts verlag Göttingen.

Al-Hibri, A. Y. (2000). An introduction to Muslim women's rights. *Window of Faith, 51,* 51–71.

Barlas, A. (2002). *"Believing Women" in Islam: Unreading patriarchal interpretations of the Qur'an.* Austin: University of Texas Press.

Creswell, J. (2014). *Research design: Qualitative, quantitative, and mixed methods approaches* (4th ed.). Thousand Oaks, CA: Sage.

Federal Democratic Republic of Ethiopia (FDRE). (2007). *Summary and Statistical Report of the 2007 Population and Housing Census Results, Draft Report.* Population Census Commission, Addis Ababa, December 2008. Retrieved May 13, 2018 from https://www.scribd.com/doc/28289334/summary-and-Statistical-Report-of-the-2007

Government of Ethiopia. (1993). National Policy on Women. Addis Ababa, ET: Author.

Government of Ethiopia. (1995). Constitution of Ethiopia. Addis Ababa, ET: Author.

Hassan, H. (2006). *Marriage: Islamic discourses.* In S. Joseph (Ed.), *Encyclopaedia of women and Islamic cultures: Family, body, sexuality and health* (Vol. 3 pp. 246–249). Boston, MA: Brill.

Hatch, R., & Schumm, W. (2003). Religion. In J. J. Ponzetti (Ed.), *International encyclopaedia of marriage and gender* (Vol. 3, pp. 1316–1323). New York, NY: Macmillan.

Jawad, H. (1998). *The rights of women in Islam: An authentic approach.* New York, NY: St. Martin's Press.

Keddie, R. N. (2012). *Women in the Middle East: Past and present.* Princeton, NJ: Princeton University Press.

Knoema. (n.d.). *Ethiopia—Male to female ration of total population.* https://knoema.com/atlas/Ethiopia/topics/Demographics/Population/Male-to-female-ratio

Mir-Hosseini, Z. (2006). Muslim women's quest for equality: Between Islamic law and feminism. *Critical inquiry, 32,* 629–645.

Patton, Q. M. (2002). *Qualitative research and evaluation methods* (3rd ed.). London, UK: Page

Roald, A. (2001). *Women in Islam: The western experience.* London, UK: Routledge.

Saheeh International. (2004). *The Quran: English meaning.* London, UK: Al-Mundata Alislami.

Syed, A. (2004). *The position of women in Islam: Progressive view.* New York, NY: State University of New York Press.

UN. (1948). Universal Declaration of Human Rights. New York, NY: Author.

UN. (1979). Convention on the Elimination of All Forms of Discrimination against Women. New York, NY: Author.

UN. (1993). Declaration on the Elimination of Discrimination against Women. New York, NY: Author.

Wadud, A. (1999). *Qur'an and woman: Reading the sacred text from a woman's perspective.* New York, NY: Oxford University Press.

Wadud, A. (2006). *Inside the gender jihad: Women's reform in Islam.* Oxford, UK: Oneworld.

The Implications of a Patriarchal Culture for Women's Access to "Formal" Human Rights in South Africa: A Case Study of Domestic Violence Survivors

Shahana Rasool

This chapter shows how patriarchy violates women's human rights and creates an environment of fear that impedes their help seeking. Patriarchy in this study refers to the hegemonic belief in male rights, ownership, and control over women (Pendergast & McGregor, 2007). The narratives of all 17 women interviewed in the study support the feminist argument that the use of power and control in abusive relationships, largely by men against women, has a direct bearing on women's help-seeking behaviour after women are abused. While there are other factors that contribute to abused women's reluctance to seek help, those are discussed elsewhere (Rasool, 2012, 2015). Woman abuse / domestic violence, in this chapter, refers to the physical and/or emotional violence by an intimate male partner (i.e., husband, partner, or boyfriend) as reported by the women.

Pendergast and McGregor (2007) define patriarchy as "any . . . system that grants privileged status to males and permits or encourages their domination of women" (p. 3). Patriarchy has historically been associated with an aggressive, "macho" masculinity. Some theorists contest a static notion of patriarchy and argue that masculinities and patriarchy are not fixed or homogenous and that they often differ across history and cultures (Salisbury & Jackson, 1996). Walker (2005) contends that in South Africa, "contemporary expressions of masculinity are embryonic, ambivalent and characterized by the struggle between traditional or conventional male practices and the desire to be a modern, respectable, responsible man" (p. 225). Although it is acknowledged that notions of masculinity and patriarchy are historically and socially located and are fluid, the narratives of the women in this study about their experiences of abuse largely conform to historical descriptions of patriarchal masculinities that are "steeped in violence and authoritarianism" (Walker, 2005, p. 227).

Abuse of women, as illustrated in this study, is an extreme consequence of the enactment of patriarchal attitudes that affirms notions of male ownership over women, which creates a major stumbling block to the attainment of women's rights. Women's accounts of abuse show how the violation of their human rights in the private sphere impedes help seeking in the public domain. Lister (2003) confirms that

> male violence inside and outside the home, together with the fear it creates, serves to undermine women's position as citizens. If women cannot move and act freely in the public sphere and/or are intimidated in the private sphere because of the threat of violence, then their ability to act as citizens is curtailed. (p. 113)

Women's rights, namely the rights to human dignity, equality, freedom of movement, and freedom of expression and association, as well as their right to be protected against all forms of violence, have been violated in domestic violence situations. Domestic violence prevails even though all the human rights referred to above are enshrined in South Africa's Constitution and the Bill of Rights (Government of South Africa, 1996) and undergird social policy and legislation to protect women against abuse. The Constitution provides for the "protection and security of the person which includes the right of everyone to be free from all forms of violence from either public or private sources" (Government of South Africa, 1996, Section 12[1][C]). The Constitution acknowledges that violence occurs in both the public and private domains and requires state action. Nevertheless, violence in intimate partner relationships curtails the rights of women and prevents them from accessing help.

Abused women's narratives illustrate their lived experiences of patriarchy, and how these manifest themselves in domestic violence in the private sphere, which serves to impair their human rights. While the threat posed by patriarchy in the public sphere in South Africa may be weakening for some women, due to the promotion of gender equality in legislation and policy as well as increased access to opportunities in post-apartheid South Africa, the narratives of abused women in this study demonstrate that for other women, patriarchy is rife in the private sphere. Women's encounters of violence illustrate the limits of formal rights, policies, and legislation that are premised on the assumption that women will readily disclose abuse and seek help in situations of domestic violence. Despite these limitations, I argue that rights provide an important stepping-stone in advancing gender equality and in protecting women from violence. However, public policies and legislation need to take account of the lived experiences of abused women, in order to devise appropriate and effective measures to protect them and to assist them in claiming their rights.

Methodology

This chapter is based on a qualitative study conducted with abused women. The purpose of the study was to understand help-seeking patterns; hence women who had disclosed abuse and sought help on numerous occasions for abuse were accessed through shelters in Johannesburg and Cape Town. Non-probability, purposive sampling was used to access 17 survivors of woman abuse who volunteered to participate. Shelter workers referred adult women living in shelters, and who had experienced abuse in a heterosexual, intimate partner relationship, to the researcher. All ethical requirements of research were adhered to. Pseudonyms are used to protect the anonymity of participants.

Analysis of the data was based on an approach outlined by Mandelbaum (1973) in conjunction with guidelines provided by Rubin and Rubin (2005). The data was entered into ATLAS.ti for coding and organizing. Trustworthiness is assured by providing thick descriptions (Geertz, 1973) of the narratives.

The women interviewed came from all over South Africa even though interviews were conducted in shelters based in Johannesburg and Cape Town. The age of the women ranged from 19 to 46. Most of the women in the study were married at the time of the interview and the majority had a high school education. All the women had children. Almost an equal number of women were employed (8) and unemployed (9). In many respects the women interviewed were quite diverse, but most came from middle- to lower-income communities. The following sections highlight how intimate partners curtailed the rights of the women.

Curtailment of Women's Rights

The power and control strategies utilized by abusive men violate the rights of abused women and fundamentally limit their possibilities for seeking help. Women's ability to seek help is seriously hampered by the varying strategies employed by men to prevent them from having contact with people, including constantly watching them, not allowing them to speak freely or go anywhere by themselves, incarcerating them, physically and sexually violating them, or sabotaging their relationships with others. Isolating women from social networks such as family and friends is one of the most powerful control tactics that impedes help seeking. The central premise of seeking help rests on a person having contact with people outside of the household or private sphere. If women are constantly being watched and their contact with other people is limited, the space for disclosing abuse or violence or obtaining help in the public domain is significantly reduced. In the following sections, women speak of the curtailment of their rights to freedom of expression, association, and movement that affected their capacity to seek help and hence their right to human dignity. The South African Constitution (Government of South Africa, 1996) accords a central place to the value of human dignity in South Africa's rights-based approach to gender-based violence (Section 10). The narratives of women show how their physical integrity and basic freedoms have been violated by domestic violence.

Curtailing Freedom of Expression and Association—"I must sit and just be serious, not laugh, not talk to [anybody]."

Controlling abused women's speech is tantamount to limiting their right of expression. Section 16.2 of the Constitution (Government of South Africa, 1996) guarantees the right of individuals to free expression, which in principle includes "every act by which a person attempts to express some emotion, belief, idea or grievance" (Currie & De Waal, 2005, p. 362), including conduct that seeks to communicate something. Currie and De Waal (2005) take a broad reading of the purpose of this provision in the Constitution, rather than a narrower focus on the freedom of the press, for instance. They argue that state intervention is permissible in intimate partner and/or family associations, if this provision is read in the context of the protection of families, children, and the elderly against abuse and if it is read together with the right to dignity and equality (Currie & De Waal, 2005, p. 432).

The narratives reflect how women's rights to free expression and association are curtailed in abusive relationships. If women are not allowed to "speak" and disclose abuse, seeking help is challenging and requires ingenuity on the part of women to find strategies to escape. A participant, Bongi, related that when she was dating the abuser, he did not want her to greet or look at anyone. It later reached the stage where she was "banned" from speaking to her male friends, and two weeks after that she was told by the abuser that she was "not even allowed to speak to girls." In some situations, the abusers allowed women to talk to others but wanted to know about the content of their conversations. Catherine said the following in this regard: "Every time I talk to . . . friends . . . he asks me: 'What are you talking about? You must tell me now.' I'm scared [so] . . . I tell him [what we talked about]." This scenario, where communication is possible, seems less extreme than when women are not allowed to talk at all. This was confirmed in a South African study that found that one of the principal ways in which men curtailed women's freedom of expression and association was by controlling "who their girlfriends were with [which] extended to attempting to dictate which friends they associated with" (Wood & Jewkes, 1998, p. 24). Controlling women's contact with others restricts their opportunities for disclosing abuse and seeking help.

Although male partners tried to restrict women's speech, some of the women displayed extreme resourcefulness in dealing with their partners' power and control. Fatima explained how her ability to communicate with others was limited by her partner, because she was not allowed to speak to customers, although she was expected to work in her partner's shop. Fatima resisted this by making an agreement with regular visitors about how she would interact with them when the abuser was present. She told of how a man who ran the butcher shop next door to their business would visit their store and speak to her, but the abuser did not want her to speak to him. So she told this man, "Nathan do me one favour, don't come in here when Faheem is here, or just excuse me [if] . . . I don't talk to you or I don't greet you." In this way Fatima was trying to maintain her relationships with the neighbour, while still placating the abuser. She was not disclosing the abuse per se or directly challenging the status quo of the abuser, but she was keeping the door for communication open in the absence of the abuser. Fatima used "weapons of the weak" (as explained below) (Säävälä, 2001) that allowed her to maintain some of her relationships with others. As Säävälä (2001, p. 201) points out, "The use of 'weapons of the weak'— gossiping, pouting, denying proper food or sex, slowing down actions, not passing on information, quarrelling, etc—[is] not geared to building up a dissident mentality among women . . . but simply [to] maximize their space to manoeuvre in a situation where gender relations *per se* are un-challenged" (p. 201). Several women in this study displayed acts of agency and resistance, within the confines of the authority asserted by men and to the extent that this was possible within their circumstances, which conforms with what Säävälä (2001) describes as "weapons of the weak." This is highlighted when women leave. Leaving and going to a shelter represented an enormous act of courage on the part of all the women in this study

Isolation

Intimate partners also used isolation to restrict the contact women had with other people, including family members, and this compounded the difficulties women had in reaching out for help and disclosing abuse. Annella described how the abuser kept her away from her family: "I seldom went to see my mum. He never took me to my parents. [We] always rode past my mother's house. Since I got married I never spoke to my mother. [I was] very isolated from them." Similarly, Fatima related how her partner kept her away from family and potential systems of support when she said, "He didn't take me to my family. He kept me away from them. I had no friends." I have illustrated elsewhere the importance of family and friends as potential helpful resources in help seeking and escaping abuse (Rasool, 2012, 2015).

In cases where women are not isolated from their families, some abusers make sure that they are constantly present when there are other people around or when women go out, particularly after an abusive incident. In some cases, the men dictated what the women were permitted to say. In Catherine's case, the abuser stopped her from going to church, which could have been an important source of succour and help. When members of the congregation came to inquire about her absence from church, her partner made sure he was present. She related the following:

> There was a pressure . . . because my husband is sitting there. I must say to them [I'm sick]. I can't tell them [the truth]. It's all . . . an excuse. . . . It's horrible; it's horrible to lie to . . . good people. . . . Yes, that's my life.

Similarly, Shamima had "a black eye" as a result of the abuse, but she was forced to lie to people at work. The abuser made sure he was present the first time she had contact with her work colleagues after the incident to control what she said. She revealed the following:

> He actually told me . . . to tell my boss that "on my way home the previous day I was robbed, people took . . . my cell phone and, and they beat me like that." [He did not allow me to go inside the office], he said that, "I must sit in the car and he's going to call my boss, my boss must come to the car." I don't know, maybe to see that I am going to tell him this story that he thought up. And that was just after we came from the hospital [where] they took scans and stuff.

Abusers manipulated and controlled where women could and could not go, and they ensured that they were present when opportunities for disclosing abuse and seeking help emerged. Women were also forced to lie about what was happening. Within this context, help seeking becomes extremely difficult, as Fatima states: "I couldn't reach out for help because he was there, taking control of me."

Abusers use a combination of tactics to prevent women from disclosing abuse and seeking help, including isolation and preventing them from speaking to others by limiting contact with people through controlling their movements, which is discussed below.

Curtailing Freedom of Movement—"My house was . . . a prison."

One of the most egregious ways in which abusers violate the rights of women is by limiting their freedom of movement. Many women interviewed described how abusers restricted their movements and controlled their interaction with others, which was a serious hindrance to participation in public life. Some women were not allowed to leave the house or have visitors, which limited their possibilities for accessing social rights, such as social services and social benefits.

Five of the women interviewed indicated that they were not allowed to go out, especially without the abuser. As Annella stated, "I never went out of the house. I was always indoors." For another participant, the extent of the isolation was so intense that she was locked in the house and not allowed to open the windows or curtains. She was not even allowed to look out of the window. Controlling the movements of women in these ways and keeping them away from people substantially reduces their chances of being able to build relationships with others in order to disclose something as private and sensitive as domestic violence. Jemina, a woman originally from Cape Town but living in Johannesburg at the time of the interview, described how her partner was constantly watching her to the extent that she was not allowed to do anything independent of him. She stated:

> [He] locked me up [and he] always fetched me at work. He'd drop me at home and [he would] not let me go anywhere. When we [got] home he [would] start hitting me. He was always [there]. When I open my eyes, he was standing in front of me. [I] could never go anywhere without him. If you lock

someone up in the house what [can you do] if something happens in the house? [He would] always leave money but [there was] no way to get out to buy something.

The control the abuser exerted over every aspect of Jemina's life was so intense that she felt as though she was being permanently watched; for her it was almost like the "Big Brother" effect. Disclosing abuse and seeking help under these conditions is extremely difficult. Attribution theorists (Metalsky & Abramson, 1981; Weiner, 2000) argue that the locus of control is one dimension that people consider when seeking help. In these situations, women seem to perceive the locus of control as external to them, situated in the abuser, which hinders help seeking. Nevertheless, despite the overwhelming control exerted by the abuser over her life, Jemina did manage, at some points, to subvert the abuser's control and reclaim her agency in little ways, by for example sending "the child through the burglar guards to play outside," or finding means to get out of the house when he locked her up for the weekend, and returning before he could suspect that she had left. These acts of agency and challenging the abuser's power supports Gondolf and Fisher's (1988) survivorship theory, expanded on below, which suggests that abused women employ a range of strategies to resist within the limits of the abusive relationship.

Catherine, another participant, was also literally locked up in the house, which impeded her access to services. It took her a month from the time she was given information about the shelter until she was able to develop a strategy to escape from her partner. When I asked her why it took her so long to leave she said, "Because I couldn't get out of the house. He locked the doors. I . . . [couldn't] go out." When I probed as to how she finally escaped, she said, "When he went to another friend, then I ran with my two children, the other one is big . . . the eldest one helped me pack." She explained that she was unable to pack all her belongings and left most of her possessions behind. Catherine's situation provides a clear example of how help seeking for domestic violence in the public domain is deterred by abusers isolating women and controlling their movements.

The process of getting out of an abusive relationship, when one's movements are constantly being monitored, is extremely complex. Women used their knowledge of what would help to convince the abuser to let them out of the house to escape. Catherine said that initially she lied to the abuser about where she was going, to get out of the house to obtain professional help. To get help she cleverly told her partner that she would bring him money to support his drug habits, as she knew he would not let her out otherwise, as she related:

> I found a way to lie to him. [I told him,] I want to go there [to] bring something for you. I'm going to bring money for you. . . . I could only go out if I bring him something. You see if I don't bring him something he [will] hit me. He beats me up and he rapes me.

Catherine's narrative illustrates how women's real fear, associated with their previous experiences of physical and sexual violation, inhibits help seeking. However, it also shows how desperate they are to get out and, when they are ready to leave, that they will find inventive ways to escape. She knew that the only way she would be allowed to escape the abuser's "gaze" was if she gave him money to support his drug habits. She utilized the "weapons of the weak" to acquire freedom for herself. Catherine's situation epitomized the struggle women encounter between challenging patriarchy while at the same time remaining compliant. Feminists argue that challenging existing power relations is critical to the reconstruction of gender ideologies and notions of masculinity (Addis & Mahalik, 2003). However, such challenges are severely constrained in a patriarchal context like South Africa, where despite constitutional and legal sanctions against domestic abuse and violence, social and cultural ideas that perpetuate violence against women remain embedded in the practices of society (Rasool, 2012, 2015; Rasool & Suleman, 2016), even in institutions that should be protecting women.

Three women from Cape Town described how the control of their movements profoundly limited their ability to seek help. These women reflected on how they were expected to be at the "beck and call" of the abusers 24 hours a day:

Nita: If he want[s] that, he want[s] that, if he want[s] me to sit there while he's asleep I must sit there. If he wake[s] up I must still be there.

Rehana: [I must] sit and just be serious, not laugh, not talk to [anybody]. . . . I must sit there [where] he wants [me to sit]. When he comes home he must . . . [see] my face, when he goes out he must see me there. . . . I must just be there like an ornament all the time. [I'm not allowed to move]. If he puts me there I must be there.

Fatima: I used to hate sitting [there with a sour face] and when people [used to] come in I can't even smile. [I had to] sit like this with this sour face. Oh! I couldn't take it . . . I haven't been myself. . . . since I'm with this man. I really haven't been myself.

These women expressed frustration about the level of control exerted by the abuser and the way the abuser treated them like objects rather than autonomous human beings. Abusers expect women to be completely compliant with their wishes, thereby thwarting their identity and sense of self, which is indicative of the way in which women's dignity was compromised by their partners. Women expressed frustration and anger about having to be unnatural and unfriendly to everyone. South African research confirms the connections between violent masculinities and domestic violence with the end result of intimate femicide (Mathews et al., 2015). Researchers in Britain found that over half of their male respondents indicated that they saw women as sexual objects that exist "merely" as recipients of men's sexual attention. "Women were not viewed as autonomous beings with preferences and interests of their own" (Beech et al., 2006, p. 1641). Abusers became so controlling that women had to limit their self-expression to prevent abuse. Not being free to speak has a profound effect on abused women's sense of self and their ability to be who they are, thereby compromising their right to human dignity.

To deal with the abuse, women seem to have changed their behaviour such that they presented themselves as unfriendly and non-talkative, in order to placate the abuser in the hope that this would prevent abuse. However, this strategy increased their isolation and thus their vulnerability to abuse because their relationships with people in their environment were negatively affected by their behaviour and their opportunities for disclosing abuse and receiving help were curtailed.

Abused women found the control over their speech and movements extremely frustrating, since it not only infringed on their sense of self but essentially objectified them. Paulina's situation illustrates clearly the extent to which abusers see women as objects or animals to be dominated. Paulina lived in a shared house in one of the townships of Johannesburg. The abuser's control was so absolute that he even dictated when she could go to the toilet. She recounted the horrendous treatment received from her partner:

> My life was very bad. He was treating me like a dog. I couldn't even go to the toilet. I couldn't even go to the kitchen when there [are] people [there]. I couldn't even sit with the people. I was always sitting in the room, because as soon as I go out and talk to the people . . . he is swearing [at] me. I must make sure [that] when he comes from work, I am finished with the toilet . . . because if I go, he is gonna tell me "ya, you never went to the toilet, I know who was screwing you in the toilet." This was said in front of my kids.

Paulina's movements were extremely limited at a micro level. The abuser's inhumane treatment of her extended to the abuser urinating on her or deliberately urinating around the house and expecting her to clean it up. This type of behaviour is cruel, inhumane, and degrading, and it violated Paulina's dignity. These extreme levels of control and display of male power were aimed at regulating abused women's contact with other people. Ultimately, having limited contact with other people reduced the possibilities of developing relationships of trust with others, which made disclosing abuse and seeking help in the public domain difficult.

Male partners also used accusations of infidelity to control women's movements and prevent them from talking to others. Jealousy is often an expression of the male belief that they own the women in their lives

(Serran & Firestone, 2004). South African research by Mathews et al. (2011) has indicated that jealousy and mistrust were contributors to men killing women in intimate partner relationships. Research in Britain also confirmed that sexual jealousy was an important predictor of male violence against women (Russell & Wells, 2000). As in Paulina's case, other women also experienced unfounded accusations of affairs. Joslyn explained that when she went to have a bath, the abuser would suggest she was cleaning herself because she was seeing another man. Similarly, Catherine described how she hardly ever left the house because when she did, the abuser would "check" her vagina to establish whether she had cheated on him. She related the following incident:

> I don't like . . . to talk about that, but I'm going to tell you. He . . . is a man who . . . rapes me. All the time he rapes me forward and back. Then . . . he take[s] his finger and he feel[s] if there was not another man by me. You see that's why I don't go out. I was so scared he [would] do these things to me.

In Catherine's situation, the abuser controlled her movements through fear, constant accusations of affairs if she left the home, and through checking her vagina.

Further, accusations of infidelity appear to intensify when women assert themselves, suggesting that abusers use them as a control mechanism in domestic violence situations. Shamima indicated that when she challenged her partner, the abuse intensified, and he suggested that the only reason she was standing up to him was because she was having an affair. She stated:

> When I put my foot down, when I said to him, I'm not going to allow him to do it to me any longer, he used to say that, "I can see that you don't love me anymore and I can see that you've got someone else, that's why you don't want me." That's when the abuse started to get worse. It used to happen so frequently . . . on a daily basis. Every night when he used to come home from work then I used to think and

wonder what is this guy going to do. When he first walks in the door, is he first going to scream at me, then he's going to hit me . . . or what's going to happen. . . . I had that fear in me.

When Shamima reported her partner's abusive behaviour to the police he accused her of doing so because she wanted to continue with her affair. The abuser apparently told her, "I want to put him away so that my lover can come to me, he even used to tell my daughter, 'Your mummy got another daddy for you.'"

Serran and Firestone (2004) confirm that accusations of infidelity are likely when partners make a "unilateral decision to terminate the relationship" (p. 7) and when abusers feel they are unable to control their women; in some instances, this leads to femicide. The issue of male insecurity and jealousy is a serious one because research indicates that "spousal homicides have evidently been precipitated by the husband accusing the wife of sexual infidelity and/or by her decision to terminate the marriage" (Serran & Firestone, 2002, p. 3). The abusers' accusations of infidelity, often linked to jealousy, insecurity, and/or manipulation, led women to reduce their contact with others, to prevent the recurrence of accusations or vaginal testing, thereby limiting the possibilities of them seeking help.

In summary, women's lived experiences of abuse, described so vividly above, illustrate how abuse is an attack on the dignity of women and curtails human rights in fundamental ways. All the women experienced physical, sexual, emotional, and psychological abuse in their intimate partner relationships. The Domestic Violence Act (DVA) (Government of South Africa, 1998) makes provision for people, regardless of gender, to seek protection orders preventing their partners from abusing them. However, the freedom of movement of women in this situation is restricted, and their capacity to reach out for help and to take the extra step toward claiming their right to protection under the DVA, in intimate partner relationships, is limited.

Conclusions

The accounts of women in this study underscore the link between the private domain (home) and public domain (community, state). Despite the enormous challenges to patriarchy that have occurred over the last few decades and the strides women's movements have made at the public level in advancing gender equality in South Africa (Vetten & Ratele, 2013), little has changed in the lives of many survivors of abuse in the private domain. These patriarchal attitudes continue to support a historically "macho" masculinity that encourages abuse, as highlighted in the narratives of the women interviewed.

Women's narratives of abuse indicate clearly why they do not readily claim these rights to protect themselves from violence in the home. The way in which men exert power and control over women in abusive relationships threatens the constitutional rights of women, including their right to dignity, equality, bodily integrity, and freedom of expression, association, and movement, as well as the right to be free from all forms of violence from either public or private sources (Government of South Africa, 1996). Until patriarchy is challenged at the root, that is, within the private sphere, public policy and political gains will have a limited impact on the lives of abused women.

These women's stories lead to a questioning of the utility of rights in situations of domestic violence where these are perceived to be "paper rights." A major gap exists between rights discourses as embedded in the Constitution and the lived experiences of abused women in the private domain. With abused women being restricted and oppressed in the private realm, the possibilities of them exercising the constitutional rights afforded to them in the public domain, through policy and legislation, is severely compromised. However, while rights in and of themselves are not adequate to change the culture that perpetuates woman abuse, they provide the basis for change. Rights serve to give women a voice in the face of the denial of their humanity and provide some way of supporting those who can find creative ways to claim these rights, in conjunction with women's rights organizations that support them. The question must be posed in the South African context as to whether there is adequate commitment to giving effect to these rights, since funding of human and women's rights organizations is dwindling; policy bureaus that were set up to monitor and evaluate women's rights have become less effective, and the strength and role of the women's movement is in question.

More work needs to be done to encourage family, friends, and neighbours who find out about woman abuse to help survivors navigate their way out of the abusive relationships. Family and friends are located in the private domain, and instead of privatizing abuse, they need to act in ways that condemn the abuse and assist women with accessing appropriate services. Further, legislative frameworks require better implementation mechanisms that account for the real danger and challenges women face when trying to leave, which contributes to their ambivalence and reluctance to report abuse. In addition, spreading knowledge of the role of shelters and how they can assist abused women practically is required, so that abused women think about social workers and shelters as viable options for help seeking.

REFERENCES

Addis, M., & Mahalik, J. (2003). Men, masculinity, and the contexts of help seeking. *American Psychologist, 58*(1), 5–14.

Beech, A., Ward, T., & Fisher, D. (2006). The identification of sexual and violent motivations in men who assault women: Implications for treatment. *Journal of Interpersonal Violence, 21*(12), 1635–1653.

Currie, I., & De Waal, J. (2005). *The Bill of Rights handbook* (5th ed.). Cape Town, ZA: Juta.

Geertz, C. (1973). *The interpretation of cultures: Selected essays.* New York, NY: Basic Books.

Gondolf, E. W., & Fisher, E.R. (1988). *Battered women as survivors: An alternative to treating learned helplessness.* Lexington, MA: Lexington Books.

Government of South Africa. (1996). Constitution of the Republic of South Africa (Act 108 of 1996). Pretoria, ZA. https://www.gov.za/sites/default/files/images/a108-96.pdf

Government of South Africa. (1998). Domestic Violence Act (Act 116 of 1998). Pretoria, ZA. https://www.justice.gov.za/legislation/acts/1998-116.pdf

Lister, R. (2003). *Citizenship: Feminist perspectives* (2nd ed.). New York, NY: Palgrave MacMillan.

Mandelbaum, D. G. (1973). The study of life history: Gandhi. *Current Anthropology, 14*(3), 177–206.

Mathews, S., Jewkes., R., & Abrahams, N. (2011). "I had a hard life": Exploring childhood adversity in the shaping of masculinities among men who killed an intimate partner in South Africa. *British Journal of Criminology, 51*(6), 960–977.

Mathews, S., Jewkes, R., & Abrahams, N. (2015). "So now I'm the man": Intimate partner femicide and its interconnections with expressions of masculinities in South Africa. *British Journal of Criminology, 55*(1), 107–124. https://doi.org/10.1093/bjc/azu076

Metalsky, G. I., & Abramson, L. Y. (1981). Attributional styles: Toward a framework for conceptualization and assessment. In P. C. Kendall & S. D. Hollon (Eds.), *Assessment strategies for cognitive-behavioral interventions* (pp. 13–58). New York, NY: Academic Press.

Pendergast, D., & McGregor, S. (2007). *Positioning the profession beyond patriarchy.* East Lansing, MI: Kappa Omicron Nu. http://www.kon.org/patriarchy_monograph.pdf

Rasool, S. (2012). "Do We Accept the Unacceptable?" The Privatisation of Women Abuse by Informal Networks in South Africa. *Journal of Gender and Religion in Africa, 18*(2), 143–149.

Rasool, S. (2015). The influence of social constructions of family on abused women's help-seeking after domestic violence. *South African Review of Sociology, 46*(4), 24–38.

Rasool, S., & Suleman, M. (2016). Muslim women overcoming marital violence: Breaking through 'structural and cultural prisons' created by religious leaders. *Agenda, 30*(3), 38–49.

Rubin, H., & Rubin, I. (2005). *Qualitative interviewing: The art of hearing data.* London, UK: Sage.

Russell, R. J. H., & Wells, P. A. (2000). Predicting marital violence from the Marriage and Relationship Questionnaire: Using LISREL to solve an incomplete data problem. *Personality and Individual Differences, 29*, 429–440.

Säävälä, M. (2001). *Fertility and familial power relations: Procreation in South India.* Richmond, UK: Curzon Press.

Salisbury, J., & Jackson, D. (1996). *Challenging macho values: Practical ways of working with adolescent boys.* London, UK: Falmer Press.

Serran, G., & Firestone, P. (2004). Intimate partner homicide: A review of the male proprietariness and the self-defense theories. *Aggression and Violent Behavior, 9*, 1–15.

Vetten, L., & Ratele, K. (2013). Men and violence. *Agenda: Empowering women for gender equity, 27*(1), 4–11. Retrieved June 19, 2016 from http://www.academia.edu/download/44021202/Men_and_violence.pdf

Walker, L. (2005). Men behaving differently: South African men since 1994. *Culture, Health & Sexuality, 7*(3), 225–238.

Weiner, B. (2000). Intrapersonal and interpersonal theories of motivation from an attributional perspective. *Educational Psychology Review, 12*(1), 1–14.

Wood, K., & Jewkes, R. (1998). *Love is a dangerous thing: Micro-dynamics of violence in sexual relationships of young people in Umtata.* Pretoria, ZA: Medical Research Council. http://www.mrc.ac.za/gender/finallove.pdf

Child Marriage Among the Apostolic Sects in Zimbabwe: Implications for Social Work Practice

Munyaradzi Muchacha, Abel Blessing Matsika, and Tatenda Nhapi

Child marriage is a major global child rights challenge, especially in the Global South, where its prevalence is high. For example, in South Asia and sub-Saharan Africa, where its prevalence is higher than in the rest of the world, an estimated 45 percent and 39 percent of girls, respectively, are married before the age of 18 (UNICEF, 2016a). Zimbabwe is greatly affected by this problem; for instance, an estimated 32 percent of girls in that country are married before the age of 18 (UNICEF, 2016a). Child marriage also affects boys, but it mainly affects girls due to structural and gender inequalities as well as harmful social norms that encourage the marriage of the girl child (Muchacha & Matsika, 2017). Child marriage is considered a major violation of child rights; it contravenes rights such as health, education, and freedom from abuse and exploitation (UN Fund for Population Activities [UNFPA], 2012). In addition, it is strongly linked to social problems such as birth complications, high infant and maternal mortalities, gender-based violence, and spread of sexually transmitted diseases (UNFPA, 2012). It is contrary to various social work values such as social justice, equality, empowerment, and liberty (Muchacha & Matsika, 2017).

Fortunately, recent years have witnessed a surge in interventions by local and international organizations, governments, and the international community to tackle child marriage (UN, 2017). Such efforts include the development and implementation of international policies, creation and strengthening of laws against child marriage, international conferences, and global campaigns (UNFPA, 2012). Most of these interventions are informed by the United Nations Convention on the Rights of the Child (CRC) (UN, 1989), which outlines an ideal standard of childhood and child care that every child across the world should have and sets out the obligations of the state and related actors to ensure these envisaged ideals. Indeed, the CRC has played and is playing a crucial role in improving life chances of children by enabling access to various services for children such as health and education (Twum-Danso, 2008a).

Nonetheless, critics of this international human rights norm argue that it advances a "Eurocentric" form of childhood that contradicts the lived realities of children in Africa and other parts of the Global South (Twum-Danso, 2008b). For instance, the CRC views childhood as age specific, and children as asexual, innocent, and deserving a special form of care to successfully transition into a better adulthood (Twum-Danso, 2008b). Yet many scholars, especially from childhood studies, have clearly demonstrated that childhood is context specific and shaped by local cultures and socio-economic and political circumstances. This view contrasts with the universalization of childhood furthered by the CRC and its conduits, such as the civil society and local and international non-governmental organizations (Twum-Danso, 2008a). On the other hand, it can be argued that the African Charter on the Rights and Welfare of the Child (ACWRC) (African Commission on Human and People's Rights, 1990) enabled the "domestication" of the notion of rights to suit African contexts. Certainly, this continental child rights law makes efforts to better fit child rights to African contexts by highlighting children's responsibilities and other cultural issues. On the contrary, Twum-Danso (2008b) argues that these "modifications" did not go far enough to contextualize child rights and that in some respects, the African Charter is even more ambitious and stringent than the CRC.

The CRC and its consequential child protection systems across Africa have received criticism about their relevance and effectiveness in addressing pressing childhood problems such as child marriage, sex work, female genital mutilation/cutting, and child labour. In most cases, these problems are embedded in deep-rooted and structural socio-economic, cultural, political, and religious issues and complexities (Sibanda, 2011). Hence, some scholars argue that most low-income countries cannot afford the childhood standards espoused by this international law regime and are calling for contextualization to better suit the peculiar dynamics in African contexts (Laird, 2005).

This chapter contributes to the growing body of literature that explores this contestation, and the need for the alignment of international human rights norms and practices, which are central and advanced by the social work profession, with the lived realities in Africa. It does this by exploring the contravention of children's rights to health, education and freedom from abuse and exploitation when child marriage is common (Human Rights Watch, 2016). However, caution should be taken against stereotyping the sects included in this study, on the basis of their beliefs and practices. The fact that child marriage is also significantly shaped by poverty in Zimbabwe, and across the Global South, must be acknowledged. The chapter then highlights the child protection challenges that social workers face in dealing with child marriage in Zimbabwe. It is fair to say that the persistent uncritical promotion of the rights discourse and the so-called Western forms of social work will not succeed in effectively tackling child marriage. Therefore, in agreement with other scholars across the African continent, we encourage the social work profession in Zimbabwe to contextualize the promotion of human rights through approaches such as dialogue to better address child marriage among the Apostolic Sects. Further, it is also essential to prioritize poverty alleviation given its close link to child marriage.

Conceptualizing Child Marriage

Child marriage is defined as the marriage of any person below the age of 18, in line with the CRC, which views a child as anyone below the age of 18 (UNFPA, 2012). There are large tensions between the rights- and age-based international definitions of child marriage and what different communities in Africa and across the Global South consider as the appropriate stage for one to get married. For example, some communities in Zimbabwe consider the beginning of menstruation and one's maturity as the appropriate "stage" for marriage and not age (Sibanda, 2011). This maturity is measured by variables such as ability to perform household chores well (Sibanda, 2011). Further, in many African countries there are tensions between criminal and customary laws, thereby creating different minimum ages of marriage (Melchiorre, 2013). Despite these problems, the age-based definition is preferred by most actors since it allows standardization and is in line with the CRC, which most countries have ratified and are obliged to fully implement.

Several international human rights laws and policies highlight the illegality of child marriage. For instance, the Convention on the Elimination of All Forms of Discrimination against Women (CEDAW), ratified by 187 countries, specifies:

> The betrothal and the marriage of a child shall have no legal effect, and all necessary action, including legislation, shall be taken to specify a minimum age for marriage and to make the registration of marriages in an official registry compulsory. (UN, 1979, Article 16[2])

Relatedly, the Universal Declaration of Human Rights (UN, 1948) provides that any marriage should involve the free and full consent of both partners, and consequently, children are viewed as not mature enough to make well-informed choices and consent to marriage (Muchacha & Matsika, 2017). While the CRC makes no explicit reference to child marriage, many of its articles urge state parties to protect children from all forms of exploitation, harm, and violence, which include child marriage. More precisely, the ACWRC is very emphatic about the illegality of child marriage, and its Article 21 clearly stresses that governments should address harmful cultural practices such as child marriage (African Commission on Human and Peoples' Rights, 1990). The ACWRC defines a child as any "human being below the age of 18 years" (Article 2). In addition, there are various resolutions by international bodies such as the Human Rights Council and the Security Council emphasizing that child marriage is a human rights violation and calling upon state parties to strengthen their efforts against this social problem (UN, 2017).

Causes of Child Marriage

Child marriage has several causes, which include but are not limited to poverty, cultural practices, religion, early pregnancies, and gender inequalities (Sibanda, 2011). International research highlights that child marriage is mainly caused by poverty, which contributes to limited access to education and other services, poor standards of living, and lack of viable livelihood choices (UNFPA, 2012). Child marriage emerges as a social safety net for vulnerable girls and a way for families to reduce the burden of child care (UNFPA, 2012). As such, child marriage is prevalent among poor households, and thus is more prevalent in the poorest countries of the world. Early child pregnancies are also viewed as a major cause of child marriage because it is a social norm in Zimbabwe, and many other African countries, that a person gets married to the person responsible for the pregnancy, even if the pregnancy was unplanned (Sibanda, 2011). Furthermore, in many societies across the globe child marriage is a consequence of traditional, religious, and cultural norms that are considered harmful to the care and well-being of children (UNICEF, 2016b). More broadly, most of these cultural, traditional, and religious norms are underpinned by patriarchy and gender relations that marginalize and restrict opportunities for girls and women (UNICEF, 2016b). For instance, in many countries the marriage age for boys and girls is different and it is mostly men who decide who and when girls should marry (UNFPA, 2012).

The Apostolic Sects: History, Practices and Child Marriage in Zimbabwe

The Apostolic Sects (also known as African Initiated Churches, Spirit led churches, Indigenous churches) are the largest religious group in Zimbabwe (Maguranyanga, 2011). They have an estimated three million members, while the total population of Zimbabwe is 14 million people (Maguranyanga, 2011). The Apostolic Sects have a long history in Zimbabwe, having emerged during the colonial era mainly through the pioneering work of charismatic leaders such as Johanne Marange and Johanne Masowe (Hallfors et al., 2016). The earliest churches were mainly composed of the family members of the charismatic leaders, but these churches have since expanded across Zimbabwe and sub-Saharan Africa (Machingura, 2011). Due to conflicts, there are now several and many types of Apostolic Sects, which share different kinds of doctrines. The earliest sects emerged as a counter and alternative to the domination of Christianity promoted by the state and missionaries, which was regarded as aligned to colonialism (UNICEF, 2015). The Apostolic Sects' practices and beliefs are a mixture of Christianity and African Traditional Religion (Machingura, 2011). This fusion allows these churches to resonate with the world views and lived experiences of many locals, leading to their huge popularity and acceptance (Maguranyanga, 2011). Further, in recent years, these sects have witnessed a significant expansion in Zimbabwe as a result of the recent economic crisis, which motivates many to seek prophecies and other spiritual solutions.

Apostolic beliefs

The Apostolic Sects share a common overarching spiritual concept called *mweya*, a religious practice akin to the Holy Spirit in English (Maguranyanga, 2011). They use *mweya* to communicate with and receive messages from God, and to prophesy (Maguranyanga, 2011). It is also a tool for healing, and most sects prohibit the utilization of formal health services. As such, *mweya* is a major spiritual aspect that differentiates the Apostolic Sects from most Christian denominations in Zimbabwe (Mpofu et al., 2011). Although most Apostolic Sects share this belief system, caution should be taken against viewing these sects as homogenous. As earlier pointed out, there are various Apostolic Sect denominations, and they have a wide range of religious practices. To this effect, Maguranyanga (2011) offers a potentially useful way of categorizing the Apostolic Sects into two major groups, ultra-conservative and liberal. The ultra-conservative Apostolic Sects have religious doctrines that are regarded as "radical," such as prohibition of access to conventional health care, education, and the formal labour market. Failure to abide by these moral codes is met with sanctions and shaming (Hallfors et al., 2016). Liberal sects are those such as Zion Christian Churches that allow access to health care, education, and the formal labour market(Maguranyanga, 2011).

Child marriage in the Apostolic sects

It is commonly argued that child marriage in Zimbabwe is disproportionally high among the Apostolic Sects, in particular among those perceived as "ultra-conservative" as evidenced by Human Rights Watch (2015). The Multiple Indicator Monitoring Survey (2014) and Zimbabwe Demographic Health Survey (2010–2011), highlighted that child marriage was highest among the Apostolic Sects compared with other church denominations in Zimbabwe (as cited in UNICEF, 2016b). A participant in the work of Hallfors et al. (2016, p. 184) pointed out that "the church does not have problems with that [child marriage]. It is common in our church (Johane Masowe Apostolic)" (p. 3.3, para. 2). Sibanda (2011) observed that most child marriages within the Apostolic Sects are facilitated by *mweya*, which directs and helps males to choose and marry a girl child. Hallfors et al. (2016) argued that given that *mweya* is a supernatural concept that cannot be verified or questioned, some men were deceptively using it to marry any girl they wished (UNICEF, 2015). Relatedly, a participant in a study by Human Rights Watch (2016) reported that as soon as a girl reaches puberty any man in the church can claim her as a wife. These marriages may be necessitated by church doctrines that prohibit use of family planning and encourage large families and expansion of the Apostolic community in line with the Bible, which says that human beings should multiply like sand (UNICEF, 2015). Nonetheless, Hallfors et al. (2016) noted that there are some Apostolic Sects that prohibit child marriage, where it is punishable through sanctions. This displays the diversity among the Apostolic Sects, and nuanced efforts should be made to understand why some sects accept child marriage while others prohibit it.

It is important to highlight that child marriage is also prevalent among the Apostolic Sects that prohibit it (Hallfors et al., 2016). This is mainly because of poverty, which is generally regarded as the major cause of child marriage in Zimbabwe. Poverty is also a central aspect of the pathway to child marriage even among the ultra-conservative sects (Hallfors et al., 2016). This is not surprising, given that Zimbabwe is experiencing a protracted socio-economic crisis, affecting almost everyone, which has caused high unemployment, poverty, and poor standards of living (Sibanda, 2011). Poverty compels vulnerable families to pursue child marriage as a form of social safety net. For instance, Hallfors et al. (2016) noted that most children among the Apostolic Sects who got married had dropped out of school due to lack of funds for school fees.

Child Protection in Zimbabwe: Practice Challenges

Zimbabwe has a child protection system, imported from the West during the colonial era, that is undergirded by rights and various laws meant to protect children from what is considered risk and harm (Muchacha et al., 2016). The new Constitution of Zimbabwe (Government of Zimbabwe, 2013a) is clear that a child is any person who is below the age of 18, and it also provides for various rights such as education, health, housing, and other social services. Relatedly, a Zimbabwe constitutional judgment on child marriage of 2016 ruled that this practice is illegal and a major violation of children's rights. It stated that "with effect from 20 January 2016, no person, male or female may enter into any marriage . . . before attaining the age of 18 years" (Nemukuyu, 2016, para. 6). This ruling, therefore, overrules all the acts of parliament that are discriminatory against girls and "permissive" of child marriage. For example, the Children's Act (Government of Zimbabwe, 2013b, Chapter 5:06) stipulates that the minimum age of sexual consent and marriage for girls is 16 years. Likewise, the Marriage Act (Government of Zimbabwe, 2006, Chapter 5:11) allows girls aged 16 to marry, yet sets 18 as the minimum age for boys.

Indeed, laws are very indispensable to promote a fair, just, and equal society, and they are pertinent to address child marriage. However, a growing concern regarding the child protection system in Zimbabwe, and across the world, is that legalistic solutions are being emphasized. A legalistic approach assumes that a legal ban will end social problems (Laird, 2005); see, for example, the impression given by the earlier mentioned constitutional ruling. Yet there is very limited implementation of such laws, as evidenced by the rarity of cases of prosecution for child marriage cases (UNICEF, 2016b). A legalistic approach is also limited by the fact that, in Zimbabwe, access and use of legal systems is mediated by family ties and consensus, especially regarding cases that are embedded in social relations and norms, such as child marriage. As UNICEF (2016b) further noted, it is very unlikely for an Apostolic Sect girl to report to the police if she is forced to marry an older man, due to various potential negative consequences such as condemnation by family members, disruption of family ties, and church sanctions. As such, Laird (2002) cautions:

> The belief systems and social circumstances, which result in adverse practices against children cannot simply be legislated out of existence. They must be addressed through interventions, which engage with both traditional norms and economic realities. (p. 901)

For example, the Zimbabwean government has tried at several intervals to use force to compel the Apostolic Sects to stop child marriage, and to comply with government laws and policies on education and health, but such efforts have not yielded much in the way of results (Maguranyanga, 2011). Efforts to enforce laws among the Apostolic Sects are obstructed by the fact that these communities are hard to reach and secretive (Maguranyanga, 2011). On the other hand, the government is inhibited from fully applying these child protection laws because the Apostolic Sects are a major portion of the electorate, and further clashes may have a negative bearing on electoral outcomes (UNICEF, 2015). These laws are not positioned to tackle the religious and cultural factors that surround child marriage, or to effect sustainable behaviour and social change (UNICEF, 2015). Rigid legal enforcement may lead to the hardening of religious stances and cases of child marriage being hidden within such communities. As Boyden et al. (2013) contend,

> it is not at all obvious that an abolitionist approach backed by punitive measures like imprisonment and fines is suitable for addressing practices of such social significance and intricacy as female genital mutilation and early marriage. (p. 515)

The child protection system in Zimbabwe, and similar Global South contexts, receives strong criticism for being too individualistic and paying limited attention to structural challenges that children encounter (Muchacha et al., 2016). Yet, poverty is a major cause of child marriage and related concerns: an estimated half of the Zimbabwean population lives below the poverty line, and children are more affected (Muchacha et al., 2016). As Boyden et al. (2013) rightfully state, "conceptions of risk and on generic interventions designed without full consideration of local . . . contexts are unlikely to become effective as rapidly as intended" (p. 515). The government child protection system and practice in Zimbabwe is hampered by limited resources, especially human and financial resources (Muchacha et al., 2016). For instance, in comparison with its southern African neighbours, Zimbabwe has the largest child to social worker ratio in this region (Wyatt et al., 2010). This illustrates the inadequacy of this child protection system in addressing structural child protection issues, such as child marriage, that are widespread (Sibanda, 2011).

Since the late 1990s, when it adopted the Economic Structural Adjustment Programs, the Government of Zimbabwe has increasingly retreated from providing social safety nets, producing a vacuum that is being filled by non-governmental organizations (NGOs) (Muchacha et al., 2016). These actors are now a central part of the child protection system and are arguably providing more services than the government. For instance, there are over 24 NGOs in Zimbabwe that are focused on addressing child marriage (Girls not Brides, 2002). Their major intervention to address child marriage in Zimbabwe consists of campaigns to raise awareness and contribute to behaviour change. Indeed, this intervention is crucial in promoting knowledge and an enhanced understanding pertaining to human rights and the effects of child marriage and related practices (Boyden et al., 2013). However, the conventional information dissemination approach favoured by most NGOs, which includes campaigns, posters, and road shows, has been criticized for being top down, ethnocentric, and incapable of facilitating meaningful behavioural and social change (Myers & Bourdillon, 2012). Given these practice challenges, there is need for the child protection system in Zimbabwe to be reformed and contextualized in order to effectively engage with its socio-economic, political, cultural, and religious contexts.

Contextualizing Human Rights to Sensitively Address "Harmful" Religious Practices

While human rights or similar notions are cardinal values for a just society, they should be promoted and implemented in a manner that appreciates the local socio-economic, religious, and cultural circumstances (Myers & Bourdillon, 2012). Rejecting human rights on the basis that they are Western and not universally applicable is counterproductive since they have an important goal of promoting human dignity and worth, a value many cultures across the world hold (Hugman, 2012). These values are central to the Afrocentric paradigm. Furthermore, the "universality vs. relativity dichotomy does not help us to protect children on the ground. Hence, it is necessary to move beyond the binary debate relating to the universality and relativity of children's rights and engage with children's local realities" (Twum-Danso, 2008b, p. 1).

A vital step in the contextualization of human rights is the recognition that cultures in Zimbabwe and around the world have ways to affirm the notion of worth and dignity of human beings (Hugman, 2012). Consequently, the ways in which these communities recognize the worth and dignity of human beings can be of great value in addressing child marriage. For instance, in Zimbabwe, as with many sub-Saharan countries, most local communities subscribe to the notion of *Ubuntu/hunu,* a philosophy that the "universe is built upon the principles of coexistence characterized by harmony, peace, interdependence, love and justice" (Lubombo, 2015, p. 37). These communities utilize *Ubuntu/hunu* as a reference to address various issues such as domestic violence, disputes, and even the care of children (Muchacha & Matsika, 2017). Social workers in Zimbabwe might explore how this notion relates to human rights, and how it could be a reference point in addressing child marriage among the Apostolic Sects, as argued by Chitando et al. (2014). In practice, this involves reflecting on how child marriage compromises *Ubuntu/hunu* or similar notions. Potential answers to this question are that it contributes to deprivation of girls' education, birth complications, and maternal mortalities. This approach avoids the domination of human rights rhetoric, which may be viewed as foreign, while achieving the same goals of advancing fairness and social justice (Chitando et al., 2014).

A critical aspect of the contextualization of rights is dialogue: this is a "shift from persuasion and the transmission of information from outside technical experts to dialogue, debate and negotiation on issues that resonate with members of the community" (Figueroa et al., 2002, p. ii). In practice, this would entail actively involving the Apostolic community in problem identification, the communication process, and action, monitoring, and evaluation. In this process social workers and the Apostolic Sect communities engage as equals. This dialogue and debate must explore what is needed for children's well-being, how that relates to the notion of children's rights, how child marriage affects children, how the Apostolic Sect practices violate child rights, and how this community can work together to address this problem. The role of social workers or other actors in these dialogues is to identify and engage gatekeepers and promote active participation, mutual learning, and collective decision making among the participants (Figueroa et al., 2002). Furthermore, social workers need to promote the active participation and inclusion of marginalized and disadvantaged members, considering that "quite often there are marginalized people, including children and the poorest of the poor, who either do not attend such gatherings or remain voiceless when they do attend" (Wessells, 2015, p. 5).

Engaging the Apostolic Sects Leadership

The Apostolic Sects leaders are the custodians of the Apostolic religion; they engage in various functions such as preaching, prophesying, healing, and governance of the church. As such, they wield huge influence, and their directives are usually followed and respected. Therefore, social workers in Zimbabwe need to actively engage this leadership to find solutions. The expected outcome of this engagement is to see the Apostolic Sect leadership becoming champions and role models against child marriage, thereby influencing members to follow suit. As UNICEF (2015) suggests, "Identify influential role models (positive agents of change) within the Apostolic community and broader local community and use them to facilitate relationship building and dialogue" (p. xii). The engagement of faith leaders in addressing social problems within faith organizations is considered a "best practice" in addressing religious practices that are considered harmful to the well-being of the members (Maguranyanga, 2011). This approach would allow the Apostolic leaders to be the facilitators of social change, contrary to interventions by practitioners that are usually short term and interpreted as external.

Consequently, this approach of centralizing the role and influence of faith leaders in social change endeavours has been adopted to deal with various concerns such as gender-based violence, access to HIV/AIDs treatment and prevention, and health care services in general. For instance, organizations such as UNICEF in Zimbabwe are working closely with the Apostolic Sects leadership to facilitate access to maternal and neonatal health services (UNICEF, 2015). Because of this engagement and dialogue, these development organizations have managed to assist the Apostolic churches in developing a gender equality policy to address gender-based violence. This was achieved through the representative organization of 160 Apostolic churches in Zimbabwe, the Union for the Development of Apostolic Churches in Zimbabwe. Social workers in Zimbabwe can engage similar representative organizations such as the Apostolic Christian Council to mobilize member churches to address child marriage (Machingura, 2014). Paramount to this engagement is a non-judgmental and respectful approach to the Apostolic Sect leadership and practices. If one fails to respect these crucial values, resentment and resistance may occur (UNICEF, 2015).

Promoting the Participation of the Apostolic Sect Communities in the Development of Child Marriage Policies and laws

Following the constitutional ruling on child marriage in January 2016, there have been calls for the Government of Zimbabwe to partner with donors, community leaders, adolescents, and civil society in developing a national action plan to end child marriage (Human Rights Watch, 2016). Parliament should also initiate processes to develop a child marriage law in line with the South African Development Community (SADC) Child Marriage Model Law, which sets a consistent standard for how legislation should deal with child marriage and protect children already in marriage (Newlands, 2016). This is encouraging progress indicative of the political will and concerted efforts to address child marriage. Such policy-making processes are often dominated by experts and policy makers, and to a limited extent the community that they seek to save. While the contribution of technocrats is invaluable, such policies usually encounter resistance and backlash as they lack perspectives from the community. Fortunately, the Parliament of Zimbabwe has a participatory mechanism to mainstream community perspectives in the development of the laws, which is the parliamentary bills hearings. Given this crucial platform, the role of social workers and other actors should be to encourage the participation of communities in such processes, and advocating that parliament ensure that this platform reaches secluded communities such as some Apostolic Sects. Relatedly, such participation must be enhanced in the development of policies such as the National Action Plan.

Poverty Eradication

As earlier argued, child marriage within the Apostolic Sects happens in a context of poverty, which limits access to education, and generally increases girls' economic vulnerability. Even if religious and other issues surrounding child marriage among the Apostolic Sects are effectively addressed, child marriage is likely to continue if poverty is not addressed. As such, Muchacha and Matsika (2017) argue that developmental social work can be a useful and relevant practice to address child marriage given that its main thrust is to address poverty. The limited space here does not allow a nuanced conceptualization and outline of this approach. Nevertheless, broadly speaking, developmental social work practice is a radical shift from individualistic and curative interventions toward those focused on promoting structural reforms, equality, and social justice. It is strength based, participatory, and aimed at sustainable empowerment of the communities so that even if they do not receive support from the state and related actors they can sustainably meet their needs (Muchacha & Matsika, 2017). The role of social work in this context is to enable equitable access to the social safety nets for education and health among the Apostolic Sects. Equally important, most of the Apostolic Sect communities are involved in informal sector livelihoods such as carpentry, weaving, blacksmithing, street vending, and farming, which are their major sources of income (Maguranyanga, 2011). The role of social work should be to assist in strengthening these livelihoods to ensure their sustainability, productivity, and viability in order to reduce poverty. This can be achieved through functions such as enabling access to lucrative markets for the products produced by these communities, empowerment training in financial management, and facilitating access to pro-poor microfinance initiatives. In addition, efforts need to be made to ensure that proceeds from these livelihoods are used for goals that enhance the rights and well-being of children, such as access to education and food, which is crucial in reducing child marriage.

Conclusion

This chapter has explored child marriage among the Apostolic Sects and the implications for social work. It has argued that while child marriage among the Apostolic Sects may be linked to their religious practices such as *mweya* and spiritual dreams, it is also reinforced by widespread poverty, which is mainly emanating from the protracted socio-economic crisis affecting this sub-Saharan country. We have also argued that the child protection system in Zimbabwe, which is undergirded by the notion of rights, is not adequately positioned to address child marriage among the Apostolic Sects or the general population of Zimbabwe, due to its overemphasis on legalistic and individualistic interventions and neglect of structural interventions. It is not capable of effectively engaging and tackling the complex religious, political, and economic factors that surround child marriage. To remedy this, we have argued for the conceptualization of rights through recognition of local socio-cultural practices and for dialogue to promote sustainable social change in the interests of children. Similarly, we have argued for the active engagement of the Apostolic Sect leadership, as they are the custodians of the Apostolic Sects religion and role models, and their views are respected by their followers. Addressing poverty, child marriage, and other child protection concerns calls for a strong political will, resolve, and action since these social problems require political and governance solutions. To this effect, social workers in Zimbabwe need to continually lobby political actors to promote economic policies that help the poor and are aimed at promoting equitable access to social safety nets. These advocacy efforts should also push the government to fulfill its international obligations regarding gender justice and the rights and well-being of children.

REFERENCES

African Commission on Human and Peoples' Rights. (1990). African Charter on the Rights and Welfare of the Child. https://www.achpr.org/public/Document/file/English/achpr_instr_charterchild_eng.pdf

Boyden, J., Pankhurst, A., & Tafere, Y. (2013). *Harmful traditional practices and child protection: Contested understandings and practices of female child marriage and circumcision in Ethiopia.* Oxford, UK: Young Lives.

Chitando, E., Taringa, N. T., & Mapuranga, T. P. (2014). On top of which mountain does one stand to judge religion? Debates from a Zimbabwean context. *Journal for the Study of Religion, 27*(2), 115–136.

Figueroa, M. E., Kincaid, D. L., Rani, M., & Lewis, G. (2002). *Communication for social change: An integrated model for measuring the process and its outcomes.* http://www.communicationforsocialchange.org/pdf/socialchange.pdf

Girls not Brides. (2002). *Child marriage around the world.* http;//www.girlsnotbrides.org/child-marriage/Zimbabwe

Government of Zimbabwe. (2013a). Constitution of Zimbabwe. Harare, ZW. https://zimlii.org/zw/legislation/act/2013/amendment-no-20-constitution-zimbabwe

Government of Zimbabwe. (2013b). Children's Act. Harare, ZW. https://www.justice.gov/sites/default/files/eoir/legacy/2013/11/08/childrens_act.pdf

Government of Zimbabwe. (2006). Marriage Act. Harare, ZW. http://unstats.un.org/unsd/vitalstatkb/Attachment187.aspx?AttachmentType=1

Hallfors, D. D., Iritani, B. J., Zhang, L., Hartman, S., Luseno, W. K., Mpofu, E., & Rusakaniko, S. (2016). "I thought if I marry the prophet I would not die": The significance of religious affiliation on marriage, HIV testing, and reproductive health practices among young married women in Zimbabwe. SAHARA-J: Journal of Social Aspects of HIV/AIDS, 13(1), 178–187.

Hugman, R. (2012). *Culture, values and ethics in social work: Embracing diversity.* London, UK: Routledge.

Human Rights Watch. (2015). *Zimbabwe: Scourge of child marriage—Set 18 as minimum age; Adopt national action plan.* https://www.hrw.org/news/2015/11/25/zimbabwe-scourge-child-marriage

Human Rights Watch. (2016). *Dispatches: Ending child marriage in Zimbabwe.* https://reliefweb.int/report/zimbabwe/dispatches-ending-child-marriage-zimbabw

Laird, S.E. (2005). International child welfare: Deconstructing UNICEF's country programmes. *Social Policy & Society, 4*(4), 457–466.

Lubombo, M. (2015). *Towards an Ubuntu framework for mainstreaming participation of people living with HIV (PLHIV) in social change communication for HIV prevention in South Africa.* (Unpublished doctoral dissertation). University of KwaZulu-Natal, Durban, ZA.

Machingura, F. (2011). A diet of wives as the lifestyle of the Vapostori sects: The polygamy debate in the face of HIV and AIDS in Zimbabwe. *Africana, 5(2),* 185–210.

Machingura, F. (2014). The martyring of people over radical beliefs: A critical look at the Johane Marange Apostolic Church's perception of education and health (family planning methods). In E. Chitando, M.R. Gunda., & J. Kugler (Eds.), *Multiplying in the spirit* (pp. 175–198). Bamberg, DE: University of Bamberg Press.

Maguranyanga, B. (2011). *Apostolic religion, health and utilisation of maternal and child health services in Zimbabwe.* Research report. Collaborating Centre for Operational Research and Evaluation. Harare, ZW: UNICEF and M Consulting Group.

Melchiorre, A. (2013). *A minimum common denominator? Minimum age for marriage reported under the Convention on the Rights of the Child.* http://www.ohchr.org/Documents/Issues/Women/WRGS/ForcedMarriage/NGO/AngelaMelchiorre.pdf.

Mpofu, E., Dune, T. M., Hallfors, D. D., Mapfumo, J., Mutepfa, M. M., & January, J. (2011). Apostolic faith church organization contexts for health and wellbeing in women and children. *Ethnicity & Health, 16*(6), 551–566.

Muchacha, M., Dziro, C., & Mtetwa, E. (2016). The implications of neoliberalism for the care of orphans in Zimbabwe: Challenges and opportunities for social work practice. *Aotearoa New Zealand Social Work, 28*(2), 84–93.

Muchacha, M., & Matsika, A. B. (2017). *Developmental social work: A promising practice to better address child marriage in Zimbabwe.* https://link.springer.com/article/10.1007/s41134-017-0042-3

Myers, W., & Bourdillon, M. (2012). Introduction: Development, children, and protection. *Development in Practice, 22*(4), 437–447.

Nemukuyu, D. (2016). *Zimbabwe Constitutional Court bans under-18 marriages.* http://nehandaradio.com/2016/01/21/concourt-bans-u18-marriages/

Newlands, A. (2016). SADC Model Law: One step closer to ending child marriage in Southern Africa. https://www.girlsnotbrides.org/sadc-model-law-one-step-closer-to-ending-child-marriage-in-southern-africa/

Sibanda, D. (2011). *Married too soon: Child marriages in Zimbabwe.* Harare, ZW: Research and Advocacy Unit.

Twum-Danso, A. O. (2008a). A cultural bridge, not an Imposition: Legitimizing children's rights in the eyes of local communities. *Journal of the History of Childhood and Youth, 1*(3), 391–413.

Twum-Danso, A. O. (2008b). *Searching for a middle ground in children's rights: The implementation of the Convention on the Rights of the Child in Ghana* (Unpublished doctoral dissertation). University of Birmingham, Birmingham, UK.

UN Fund for Population Activities (UNFPA). (2012). *Marrying too young*. New York, NY.

UNICEF. (2015). *The Apostolic Maternal Empowerment and New-born Intervention (AMENI) model: Improving maternal and new-born child health outcomes among apostolic religious groups in Zimbabwe*. Harare, ZW.

UNICEF. (2016a). *The state of the world's children 2016*. https://www.unicef.org/sowc2016/.

UNICEF. (2016b). *Extended analysis of Multiple Indicator Cluster Survey (MICS) 2014: Child protection, child marriage and attitudes towards violence*. Harare, ZW.

UN. (1948). Universal Declaration of Human Rights. New York, NY.

UN. (1979). Convention on the Elimination of All Forms of Discrimination against Women. http://www.ohchr.org/Documents/ProfessionalInterest/cedaw.pdf

UN. (1989). Convention on the Rights of the Child. http://www.ohchr.org/Documents/ProfessionalInterest/crc.pdf

UN. (2017). Resolution adopted by the General Assembly on child, early and forced marriage. http://www.un.org/en/ga/search/view_doc.asp? symbol=A/RES/71/175&referer=http://www.un.org/en/ga/71/resolutions.shtml&Lang=E

Wessells, M. G. (2015). Bottom-up approaches to strengthening child protection systems: Placing children, families, and communities at the center. *Child Abuse & Neglect*, *43*(1), 8–21.

Wyatt, A., Mupedziswa, R., & Rayment, C. (2010). Institutional capacity assessment. Harare, ZW: UNICEF and Ministry of Labour and Social Services.

"Everybody Here Knows This, If You Want to Go to School then You Must Be Prepared to Work": Children's Rights and the Role of Social Work in Ghana

Ziblim Abukari

Ghana is a signatory to many international conventions that seek to promote and protect the rights of children and was the first country to ratify the UN Convention on the Rights of the Child (CRC) (UN, 1989). At the continental level, the country also ratified the African Charter on the Rights and Welfare of the Child (African Charter) (African Commission on Human and Peoples' Rights, 1990) as a further demonstration of its commitment to protecting the rights and well-being of children. The Ghanaian government has enacted several legislative items since 1990 to streamline children's rights and welfare policies in the country. For example, Article 28 of the 1992 Constitution guarantees the rights of children to parental care and protection against exposure to physical and moral hazards, including engaging in work that threatens their health and educational development (Government of Ghana, 1992). These rights align with the tenets of international human rights instruments such as the CRC and the African Charter. Similar legislation pertaining to human rights and the rights of children that has been enacted in recent years includes the Criminal Act (Amendment) Act 1998 (Act 554), the Children's

Act 1998 (Act 560), Child Rights Regulations 2002 (LI 1705), and the Juvenile Justice Act 2003 (Act 653) (Manful & Manful, 2014).

Ghana's embrace and ratification of international conventions and enactment of national laws that protect both children in need and juvenile justice signals the government's commitment in principle to strengthening the legal framework for child protection. However, recent analysis of the legal instruments of child protection suggests that many of the children's rights and protection laws and policies are not properly coordinated, and the provisions in the Children's Act are not working as envisaged (Manful & Manful, 2014). Some have also pointed out the striking similarities between the Children's Act of Ghana and the UK crisis intervention model, which tends to rely on formal investigations and court-ordered interventions, practices that are incongruent with the family-centered and consensus-based approaches to decision making in Ghana (IFSW, 2011). While this is intriguing, it is not surprising because Ghana, like many countries in sub-Saharan Africa, inherited or adopted the child protection policies of their former colonizers, which to a large extent are ineffective because they do not reflect unique Ghanaian traditions, cultures, values, and resources.

The goal of this chapter is to examine the existing child protection laws in Ghana within the context of the CRC and the African Charter and the degree to which they enhance the rights of children as prescribed in these conventions. An additional impetus for this chapter is to critically examine the compatibility of these conventions with Ghanaian child-rearing practices. Traditional child protection practices prior to colonialism, including traditional child fostering, are examined, as some are still being practised today. The chapter also reviews the role of social work education and practice in promoting children's rights within the Ghanaian context given that many people, including child welfare professionals, seem to object to the universal notions of childhood being imported from Western cultures. Progress and challenges in children's education and protection against child labour are also examined.

Traditional Child Protection Practices Prior to Colonization

The traditional Ghanaian notion of the child and childhood is varied and contradictory at best. On the one hand, children are considered the future leaders of the nation and are held in high regard. As Boakye-Boateng (2010) observed, within the context of Afrocentric tradition, children are recognized as the custodians of tomorrow, and society's continuous existence hinges on its ability to socialize them in the art of survival and perpetuation. According to Onwauchi (1972), African children, prior to colonization, were educated by elders in their traditional customs, values, tales, and myths as well as moral and ethical codes of behaviour and social relationships. Some of these teachings also involved religious rituals and practices that instilled the ideas of love, respect, and obedience toward parents and elders. Through apprenticeship and participation in cultural rituals, Onwauchi (1972) observed, children develop communication skills and the art of survival, as expressed in the local culture. As part of this socialization, male children from seven years of age begin to engage in age-appropriate work of the father while female children learn household chores of the mother. There also existed a traditional African system of fostering (more on this later) that ensured the provision of material and spiritual support for the development of children (Boakye-Boateng, 2010).

Similarly, in their argument against the universal notion of childhood, Ndofirepi and Shumba (2014) observed that "the notion of 'child' is not a natural or universal category predetermined by biology, nor is it something with a fixed meaning"; instead, "childhood is historically, culturally, and socially variable" (p. 233). In the African context, children are perceived both as biologically fragile beings in need of protection and nurturance and social beings with prescribed social functions and relationships (Boakye-Boateng, 2010). Laird (2015) highlighted the pervasiveness of this resistance to universalized childhood in her study of child neglect in sub-Saharan Africa. Mwachilale (as cited in Laird, 2015) quoted a Malawian member of parliament's contribution to a debate for a childcare and protection bill as part of Malawi's efforts to implement the CRC. In his opposition to the bill he stated:

Malawi is located in the east of Central Africa and not to the east of Europe. We need to make some necessary departures from the way our friends in Europe do things. . . . Are we serious, if parents are punished for asking their children to feed goats, assisting them on tobacco work or for bringing up their children in that way. (p. 2)

This was ultimately an objection to what the MP perceived as an imposition of alien child-rearing practices on him and his country.

Beside these constructions of childhood existed an informal system of child fostering in pre-colonial Gold Coast, now Ghana. It was customary for the extended family, through kinship, to provide foster care to their family members whose parents were unable to do so (Goody, 1982; Kuyini et al., 2009). Afrocentric child fostering served other purposes in addition to care and protection of vulnerable children. For example, according to Oppong (as cited in Frimpong-Manso, 2014), among the Dagomba in northern Ghana, cultural practices such as *zuguliem* (a traditional practice where drummers assume the role of rearing their daughters' and sisters' children and train them in their profession) gave children an opportunity to learn a trade.

The practice of parents placing children in another family is a tradition in many societies worldwide. But existing literature suggests that the practice is more widespread in West Africa (Isiugo-Abanihe, 1985; Kuyini et al., 2009; Pilon, 2003). Within the West African region, child-fostering purposes vary across cultures. According to Goody (1982), this is because the practice serves distinct purposes depending on the cultural context and depending on the child's gender. Some of the purposes for child fostering, according to Goody (1982), include schooling, illness, death, divorce, mutual help among family members, socialization, and strengthening of family ties. The purposes can be grouped into two broad categories: kinship fostering (fostering within the family), and non-kinship fostering outside the family or between families (Isiugo-Abanihe, 1985; Kuyini et al., 2009; Pilon, 2003). In a study of child fostering in West Africa, Isiugo-Abanihe (1985) categorized the types and motivations of traditional child fostering into four distinct groups. These are crisis fostering, alliance and apprentice fostering, domestic fostering, and educational fostering. Since traditional child fostering is not the focus of this chapter, two categories are briefly highlighted here.

Crisis fostering

Crisis fostering is usually necessitated by a crisis such as death, the dissolution of the family, or perceived danger (Goody, 1982; Isiugo-Abanihe, 1985; Pilon, 2003; Serra, 2009). According to Goody (1982), "where fostering follows the dissolution of the conjugal family . . . 'crisis' fostering is used to distinguish it from 'voluntary' or 'purposive' fostering, which is initiated while the parents' marriage is intact" (p. 43). This form of fostering has played and continues to play a critical role in protecting children in times of crisis, since institutional child fostering remains at the peripheral level, serving less than 1 percent of children in Ghana (Ministry of Gender, Children and Social Protection, 2015). In her study of children orphaned on account of AIDS in the Manya Krobo District of the Eastern Region of Ghana, Ansah-Koi (2006) noted that people who may not be related to the orphans provided foster care based on sympathy, altruism, and religious beliefs. Similarly, Pilon (2003) reported that kinship fostering has become more important in many parts of Africa because of a growing number of orphans whose parents have died of HIV/AIDS, with up to 40 percent of orphans living in traditional foster care in Burkina Faso in 2003.

Educational fostering

Unlike the other purposes of traditional child fostering, educational fostering is a more recent phenomenon necessitated by structural inequalities such as poverty and uneven access to formal educational opportunities. In this case, children are fostered out for an opportunity to obtain formal education. According to Pilon (2003), proximity to educational amenities and the readiness of a family to foster a child are key considerations in educational fostering. Similarly, Isiugo-Abanihe (1985) and Goody (1982) observed that most contemporary fostering in West Africa is associated with formal education, which is increasingly viewed as a means of social mobility. Due to the unavailability of schools, particularly in rural areas in Africa, Isiugo-Abanihe contended that young children may be sent to reside with distant relatives or non-relatives during their schooling years. However, it has also been observed that there is an ambivalent relationship between child fostering and access to formal education in Ghana (Isiugo-Abanihe, 1985; Pilon, 2003). The authors note that while some children may be fostered out to obtain formal education, child fostering may be the reason some children are out of school.

The UN Convention on the Rights of the Child and the Ghanaian Context

All African countries have ratified the CRC and incorporated its provisions into their national statutes regarding child welfare and protection. The CRC comprises 54 articles in which are enshrined children's civil and political rights, as well as their economic, social, and cultural rights. It advocates for the protection and promotion of the rights of children with special needs, of minority children, and refugee children (UN, 1989). There are four core principles that govern the implementation of these rights: non-discrimination; best interests of the child; right to life, survival, and development; and respect for the views of the child (UN, 1989).

Laird (2015) observes that the CRC provisions are based on the premise that children are dependents who require the care and protection of their parents in a nuclear family system. With regard to implementation of the CRC in lower-income countries of the world, some authors have argued that since their unsuccessful structural adjustment programs, the World Bank and the International Money Fund (IMF) have repackaged their Western-centred, patronizing approaches to emphasize "investment in human capital," which promotes early childhood development as an equalizer of opportunities (Monaghan, 2012). For example, a review of the World Bank–sponsored programs in mainly lower-income countries over a 12-year period by Sayre et al. (2015) highlighted the importance of investment in early childhood development. Focusing on five core areas of the bank's investments—education, health, nutrition, population, and social protection—the report noted that these programs not only support improved growth and development and better school outcomes but also have the potential to break the intergenerational transmission of poverty. However, implicit in this *new* approach is a push for a universal conception of childhood and child rearing with little regard to local context and traditions (Laird, 2012; Monaghan, 2012; Penn, 2012).

An independent evaluation of the World Bank's operations underscored the benefits of early childhood education investments but criticized the bank for focusing too much on child survival and physical growth to the neglect of socio-emotional development, parenting education, and maternal psychological needs (Independent Evaluation Group, 2015). The report also criticized the lack of parental involvement and alignment between the programs and the countries' needs. In the view of Jenk (2005), some international institutions, including non-profit organizations, have collectively produced "an extensive globalization of Western ideas of childhood," noting that "one particular vision of childhood has been and continues to be exported as 'correct childhood'" (p. 123). Alluding to the variations of the meaning of childhood across cultures, Jenk (2005) argues that if viewed from a social constructionist perspective, the meaning of childhood varies considerably from one society to another, with radical changes in meaning even within the same culture over time.

Laird (2015) argues that the Western hegemonic constructions of childhood that characterize children as vulnerable and needing constant care and protection from their parents and caregivers have been transmitted to Africa through international conventions such as the CRC, and make it practically difficult to distinguish between parental neglect and appropriate traditional practices of child rearing in Africa. The contradiction is more conspicuous in the common adage that "children are to be seen and not heard" and was clearly expressed by some child welfare professionals in a study on the relevance of children's rights in practice in Ghana by Manful and Manful (2014): "Children's rights is about allowing children to be involved in issues that adults are to take care of; it will make children in the Home indiscipline[d] and uncontrollable, we can't allow that to happen." Another respondent added, "Children's rights, allowing children to be involved in every issue is a 'white man's' idea; it has nothing to do with us" (p. 323). These paternalistic images of the child and perceptions of child welfare workers confirm that they object to any form of the Anglo-Eurocentric ideals of childhood and child-rearing practices being imposed on them and highlight the complexities of enforcing child protection laws in Ghana, and the continent, if the laws do not reflect indigenous cultural mores and values.

The African Charter on the Rights and Welfare of the Child

It is an irony that all African countries unanimously endorsed the CRC, although they did not participate in the drafting of the convention. However, African governments criticized the convention for ignoring critical socio-cultural and economic realities of African circumstances (Olowu, 2002). Laird (2015) contends that it was these criticisms that led to the development and adoption of the African Charter, which ironically replicated many of the CRC provisions but added new provisions unique to the African situation. These additional provisions include "the duty to work for the cohesion of the family, to respect his parents, superiors and elders at all times and to assist them in case of need . . . to serve his national community by placing his physical and intellectual abilities at its service, to preserve and strengthen social and national solidarity" (Laird, 2015, p. 5). This list of obligations was intended to be more reflective of the collective values of the kinship system in African society and consistent with Onwauchi's (1972) description of traditional African values—and these are much broader than the narrow definitions of family obligations in the CRC. Like the CRC, the African Charter was incorporated into the national statute books of member countries. Under the African Charter, a child cannot be discriminated against based on his/her parents' or legal guardians' race, ethnicity group, or colour. The African Charter does not make any reference to a "state," unlike Article 3 of the CRC, implying that the obligation not to discriminate is binding not only on the state but other actors as well (Chirwa, 2002).

Given the disparate provisions in the CRC and the African Charter, it is not difficult to fathom why African governments have struggled to articulate children's rights and fully adhere to the obligations of these international legal instruments, because the two tend to contradict each other on several key provisions. Laird (2015) poignantly captured this contradiction when she argued that while "one version construes children as entirely dependent, requiring protection and care from their parents . . . the other conceptualizes them as holding duties to assist and meet the needs of others within an interdependent web of family relationships and community participation" (p. 5). The interdependent and collective child-rearing practices in Africa are further illustrated by Mbugua (2012) and LeVine et al. (1994) in their description of child-rearing practices in Kenya, where they observed that a child belongs not to one family, but to the extended family system and that it takes a whole village to bring up a child.

Legal Framework for Child Protection in Ghana

The first formal organization established solely for the protection of children 0–18 years of age was the Ghana National Commission on Children (GNCC) in 1979 (Addison, 2012). The GNCC was responsible for the implementation of the CRC and played key roles in advocating for various children's rights laws, including the Children's Act 1998 (Act 560), Juvenile Justice Act 2003 (Act 653), and the ratification of the African Charter on the Rights and Welfare of the Child in 2005. In 2001 the GNCC was replaced by the Ministry of Women and Children's Affairs, which was renamed Ministry of Gender, Children, and Social Protection in 2013. The establishment of a ministry devoted to women and children has pushed children and women's rights into mainstream public policy, and is seen by some as a big leap forward (Addison, 2012; Appiah, 2012). As part of this reconfiguration, the Department of Children (DOC) was also created to focus on child development and to provide guidelines to the ministries and local government organizations.

The Children's Act 1998 (Act 560)

The Children's Act of 1998 makes provisions for the rights of the child and deals with parental duties and responsibilities, maintenance, adoption, and fosterage. The law also protects children from exploitative labour and child marriage, and establishes conditions for care and protection of children. Consistent with the CRC, the Act defines a child as any person below the age of 18 years. Concerning the welfare of the child, the Children's Act makes provisions for the notion that "the best interest of the child shall be paramount in any matter concerning a child" (Article 2[1]). It also prohibits discrimination against a child based on gender, race/ethnicity, age, religion, refugee status, or ethnic origin. Regarding education, the Children's Act notes that "no person shall deprive a child access to education, immunization, adequate diet, clothing, shelter, medical attention, or any other things required for his [or her] development." It further states that "no person shall deny a child medical treatment by reason of religious or other beliefs" (Article 8[2]). Section 9(3) of the Children's Act gives the Department of Social Welfare a mandate to remove a child in need of care and protection as specified in Section 8(1) regardless of the status of the child. In addressing maintenance, the Children's Act requires parents or legal guardians to provide for the child's basic needs, including health, education, life, and reasonable shelter. Child maintenance cases may be decided in a Family Tribunal, with a child represented by a parent, probation officer, a social welfare officer, or next of kin. The Children Act also addresses child labour in Section 87, which prohibits exploitative child labour, defined in Section 87(2) as work "which deprives a child of its health, education, or development.".

The Situation of Children's Rights in Ghana

Economically, Ghana is currently one of the best-performing economies in Africa, with an annual growth rate of between 6 and 7 percent since 2005 (Cooke et al., 2016; UNICEF, 2011). The country recently achieved a middle-income status due to a significant reduction of poverty in the last two decades. Joint UN Development Programme (UNDP) Government of Ghana (2015) data shows that Ghana has largely achieved the millennium development goals of universal primary education enrolment and cutting by half the proportion of people living in extreme poverty. These are all good signs and offer hope for children's rights to better living conditions even though spatial differences remain in rural districts and northern Ghana.

The right to education

Children have a right to education, according to the Constitution of the Republic of Ghana (Government of Ghana, 1992). It states that "no child shall be deprived by any other person of medical treatment, education or any other social or economic benefit by reason only of religious or other beliefs" (Article 28[4]). The Constitution transcends the right to education to include a mandate for government to provide equal opportunities and facilities for students to realize this right. The article states that "basic education shall be free, compulsory and available to all" (Article 25). It is worthwhile noting that this is not the first time that Ghana has had an Education Act. In fact, Ghana enacted the first free, compulsory universal primary education policy (it covered primary one to six) in sub-Saharan Africa through the Education Act of 1961 (Act 87) (Foster, 1965).

Some have observed that the recent education policies in Ghana were designed to align with the provisions in international conventions such as the CRC, the African Charter, and Universal Declaration on Human Rights (Ghana NGOs Coalition on the Rights of the Child [GNCRC], 2014), thereby reinforcing the significance of education to the development of the child. The Government of Ghana's 10-year Education Sector Plan (2010–2020) contains many provisions and initiatives that suggest government's commitment to improving educational outcomes. According to the Ministry of Education (2010), the 10-year education plan aims to improve access and quality of education, promote health and sanitation, and expand pre-school and kindergarten as well as provide equal opportunities for all children to education. The last point is particularly significant because due to lack of equal access and opportunities, education has not played the role of an equalizer of opportunities since the end of colonialism more than six decades ago. Recent data suggests that even though Ghana has achieved the gross enrolment target, net enrolment is still below target at 89.3 percent. Gender parity in school enrolment has also been achieved at the kindergarten level, 99 percent at primary, 95 percent at junior high school, and lowest at 91 percent at the senior high school level (UNDP/Government of Ghana, 2015).

According to the GNCRC (2014), while the gap in gender parity in school enrolment has narrowed over the last two decades, girls still encounter difficulties in receiving an education. The GNCRC lamented that when families could not afford education of all their children, parents tended to remove their daughters rather than their sons from school. The structural inequalities, combined with cultural attitudes, exacerbate girls' lack of access to education. In their study of children's rights in Ghana, Porter et al. (2011) pointed out how remoteness and poverty commingle to hinder children's access to education, particularly for girls. Focusing on the Gomoa District of the Central Region, Porter and colleagues observed that the district has met the primary school enrolment targets and achieved gender parity in enrolment at the primary level. However, access became constricted at secondary school because students had to commute 2–4 kilometres to their nearest secondary school. They also found that only boys, not girls, had bicycles to make the daily commute.

It can be deduced that achieving the CRC objectives and that of the Children's Act will require more than providing access to education, and should include changing cultural attitudes toward girls' education and children's rights in general through education and establishing sanctions for teacher and student misconduct. A study on school and home factors that negatively impact girls' education in Malawi revealed that uneducated mothers do not believe in the benefits of girls' education, and the majority of respondents in their rural samples believed girls to be less intelligent than boys (Chimombo et al., 2000). With regard to Ghana, Sackey (2007) reviewed the determinants of school attendance from a gender perspective and concluded that parental educational levels, particularly the mother's education, had a significant positive effect on school attendance as well as changing the intergenerational socio-economic status of the family.

Several conclusions can be drawn from these studies. First, sustainable anti-poverty programs are needed to alleviate chronic poverty and enhance economic security, since poverty is a key obstacle to educational access and results in the prevalence of child labour. Second, more schools are needed in rural areas to reduce the distance to travel to school, or else government should provide transportation such as school buses to feeder schools (a policy not currently available in public schools). This is because the cost of busing may be far lower than construction of new schools. Furthermore, when parents are uneducated they do not understand the value of education and cannot perceive its long-term benefits. As a result, they tend to rely on long-held traditional gender stereotypes in favour of boys. Thus, there must be a concerted effort by government and NGOs to educate the public, particularly parents in rural areas, about the benefits of girls' education.

While the government has implemented new social protection programs such as the Livelihood Empowerment Against Poverty (LEAP), a health insurance scheme, and a school feeding program, there remains a need for a teacher training curriculum that is less authoritarian and encourages equal participation of all genders. These programs will also be more effective if there are gender-specific targets, particularly regarding girls' education and women's economic empowerment. There is also a need for policy changes on sexual harassment and teacher/student misconduct. Chimombo et al.'s (2000) study in Malawi indicated that some girls miss school or drop out because of sexual harassment by teachers and fellow students. Dunne et al. (2005) reported similar cases of sexual harassment of girls in Ghana and Botswana more than a decade ago, and the problem persists today.

Recently, a Ghanaian daily newspaper, the *Daily Graphic* (2018), reported the sexual misconduct of a headmaster of a rural district senior high school with a 16-year-old student. While this revelation was not too surprising, the reaction by the Ghana Education Service (GES) and local teachers' association was most outrageous. While the paper reported that the teacher had been suspended pending investigation, he was not charged with any crime. The paper also quoted a representative of the Ghana National Association of Teachers (GNAT) from the Central Region saying that the teacher committed no crime because the relationship was consensual, and the girl's parents knew about it. It is obvious that neither the GES nor GNAT recognized this behaviour as a crime, and an egregious violation of trust by an adult who had been entrusted with the care of minor children. This kind of attitude must change to protect young girls and help them to succeed in school.

Child labour

The adoption of the CRC in 1989 has reshaped the notion of childhood across the world and brought into sharp focus the problem of child labour. Even though the CRC has been criticized by some as an attempt to universalize or globalize the notion of childhood (Jenk, 2005; Monaghan, 2012; Penn, 2012), or export Western ideals of childhood to other countries (Laird, 2012), there is consensus about work or practices that are exploitative or harmful to children's health and development. It has been observed that the CRC, as a global children's rights instrument, has obligated countries around the world to promote and maintain the welfare of children and recognize child labour as a problem (Clerk, 2011).

Clerk (2011) also observed that the implementation of the CRC in many countries, including Ghana, has been hampered by a number of factors, including lack of consensus about how childhood should be defined. Research shows that in general child labour is more prevalent in sub-Saharan Africa, where 59 million children aged 5–17 years are engaged in hazardous work (International Labor Organization [ILO], 2017). Despite Ghana being the first country to ratify the CRC, 1.9 million children aged 5–17 were reported to be engaged in child labour in 2014, and out of this number 1.2 million were engaged in hazardous occupations, including artisanal gold mining, head porterage, and street peddling, among others (Ghana Statistical Service, 2014: Okyere, 2014).

For many contemporary Ghanaian children, engaging in an economic activity is no longer about socialization, as in earlier times, but a necessity for survival, and poverty is the primary reason for children's engagement in child labour (Ghana Statistical service, 2014; Okyere, 2014). Research also shows that more than half a million children of school age are not in school, with 26.3 percent of those who attend school engaging in economic activity while 41.6 percent of those not in school engage in child labour (ILO, 2017). These staggering statistics indicate that while progress has been made, the country still must work to fully achieve the CRC provisions. The gaps and failures of existing domestic policies were articulated by the children who participated in Okyere's (2014) study of child labour in artisanal gold mining, who opined that they needed to work to support their education. Okyere (2014) quoted a 16-year-old student who stated, "Everyone here knows this. . . . If you want to go [to school], then you must be prepared to work. They say it every day on the TV that education is the future . . . but if you don't work, no school for you" (p. 95). The children in the study acknowledged the dangers in such work but felt that they had no choice.

This case further underscores the challenges in implementing the CRC and other child welfare policies in Ghana. The laws and policies exist in principle but are either poorly coordinated or rarely enforced despite the institutional and legal framework being put in place. It is important to recognize that rectifying these problems is possible, but it will take time. Evidence shows that the overall proportion of Ghanaians who live in extreme poverty has declined by more than half in the last two decades, although nearly a quarter of the population (24 percent) still live in extreme poverty (Ghana Statistical Service, 2014; UNICEF, 2011).

With decreasing poverty, attention must be paid to strengthening the political and legal institutions as part of an effort to combat corruption, tribalism, and nepotism. As former US President Barack Obama exhorted Ghanaian and African leaders during his first visit to Africa in 2009, "Africa doesn't need strongmen, it needs strong institutions" (BBC, 2009). The need for accountability on the part of all Ghanaians regardless of class, status, or creed is obvious, and people entrusted to run social institutions, elected or otherwise, need to put the interests of children above their own. It is my opinion that the problem of children in Ghana is not entirely due to lack of resources but rather mismanagement, and stronger, more independent institutions would go a long way to curtailing this social menace.

The Role of Social Work in the Promotion of Children's Rights

The role of social work in the promotion of human rights is deeply rooted in the profession's history and origins. From the onset, the early social work pioneers sought to improve the lives of the poor, the abandoned, and the forgotten in society. This was poignantly captured by the International Federation of Social Workers (IFSW, 1988, as cited in UN, 1994) when it stated, "Social work has, from its inception, been a human rights profession, having as its basic tenet the intrinsic value of every human being and as one of its main aims the promotion of equitable social structures, which can offer people security and development while upholding their dignity" (p. 3).

Tracing the history of human rights in social work, Staub-Bernasconi (2016) identified human rights in the writings of many early pioneers, including Alice Salomon, Eglantyne Jebb, and Jane Addams. Jane Addams (cited in Staub-Bernasconi, 2016) noted: "What is all the talk about fraternity and equality, when one doesn't have the right to make it concrete in the helping relationship?" (p. 40). Contemporary human rights were formally institutionalized in social work with the publication of the text *Teaching and Learning about Human Rights: A Manual for Schools of Social*

Work and the Social Work Profession (UN, 1994) in collaboration with the IFSW in 1992 and republished in 1994. Staub-Bermasconi (2016) argues that this publication was instrumental in bringing many transformations to social work, including an international definition of social work, ethics in social work, global standards for the education and training of the social work profession, and more recently, the *Global Agenda for Social Work and Social Development: Commitment to Action.* Specifying the role of social work in the promotion of human rights, the UN (1994) states that the focus on human rights shapes the conviction that the fundamental needs of humans require that they be met not as a matter of choice but as an imperative of social justice.

In Africa, social work is a relatively young profession that continues to evolve but has a potential to play a larger role in promoting human rights, including the rights of children. Introduced to the continent by former colonial powers, the profession continues to struggle to find a niche in adopting indigenous methods to suit local needs. In this section, I focus on recommendations that will strengthen social work education and practice in Ghana and Africa to promote children's rights. The UN Centre for Human Rights (UN, 1994) made specific recommendations for teaching and learning about human rights. Although they are not specifically about children's rights, I find the recommendations useful, and they can be adapted to social work education and practice on children's rights in Ghana. The UN manual notes that teaching and learning about human rights is similar to other areas of social work because it requires application and analysis as well as personal commitment to communication and understanding. Three of the UN (1994) recommendations are outlined here: recognizing the problem, analysis, and use of reference groups.

Recognizing the problem

Education and training are the cornerstones in the promotion of children's rights. Social work's core values of dignity and worth of a person, diversity, and non-discrimination, among others, speak to an implicit human rights dimension. According to the UN (1994), the priority for teachers and students is to learn to recognize and explore these dimensions both in theory and in practice. It is important to consider client issues from three ecological systems levels (micro, meso, macro) before setting goals. Another consideration should be given to the preventive, developmental, and social-action approaches of social work intervention. The macro system level is particularly useful to Ghana because socio-economic problems are more prevalent. The ecological-level analysis is also important because there seems to be a disconnect between social workers as individuals (micro) and the larger macro system. This was evident in Manful and Manful's (2014) study of child welfare workers in Ghana on their perspectives on children's rights. The authors noted that while the child welfare workers acknowledged the importance of children's rights they felt that it was irrelevant to their work. It appears that the workers do not recognize or understand children's rights. Proper training in the form of curriculum redesign that incorporates human rights, and continuing education on current trends and developments in the field, are imperative to help such workers recognize the problem and understand their role in upholding and protecting these rights.

Analysis of the problem

The UN (1994) also notes that a conventional social work practice approach is to start from where the client is, which may be in the family or social context. In just the same manner, basic human rights issues begin with the fundamental rights of the individual as outlined in the CRC, the Ghanaian Constitution, and the Children's Act. However, unlike people in individualistic cultures who view problems confronting them as their own (Heine, 2010), individuals in collectivist cultures where family plays a central role are more likely to have an interdependent view of themselves and define their problems within the context of these interdependent relationships (Marcus & Kitayama, 2010).

In this case, the problem of children's rights in Ghana should be analyzed within the context of the interdependent relationships within the family and community. This is because the human rights and well-being of the child affect the well-being of the family and the community at large. Like the problem recognition discussed earlier, the analysis should be situated within the individual's ecological system (micro, meso, macro), because understanding the root causes is the first step in the helping process and it may be located at the individual, group, or community/societal level. Furthermore, analysis of prevailing socio-economic and political environment is critical. In the case of Ghana, government commitment to children's rights, traditional norms, and cultural attitudes all impact children's rights in various ways.

The countervailing cultural attitudes of Ghanaian child welfare workers were palpable in Manful and Manful's (2014) study, as revealed in these quotes: "We have many cultural practices that are not compatible with the rights of children, we have been socialized to believe that a good child is one who listens and [doesn't]' speak back to adults" (p. 323). Another worker added, "I cannot say children's rights is of much relevance for us because we cannot involve children in issues that affect them here, we have to emotionally protect the children from involvement in issues that might be distressful to them" (p. 323). The social workers' ignorance and disregard for children's rights may be the root cause of the problem but also reveals the irony of the CRC in Ghana and the contrasting demands in the CRC and the African Charter.

More than 25 years after the country ratified the CRC and almost 20 years after the Children's Act was passed, very few people outside of government, including some social workers, are educated enough about what these laws really mean. Based on the collectivist orientation mentioned earlier, these social workers seem to believe that children's rights are indistinguishable from that of their parents or carers, which is inaccurate. The need is therefore obvious for the inclusion of human rights content in social work education curriculum that is properly contextualized and utilizes local textbooks, Ghanaian case studies, and vignettes on children's rights in the country. Professional development in the forms of continuing education, workshops, and training for those already in the field is also needed to keep abreast of current knowledge and best practices. A cursory look at the social work program at the University of Ghana reveals some noticeable changes in the curriculum, with the inclusion of two courses on human rights: *Women and Children's Rights and Protection* and *Human Rights in Social Work Practice*. There is a third course on *Working with People in Need of Protection*. These are glimpses of hope that the curriculum is gradually being indigenized to reflect the unique needs of the local context.

Use of reference groups

Underpinning a successful intervention strategy are support elements available to the social worker (UN, 1994). The UN manual notes that support may be sought from individuals, organizations, groups, and social movements involved in human rights issues. These include self-help groups, law enforcement, NGOs, and faith-based organizations. Laird (2008) underscored the importance of reference groups, specifically mutual aid groups, in sub-Saharan Africa in providing aid to its members in times of adversity. Laird notes that the groups range from those that make regular contributions into a common fund such as *susu* (Ghana) or *esusu* (Nigeria) to those that organize for income-generating activities and skills training.

Social workers can leverage the existing strengths of these groups for public education using their existing structures. Lucas (2013) underscored the relevance of social movements to social work education in Africa and noted that because African social workers are vulnerable to victimization as individuals by the state, banding together can provide security in challenging oppression and injustice against vulnerable and marginalized groups, including children. Based on personal experience, this is already a familiar strategy for social workers in Ghana, particularly those working in non-governmental organizations. Using these community groups will be effective in educating the public about children's rights and human rights in general because there is a high level of trust between community social workers and the groups they already work with in other spheres like anti-poverty and food security programs.

Active participation in policy making

It is an irony that social workers in Ghana and many parts of the world, including Western countries, are apathetic toward the social policy-making process because, as (Lucas, 2013) puts it, the plight of social work clients is often shaped by policy makers. Because of social workers' indifference to the social policy making process, Lucas (2013) observed that the process is usually dominated by people with little understanding or concern for vulnerable groups. However, I must add that social work associations in North America and the United Kingdom are proactive advocates for policies that affect vulnerable populations. For example, the National Association of Social Workers (NASW, 2017) suggests that the social work profession was founded in social change and demonstrates this by actively engaging in social policy and legislative advocacy. In 2016–17 the NASW identified voting rights, criminal justice reform, immigration reform, and economic justice as its legislative priorities as well as several key policy issues (NASW, 2017).

Similarly, the British Association of Social Workers (BASW) has been active in campaigning on issues such as spending cuts in the voluntary and service sectors, fee capping on expert testimony by independent social workers, foster care, and refugees and immigration (BASW, 2014). Ghanaian and African social workers can emulate this by engaging in the policy-making process through advocacy and direct participation, including seeking elected positions in the national assemblies to meaningfully influence policy outcomes. Lucas (2013) further contends that while social workers deal primarily with victims of socio-economic deprivation, political intolerance, and injustices, they play no role in the formulation, development, and evaluation of programs that affect their lives.

In this regard, social workers are perceived as either silent or passive on many issues, including the distribution of resources, protection of human rights, and promotion of non-violent means of conflict resolution. Rwomire and Raditlhokwa (as cited in Lucas, 2013) put it this way: "The consequence of this constricted perception of Social Work is that in many African countries, Social Work does not proactively address structural sources of poverty, but only functions as a passive and unambitious distributor of meagre food handouts which effectively keep clients in the vicious cycle of poverty" (p. 92). It is therefore imperative for social workers in Ghana to mobilize and work with the government to create the necessary structures that put social workers at the forefront of social development.

Professionalization and professional recognition

One way for social workers in Ghana and Africa to become effective advocates is to seek professional recognition. I believe that one of the reasons why the social work curriculum has been slow to adapt is lack of standards development and licensure through which they can gain professional recognition. Like social workers in Britain and the United States who are guided by codes of ethics (e.g., BASW, 2014; NASW, 2017), Ghanaian social workers are guided by a code of ethics contained in the Ghana Association of Social Workers (GASOW) *Code of Ethics of Social Workers* (1999). The GASOW code of ethics obliges members to observe the core values of service, social justice, dignity and worth of a person, integrity, and competence. Despite this, the few social work programs in the country are not accredited, leaving the profession lurking in the periphery because of lack of professional recognition by the government and society. Participants in a study by Kreitzer et al. (2009) lamented the lack of professional identity in the form of licensing and recognition through an effective professional association.

Lucas (2013) blames the failure of social work in many African countries to meaningfully respond to the region's unique problems on its narrow focus and lack of recognition and support from governments. In his view, the lack of government support and recognition results in social workers being placed in cash-deprived ministries of social welfare to administer ineffective welfare programs, which Laird (2008) described as remnants of colonialism that have made it difficult to design programs to meet local needs.

Conclusion

Children's rights remain culturally controversial to many indigenous Africans, even among the so-called educated elite, because such rights are considered alien and antithetical to their cultural beliefs and constructions of children and child-rearing practices. The UN General Assembly unanimously adopted the Convention on the Rights of the Child in 1989 as a global standard for the protection of children against exploitation, abuse, and other harmful practices. Africa domesticated the CRC by adopting the African Charter on the Rights and Welfare of the Child, which reflected African cultural values of kinship and children's responsibilities to family and the community. At the national level, the Ghanaian government, through many children's rights legislative instruments, have brought children's rights to the mainstream. However, many children continue to engage in child labour or remain out of school. In this chapter, I outlined specific roles that social work can play to promote children's rights, including their ability to recognize a problem and analyze the problem, and being proactive in the policy-making process that affects the people they work with.

REFERENCES

Addison, R. (2012). *Addressing the needs of children in Ghana: Challenges and prospects.* Accra, GH: Centre for Policy Analysis Research Papers.

African Commission on Human and Peoples' Rights. (1990). African Charter on the Rights and Welfare of the Child. https://www.achpr.org/public/Document/file/English/achpr_instr_charterchild_eng.pdf

Ansah-Koi, A. A. (2006). Care of orphans: Fostering interventions for children whose parents die of AIDS in Ghana. *Families in Society, 87*(4), 555–564.

Appiah, E. M. (2012). *Protecting the rights of children in Ghana: The legal framework and ancillary matters.* Accra, GH: Centre for Policy Analysis Research Papers.

Boakye-Boateng, A. (2010). Changes in the concept of childhood: Implications on children in Ghana. *Journal of International Social Research, 3*(10), 104–115.

British Association of Social Workers (BASW). (2014). *The Code of Ethics for social work: Statement of principles.* Birmingham, UK: Policy, Ethics, and Human Rights Committee. http://cdn.basw.co.uk/upload/basw_95243-9.pdf

British Broadcasting Corporation (BBC). (2009). *Obama speaks of hopes for Africa.* http://news.bbc.co.uk/2/hi/africa/8145762.stm

Chimombo, J., Chibwanna, M., Dzimadzi, C., Kunkwenzu, E., Kunje, D., & Namphota, D. (2000). *Classroom, school, and home factors that negatively affect girls' education in Malawi.* Zomba, MW: Center for Educational Research and Training.

Chirwa, D. M. (2002). The merits and demerits of the African Charter on the Rights and Welfare of the Child. *International Journal of Children's Rights, 10*(2), 157–177.

Clerk, G. (2014). Child labor in Ghana: Global concern and local reality. In R. K. Ame, D. L. Agenyiga, & N. A. Apt (Eds.), *Children's rights in Ghana: Reality or rhetoric?* (pp. 15–36). Lanham, MD: Lexington Books.

Cooke, E., Hague, S., & McKay, A. (2016). *The Ghana Poverty and Inequality Report: Using the 6th Ghana Living Standards Survey.* Accra, GH: UNICEF.

Daily Graphic Online. (2018, January 23). *Head teacher in leaked sex tape did no wrong—GNAT.* https://www.graphic.com.gh/news/general-news/headteacher-in-leaked-sex-video-did-no-wrong-gnat.html

Dunne, M., Leach, F., Chilisa, B., Maundeni, T., Tabulawa, R., Kutor, N., Forde, L. D., & Asamoah, A. (2005). *Gendered school experiences: The impact on retention and achievement in Botswana and Ghana.* (Educational Papers No. 56). London, UK: Department for International Development.

Foster, P. (1965). *Education and social change in Ghana*. Chicago, IL: University of Chicago Press.

Frimpong-Manso, K. (2014). Child welfare in Ghana: The past, present, and future. *Journal of Educational and Social Research, 4*(6), 411–419. https://doi.org/10.5901/jesr.2014.v4n6p411

Ghana Association of Social Workers (GASOW). (1999). *Code of ethics of social workers*. Accra, GH. https://www.gasow.org/social-practice/code-of-ethics/

Ghana NGOs Coalition on the Rights of the Child (GNCRC). (2014). *Convention on the Rights of the Child (CRC) report*. Accra, GH. https://tbinternet.ohchr.org/Treaties/CRC/Shared%20Documents/GHA/INT_CRC_NGO_GHA_17939_E.pdf

Ghana Statistical Service. (2014). *Ghana living standards survey: Report of the 6th round*. Accra, GH. https://www.ilo.org/ipecinfo/product/viewProduct.do?productId=25515

Goody, E. N. (1982). *Parenthood and social reproduction: Fostering and occupational roles in West Africa*. Cambridge, UK: Cambridge University Press.

Government of Ghana. (1992). Constitution of the Republic of Ghana. Accra, GH. https://www.wipo.int/edocs/lexdocs/laws/en/gh/gh014en.pdf

Government of Ghana (1998). The Children's Act (Act 560). Accra, GH. http://www.unesco.org/education/edurights/media/docs/f7a7a002205e07fbf119bc00c8bd3208a438b37f.pdf

Heine, S. J. (2010). Cultural psychology. In S. T. Fiske, D. T. Gilbert, & G. Lindzey (Eds.), *Handbook of social psychology* (5th ed., Vol. 2, pp. 1423–1459). Hoboken, NJ: Wiley.

IFSW. (2011). *Social work and the rights of the child: A Professional Training Manual on the UN Convention*. Munsingen, CH.

Independent Evaluation Group. (2015). *World Bank support to early childhood development: An independent evaluation*. Washington, DC: World Bank.

International Labour Organization (ILO). (2017). *Child labor in Africa*. https://www.ilo.org/ipec/Regionsandcountries/Africa/WCMS_618949/lang--en/index.htm

Isiugo-Abanihe, U. C. (1985). Child fostering in West Africa. *Population and Development Review, 11*(1), 53–73.

Jenk, C. (2005). *Childhood* (2nd ed.). New York, NY: Routledge.

Kreitzer, L., Abukari, Z., Antonio, P., Mensah, J., & Afram, K. (2009). Social work in Ghana: A participatory action research project looking at culturally appropriate training and practice. *Social Work Education, 28*(2), 145–164.

Kuyini, A. B., Alhassan, A. R., Tollerud, I., Weld, H., & Haruna, I. (2009). Traditional kinship foster care in northern Ghana: The experiences and views of children, carers, and adults in Tamale. *Child and Family Social Work, 14*, 440–449. https://doi.org/10.1111/j.1365-2206.2009.00616.x

Laird, S. E. (2012). The construction of the child in Ghanaian welfare policy. In A. Twum-Danso Imoh & R. Ame (Eds.), *Childhoods at the intersection of the local and the global* (pp. 94–120). Basingstoke, UK: Palgrave Macmillan.

Laird, S. E. (2015). "If parents are punished for asking their children to feed goats": Supervisory neglect in sub-Saharan Africa. *Journal of Social Work,* 16 (3), 1–19. https://doi.org/10.1177/1468017315572037

LeVine, R. A., Dixon, S., LeVine, S., Richman, A., Leiderman, P. H., Keefer, C. H., & Brazelton, T. B. (1994). *Culture and care: Lessons from Africa.* Cambridge, UK: Cambridge University Press.

Lucas, T. (2013). Social work in Africa: The imperative for social justice, human rights and peace. *PULA: Botswana Journal of African Studies,* 27(1): 87–106.

Manful, E., & Manful, S. E. (2014). Child welfare in Ghana: The relevance of children's rights in practice. *Journal of Social Work, 14*(3), 313–328. https://doi.org/10.1177/1468017313477756

Marcus, H. R., & Kitayama, S. (2010). Cultures and selves: A cycle of mutual constitution. *Perspectives on Psychological Science, 5*(4), 420–430. https://doi.org/10.1177/1745691610375557

Mbugua, J. W. (2012). *Promoting child rights: Reflections on key processes of children sector in Kenya from 1989 onwards as recorded by some national civil society actors.* London, UK: Save the Children.

Ministry of Education. (2010). *Education Strategic Plan (2010–2020).* Accra, GH: Government of Ghana.

Ministry of Gender, Children and Social Protection. (2015). *Child and family welfare policy.* Accra, GH: Government of Ghana.

Monaghan, K. (2012). Early childhood development policy: The colonization of the world's childrearing practices? In A. Twum-Danso Imoh & R. Ame (Eds.), *Childhoods at the intersection of the local and the global* (pp. 56–74). Basingstoke, UK: Palgrave Macmillan.

National Association of Social Workers (NASW). (2017). *Code of ethics of the national association of social workers.* Washington, DC: Author. https://www.socialworkers.org/LinkClick.aspx?fileticket=ms_ArtLqzeI%3d&portalid=0

Ndofirepi, A. P., & Shumba, A. (2014). Conceptions of "child" among traditional Africans: A philosophical purview. *Journal of Human Ecology, 45*(3), 233–242.

Okyere, S. (2014). Children's participation in prohibited work in Ghana and its implications for the Convention on the Rights of the Child. In A. Twum-Danso & N. Ansell (Eds.), *Children's lives in an era of children's rights: The progress of the Convention on the Rights of the Child in Africa* (pp. 92–104). Abingdon, UK: Routledge.

Olowu, D. (2002). Protecting children's rights in Africa: A critique of the African Charter on the Rights and Welfare of the Child. *International Journal of Children's Rights, 10,* 127–136

Onwauchi, P. C. (1972). African peoples and Western education. *Journal of Negro Education, 41*(3), 241–247.

Penn, H. (2012). The rhetoric and realities of early childhood programmes promoted by the World Bank. In A. Twum-Danso Imoh & R. Ame (Eds.), *Childhoods at the intersection of the local and the global* (pp. 75–93). Basingstoke, UK: Palgrave Macmillan.

Pilon, M. (2003). *Foster care and schooling in West Africa: The state of knowledge.* Paris, FR: UNESCO.

Porter, G., Abane, A., Blaufuss, K., & Acheampong, F. O. (2011). Children's rights, mobility, and transport in Ghana: Access to education and health services. In R. K. Ame, D. L. Agenyiga, & N. A. Apt (Eds.), *Children's rights in Ghana: Reality or rhetoric?* (pp. 15–36). Lanham, MD: Lexington Books.

Sackey, H. A. (2007). *The determinants of school attendance and attainment in Ghana: A gender perspective.* AERC Research Paper 173, African Economic Research Forum. Nairobi, KE.

Sayre, R. B., Devercelli, A. E., Neuman, M. J., & Wodon, Q. (2015). *Investing in early childhood development: Review of the World Bank's recent experience.* Washington, DC: World Bank.

Serra, R. (2009). Child fostering in Africa: When labor and schooling motives may coexist. *Journal of Development Economics, 88,* 157–170.

Staub-Bernasconi, S. (2016). Linking two traditions of human rights in social work. *Journal of Human Rights and Social Work, 1,* 40–49.

UN. (1989). Convention on the Rights of the Child. New York, NY.

UN. (1994). *Teaching and learning about human rights: A manual for schools of social work and the social work profession.* New York, NY.

UN Development Programme (UNDP)/Government of Ghana. (2015). *Ghana Millennium Development Goals 2015 Report.* New York, NY.

UNICEF. (2011). *Report of the mapping and analysis of Ghana's child protection system: Final report.* Hong Kong, CN: Child Frontiers.

Human Rights and Medicalization of FGM/C in Sudan

Paul Bukuluki

Perpetuation of harmful practices such as female genital mutilation/cutting (FGM/C) is rooted in social motivations that do not have health benefits, and it constitutes a violation of human rights for girls and women. This chapter conceptualizes FGM/C in Africa and Sudan as a manifestation of social conventions or norms that have serious consequences for sexual and reproductive health rights (SRHR). It analyzes the drivers of FGM/C and its medicalization from a human rights perspective. It argues that FGM/C and its medicalization have socio-cultural, structural, and socio-economic drivers that need to be taken into account in SRHR policy and programming aimed at the demedicalization and abandonment of FGM/C. Social workers and health professionals in multidisciplinary teams should engage in social norm change and behavioural change interventions as well as systematic advocacy for policies and programs that address FGM/C and its medicalization in Sudan.

Background

The World Health Organization (WHO, 2018) classification describes four types of female genital mutilation/cutting (FGM/C): (1) clitoridectomy; (2) excision; (3) infibulations; and (4) other. The WHO (2019) offers the following characterization of types of FGM/C:

Type 1 is characterized by: partial or total removal of the clitoris (a small, sensitive and erectile part of the female genitals), and in very rare cases, only the prepuce (the fold of skin surrounding the clitoris) while type 2 involves the partial or total removal of the clitoris and the labia minora (the inner folds of the vulva), with or without excision of the labia majora—the outer folds of skin of the vulva. (p. 1)

The WHO (2019) further notes that FGM/C types differ in terms of severity, and in particular the type 3 (re-infibulation) that is common in Sudan is documented to be the most severe:

The most severe is type 3; often referred to as infibulation, this is the narrowing of the vaginal opening through the creation of a covering seal. The seal is formed by cutting and repositioning the labia minora, or labia majora, sometimes through stitching, with or without removal of the clitoris. (p. 1)

The WHO (2019) has described type 4 as encompassing "all other harmful procedures to the female genitalia for non-medical purposes, e.g. pricking, piercing, incising, scraping and cauterizing the genital area" (p. 1).

Although there is considerable variation in form, content, motivations, extent of genital tissue removed, instruments used, age at which FGM/C is performed, and terminology used to describe the practice, it has been aptly noted that all forms of FGM/C are characterized by "the partial or total removal of the female external genitalia or other injury to the female genital organs for cultural or other non-therapeutic reasons" (WHO, 2019, p. 1).

According to the WHO (2010), the word "mutilation" emphasizes the gravity of the act while the term "female genital cutting" is used to reflect the importance of using non-judgmental terminology with practising communities. However, the main premise of this chapter is that irrespective of who, how, when, and where it is done, FGM/C represents a gross violation of human rights and dignity of children, girls, and women. The research adopts a human rights approach as its analytical framework.

Human Rights and FGM/C

Several scholars have emphasized the health–human rights nexus and have argued for the need for complementarity between public health and human rights. One of the key protagonists for this perspective, Jonathan Mann, noted that "people could not be healthy if governments did not respect their rights and dignity as well as engage in health policies guided by sound ethical values. Nor could people have their rights and dignity if they were not healthy" (Gostin, 2001, p. 121). From Mann's perspective, health is at variance with "dignity violations," and therefore, promoting and protecting health depends upon the promotion and protection of human rights and dignity (Mann et al., 1994). Gostin (2001) took this perspective further by arguing that a health and human rights analysis requires uncovering the rights violations, failures of rights realization, and burdens on dignity that constitute the societal roots of health problems. His perspective examines how a whole human being is made vulnerable to a wide variety of pathogens and unhealthy conditions as a result of how the person is treated by society—and how this affects human rights and dignity. This observation points to the notion of social determinants of health and how they are linked to human rights, freedoms, and dignity.

Social determinants of health (SDH) and their relation to human rights are clearly articulated by the WHO (2008) Commission on SDH. The commission aptly states that "inequalities in health arise because of circumstances in which people grow, live, work and age, and the systems put in place to deal with illness. The conditions in which people live and die are, in turn, shaped by political, social and economic forces" (WHO, 2008, p. 3). There is probably no better document that heralds and advocates for human rights, especially the sexual and reproductive health rights (SRHR), than the Sustainable Development Goals (SDGs). One of the vision statements (number 8) of the SDGs aptly states:

> We envisage a world of universal respect for human rights and human dignity, the rule of law, justice, equality and non-discrimination; of respect for race, ethnicity and cultural diversity; and of equal opportunity permitting the full realization of human potential and contributing to shared

prosperity. A world which invests in its children and in which every child grows up free from violence and exploitation. A world in which every woman and girl enjoys full gender equality and all legal, social and economic barriers to their empowerment have been removed. (UN, 2015a, Article 8)

Further still, the SDGs encompass health-related strategic targets that espouse promoting women's and children's health which augment the human rights–based approach to health (UN, 2015a). Three of these targets are particularly relevant for promoting SRHR, one each under the health, gender equality, and education goals. Specifically, SDG5, "Achieve Gender Equality and Empower All Women and Girls" (p. 14) provides a clear framework for the human rights–based approach to SRHR. This is further elaborated upon in the 2015 UN Secretary General's Global Strategy on Reproductive, Maternal, Newborn, Children's and Adolescents' Health (UN, 2015b), which provides a road map to advancing the health of women, children, and adolescents, including promoting abandonment of harmful social norms that affect SRHR for women and girls. This has further added impetus to the conceptualization of FGM/C as a harmful social norm and practice that constitutes a violation of the human rights of girls and women given its short-term and long-term health consequences (WHO, 2019).

The cultural diversity–human rights paradox

Whereas FGM/C has serious health consequences and is a violation of human rights, it is not immune to the cultural diversity, cultural rights, and human rights paradox. For those who argue for the negotiation between cultural relativism[1] and human rights that tend to claim universality, the debate still goes on about how to find middle ground with respect to universalism, cultural diversity, and cultural relativism (Donnelly, 1984) in the context of FGM/C. In this case, leaning toward cultural relativism and contextualization, without taking into account the global discourses and evidence that show that FGM/C is detrimental to the health of girls and women, raises moral questions as well as issues of political correctness rather than focusing on the health and well-being of women and girls

(Nyangweso, 2016). However, it is also important to appreciate that human rights need to be translated into action in culturally sensitive ways that acknowledge cultural diversity and emphasize using cultural resources but also send a clear message that castigates harmful cultural practices. This message requires nurturing spaces for constant negotiation between cultures, rather than suffocating it in favour of the local context or universals or political correctness. This process is closely associated with what has been described as cosmopolitan localism,[2] which means taking into account global discourses (or universals like human rights) (Sachs, 2006). However, it also maintains a strong focus on the context in which people experience challenges, suffering, or illness as perceived by them. As argued by Kleinman (1978), it is important to give adequate consideration to the social and historical context, as well as the experience of suffering, in the assessment of disease. For example, it is important to avoid generalizing FGM/C to be the same and to mean the same thing in every culture or society where it is practised, because doing this would mean designing one-size-fits-all interventions. Not paying adequate attention to contextualization would also lead to falling into the trap of blind universalism like one described by Sachs (2006):

> For centuries, universalism has been at war with diversity. Science, the state and the market have dominated this campaign. . . . Science, the state and the market are based on a system of knowledge about man, society and nature that claims validity everywhere and for everybody. (p. 219)

Therefore, from this perspective, interventions against FGM/C and its medicalization as a human rights violation need to be contextualized and viewed relative to the various settings.

Medicalization of FGM/C

Medicalization of FGM/C has been defined to refer to "situations in which FGM/C is practiced by any category of health-care provider, whether in a public or a private clinic, at home or elsewhere (WHO, 2010, p. 2). "It also includes the procedure of re-infibulation at any point in time in a woman's life" (p. 2). Analysis of data from several countries shows that more than 18 percent of all girls and women who have been subjected to FGM/C in the countries from which data are available have had the procedure performed on them by a health-care provider (WHO, 2010). However, this report notes that there are large variations between countries, ranging from less than 1 percent in several countries to between 9 and 74 percent in six countries, including Sudan (WHO, 2010). Studies have shown that the categories of health-care providers that carry out FGM/C include physicians, assistant physicians, clinical officers, nurses, midwives, trained traditional birth attendants (TBAs), and other personnel providing health care to the population, in both private and public sectors (Berggren et al., 2004; WHO, 2010).

The World Health Assembly (2008) adopted the resolution WHA 61.16 on the elimination of FGM/C, in which all member states agreed to work toward the abandonment of FGM/C, including ensuring that the procedure is not performed by health professionals. This was a follow-up to earlier high-level statements by the WHO (1998) made as early as 1979 that condemned the medicalization of FGM/C at the first international conference on FGM/C, held in Khartoum, Sudan. Since then several other statements from international agencies have been issued, including a formal statement of the WHO's position to the United Nations Commission on Human Rights in 1982 (WHO, 1998). In addition, several United Nations Treaty Monitoring Bodies, including the Committee on Elimination of all forms of Discrimination Against Women (UN, 2014), have called on countries to eliminate the medicalization of FGM/C. As clearly stated in the WHO's Global Strategy to Stop Health-Care Providers from Performing FGM/C:

> Engaging health professionals to support abandonment of female genital mutilation and never to perform it is critical to success in eliminating the practice. . . . Stopping medicalization of FGM is an essential component of the holistic, human rights-based approach for the elimination of FGM. . . . By taking a stand in favour of abandonment of the practice and by refraining from performing it, health-care providers

will contribute to increased debate and questioning of the practice by communities. (WHO, 2010, p. 5)

Therefore, this chapter discusses the status and drivers of the medicalization of FGM/C in Sudan from a human rights perspective and includes research conducted between February and March 2016 concerning drivers of FGM/C medicalization among community midwives in Sudan.

Methods

The chapter is predominantly based on a document review supplemented by consultative meetings in the form of focus group discussions (FGDs) with health workers, particularly midwives, in Khartoum. The study design was phenomenological; it encouraged midwives to reflect on their own experiences in relation to FGM/C at facilities and communities where they work. The intention of the FGDs was to understand the experiences of health workers, particularly midwives, about their perceptions and experiences in relation to drivers of the medicalization of FGM/C. Two FGDs were conducted with each group consisting of 6–10 midwives. The FGDs also served as consultative meetings to generate information to facilitate development and pretest the protocol and tools for an implementation research protocol, intended to develop and test interventions to promote the demedicalization of FGM/C. The FGDs were conducted with the help of a translator fluent in Arabic and English.

FGDs were aimed at supplementing information collected through the document review process using the search engine Google Scholar, and published and unpublished reports from agencies working on FGM/C. One of the key sources of quantitative data was the secondary analysis of the 2014 multiple indicators cluster (MICS) survey report (UNICEF, 2016). The analysis of qualitative evidence from consultative meetings was thematic; it involved identification of prominent or recurring themes and sub-themes in the primary data (Dixon-Woods et al., 2005). Some verbatim extractions from key informant interview transcripts are inserted directly into the results of this chapter. The findings from secondary data were also organized into thematic categories, based on commonality of meaning. Approval to conduct interviews and FGDs was obtained from

Federal Ministry of Health given that these were part of the preliminary consultations that informed the design of a formative study.

Verbal informed consent was sought from participants using a consent form detailing the purpose of the consultations, with emphasis on voluntary participation, requesting permission to record interviews and assuring participants of confidentiality, and informing them of the risks and benefits of participation.

Results

The results of the research include the following themes: (1) magnitude of FGM/C in Sudan; (2) health consequences of FGM/C and violation of health rights; and (3) medicalization of FGM/C in Sudan, with sub-themes of the (a) perception of harm reduction, (b) power dynamics, (c) harm reduction "dilemma," (d) perception of FGM/C as a religious obligation, (e) understanding of re-infibulation to be different from FGM/C, and (f) negotiation between societal norms, values, and policies. This section presents results generated from primary sources and the review of secondary data from relevant documents.

Magnitude of FGM/C in Sudan

In Sudan, the prevalence of FGM/C among females aged 15–49 years is 86.6 percent (UNICEF, 2016 (about 8,369,890) with 77.0 percent (UNICEF, 2016) having type 3 (flesh sewn) (UNICEF, 2016) (See Fig. 10.1). The FGM/C prevalence is different within generations: 66.3 percent among those aged 0–14 years, 88.3 percent among those aged 30–34 years, and 91.8 percent among those aged 45–49 years (UNICEF 2016). The prevalence of FGM/C type 3 in 1966 was 81.9 percent compared with 2014 when it was 73.3 percent. Furthermore, secondary FGM/C (defined as recircumcision in the last 12 months) was highest among women 15–19 years (31.2 percent) compared to 20–39 years (23–24 percent). FGM/C overall prevalence in Sudan is high (86.6 percent), and the highest rates are in North Kordofan (97.7 percent), Northern State (97.5 percent), North Darfur (97.6 percent), East Darfur (97.3 percent), and River Nile (96.4 percent). There is a slight variation between rural areas (87.2 percent) and urban areas (85.5 percent) (UNICEF, 2016).

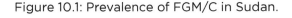
Figure 10.1: Prevalence of FGM/C in Sudan.

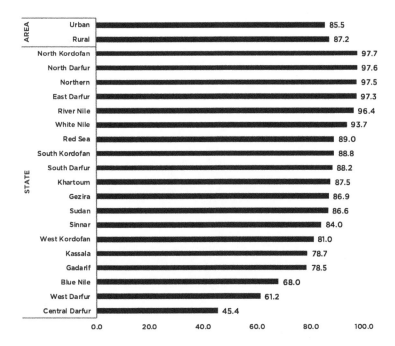

Health Consequences of FGM/C and Violation of Health Rights

The World Health Organization (2016) "Guidelines on the Management of Health Complications from Female Genital Mutilation" (pp. 6–8) provide a succinct description of the short-term and long-term consequences of FGM/C. See Table 10.1 below:

Given its harmful social and health consequences to women and girls (UNICEF, 2013), FGM/C is described as a reflection of the deep-rooted inequality between the sexes, and an extreme form of discrimination against women (WHO, 2016). FGM/C is therefore one of the cultural norms and practices that have been recognized as sitting at the intersection between violence against children (VAC) and violence against women (VAW). One of the major reasons why FGM/C is considered a human

Table 10.1: Health Consequences of FGM/C. Source: WHO (2016, pp. 6-7), Guidelines on the Management of Health Complications from Female Genital Mutilation/Cutting.

RISK	REMARKS
IMMEDIATE RISKS[1]	
Haemorrhage	
Shock	Haemorrhagic, neurogenic or septic
Genital tissue swelling	Due to inflammatory response or local infection
Infections	Acute local infections; abscess formation; septicaemia; genital and reproductive tract infections; urinary tract infections;
	The direct association between FGM and HIV remains unclear, although the disruption of genital tissues may increase the risk of HIV transmission.
Urination problems	Acute urine retention; pain passing urine; injury to the urethra
Wound healing problems	
Death	Due to severe bleeding or septicaemia
OBSTETRIC RISKS[2]	
Caesarean section	
Postpartum haemorrhage	Postpartum blood loss of 500 ml or more
Episiotomy	
Prolonged labour	
Obstetric tears/lacerations	
Instrumental delivery	
Difficult labour/dystocia	
Extended maternal hospital stay	
Stillbirth and early neonatal death	
Infant resuscitation at delivery	

[1] Also see Berg, Underland et al. (2014) and Iavazzo et al. (2013).
[2] Also see WHO (2006) and Berg, Odgaard-Jensen et al. (2014).

Table 10.1 (*continued*)

RISK	REMARKS
SEXUAL FUNCTIONING RISKS[3]	
Dyspareunia (pain during sexual intercourse)	There is a higher risk of dyspareunia with type III FGM relative to types I and II
Decreased sexual satisfaction	
Reduced sexual desire and arousal	
Decreased lubrication during sexual intercourse	
Reduced frequency of orgasm or anorgasmia	
PSYCHOLOGICAL RISKS	
Post-traumatic stress disorder (PTSD)	
Anxiety disorders	
Depression	
LONG-TERM-RISKS[4]	
Genital tissue damage	With consequent chronic vulvar and clitoral pain
Vaginal discharge and Vaginal itching	Due to chronic genital tract infections
Menstrual problems	Dysmenorrhea, irregular menses and difficulty in passing menstrual blood
Reproductive tract infections	Can cause chronic pelvic pain
Chronic genital infections	Including increased risk of bacterial vaginosis
Urinary tract infections	Often recurrent
Painful urination	Due to obstruction and recurrent urinary tract infections

[3] Also see Berg, Underland et al. (2014) and Berg, Denison et al. (2010).
[4] Also see Berg, Underland et al. (2014) and Iavazzo et al. (2013).

rights abuse is that it is nearly always carried out on minors, making it a violation of the rights of children. WHO (2016) conceives FGM/C as

> a practice that violates a person's rights to the highest attainable standard of health, right to health, security and physical integrity, the right to be free from torture and cruel, inhuman or degrading treatment, and the right to life when the procedure results in death. (p. 9)

FGM/C is a human rights violation also for the reason that it damages healthy genital tissue and can lead to severe consequences for girls' and women's physical and mental health (Vloeberghs et al., 2012). For example, several studies have shown prevalence of depression and anxiety disorders, including post-traumatic stress disorder (PTSD) among survivors of FGM/C (Applebaum et al., 2008; Kizilhan, 2011; Vloeberghs et al., 2012; Whitehorn et al., 2002).

By contributing to violation of these rights, FGM/C contravenes several international human rights instruments that promote the rights of women and girls. These include the International Covenant on Economic, Social and Cultural Rights (UN, 1966); the Universal Declaration of Human Rights (UN, 1948, Articles 1 and 3); the International Covenant on Civil and Political Rights (ICCPR) (UN 1976, Preamble and Articles 6 and 9); and the Convention on the Rights of the Child (UN, 1989, Article 19). These rights are also dealt with in the Protocol to the African Charter on Human and Peoples' Rights on the Rights of Women in Africa (African Commission on Human and Peoples' Rights, 2003, Article 5); the Joint General Recommendation/General Comment No. 31 of the Committee on the Elimination of Discrimination against Women (UN, 2014); and the Joint General Recommendation/General Comment No. 18 of the Committee on the Rights of the Child on Harmful Practices (UN, 2014).

Studies in several African countries have also revealed that the health consequences of FGM/C increase the burden of care and the economic costs of treatment. For example, a study carried out in Gambia on health consequences of FGM/C established that the practice of FGM/C has significant health consequences and economic costs as one of three patients (299 cases of871) suffered medical consequences requiring treatment

(Kaplan et al., 2011, pp. 5–6) This finding is corroborated by other studies showing that the annual costs of FGM/C-related obstetric complications ranged from 0.1 to 1 percent of government spending on health for women aged 15–45 years (Adam et al., 2010).

Other scholars have argued that FGM/C justifies acts of sexual control by devaluing bodily pleasure, thus undermining individual sexuality and reproductive rights (Nyangweso, 2016). Anthropologist Ellen Gruenbaum (2001) described FGM/C as "an expression of sexism and patriarchy" (p. 133) and conceived of it as a cultural practice that is part of and reinforces social structures that promote similar practices like polygamy and child marriage that are all designed to limit women's self-realization and well-being (Gruenbaum, 2001; Nyangweso, 2016).

Medicalization of FGM/C in Sudan

FGM/C practice has become increasingly medicalized among women (15–49 years), from 55.4 percent during 1966 to 1979 to 76 percent in the years 2000 to 2014 (UNICEF, 2016). Trained midwives (76.0 percent) perform most of the cutting compared to traditional birth attendants (18.4 percent) (UNICEF, 2016). The trend analysis of cadres that carry out FGM/C in Fig.10.2 and 10.3 below also clearly demonstrates that FGM/C is primarily carried out by health-care workers, especially midwives.

Perception of harm reduction

The major sources for data for this sub-theme were literature review and consultative meetings with midwives from two health facilities in Khartoum. From both primary and secondary sources, it was noted that the major driver of medicalization is the perception that health workers or health professionals, especially midwives, perform "milder" forms, for example, the *Sunna* type perceived as a religious rite. Health professionals are perceived to be more skilled in performing FGM/C and in reducing the health consequences arising from FGM/C. This perception thrives in the context of insufficient training of community midwives, especially in relation to ethical issues ("do no harm"), to counter existing social and religious norms and limited knowledge among health workers, particularly midwives, about the health consequences of FGM/C.

Figure 10.2: Medicalisation of FGM/C.

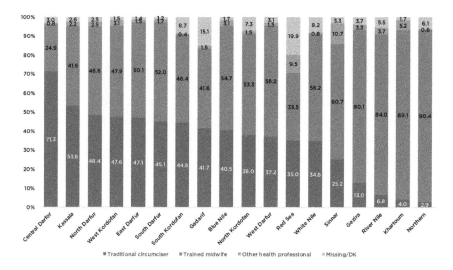

Source: Unicef—Secondary analysis of Sudan 2014 MICS Data, Feb. 2016.

Figure 10.3: Analysis of trends in medicalisation of FGM/C.

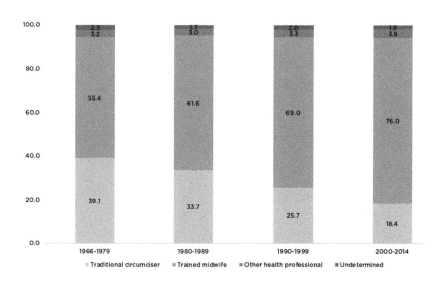

Source: Unicef—Secondary analysis of Sudan 2014 MICS Data, Feb. 2016.

Power Dynamics

Dahl (1968) has suggested that power refers to "subsets of relations among social units such that the behaviors of one or more units . . . depend in some circumstances on the behavior of other units" (p. 407). It has been described by Dahl (1968) in terms of A getting B to do something she or he would not otherwise have done. As argued by Elisheva (2004) in his commentary on Dahl's theory of community power:

> Power is exercised in a community by a particular concrete individual, while other individuals, also actual, are prevented from doing what they prefer to do. Power is exercised in order to cause those who are subject to it to follow the private preferences of those who possess the power. Power is the production of obedience to the preferences of others, including an expansion of the preferences of those subject to it so as to include those preferences. (p. 36)

This notion of power resonates with Finke's (2006) argument in the context of FGM/C, that

> from an intra-cultural perspective, the focus of FGM is not primarily on surgical intervention or the manipulation of a girl's or woman's sexual organs but rather on raising the status of the woman/(future) wife or even on initiating her into a "powerful" secret society. Even when the cutting is experienced as traumatic, the practice is not rejected. Instead, the excised body is viewed as having achieved the aesthetic norm: the genitals in their natural state are denigrated as being unaesthetic, unclean or even as harmful to health. (p. 13)

Therefore, FGM/C as a rite of passage becomes the determining factor for access to the various social institutions and resources required for normal social functioning in a society and becomes a source of inclusion or exclusion, leaving women and girls with limited options. For example, eligibility to marriage or preparation for marriage hinges on undergoing FGM/C.

Given the significance of the FGM/C as a rite of passage or a determinant of access to societal resources, the actors involved in executing FGM/C, especially mothers, circumcisers, and others, mostly elder women, enjoy their power. As explicitly stated by Finke (2006):

> Their skills with the ritual are in demand, their knowledge of how to raise the young is respected. They know the significance of virginity and the power of sexuality, which needs to be checked. Or they are bowing to the necessity of excising from the bodies of their daughters the—from their point of view—dangerous "maleness" to be found there. . . . Thus the circumcisers are proud to do their (religious) duty and join in the process of increasing the girls' eligibility for marriage. (p. 13)

During the consultative meetings with midwives it was evident that they, at the community and societal level, wield power and control over issues of sexuality and reproduction, and that they are trusted and protected by the community. The midwives noted that if you asked women and men in their community to rank powerful people in the community, midwives would be among those at the top given their significant role in relation to sexuality, reproduction, family, marriage, childbirth, and safe motherhood. They are the experts and are consulted on all aspects involving sexuality, fertility, marriage, reproduction, and FGM/C. With the increase in awareness about the health consequences of FGM/C, midwives wield even more power because they are believed to perform milder FGM/C and to contribute to harm reduction. Several midwives explain:

> The only three people are allowed to see her forbidden body parts are: her mom, the midwife and her husband, no one else is allowed. A midwife since history is known to be a secret keeper, even when women are facing issues with their husbands, they run to the midwife to solve their problems, such as sexual issues, social issues. (FGD midwives).

Another midwife states,

> Well, the midwife is an influential person; she can communicate with the Emam, El Shaiekh, with the president and actually with everyone." Another midwife elaborated: "Because she is the one the people trust on the neighborhood, the one who knows the complications and how to manage it, the midwife job it's not exclusively about deliveries, she's the one who gives education, awareness and so on.

Therefore, medicalization of FGM/C adds to the power of midwives because they are now perceived as the only ones who can do it right. It was interesting to learn from midwives that those who do not perform FGM/C were generally perceived by community members who want FGM/C as incompetent, and young, with limited understanding of the cultural, religious, and family stability values associated with FGM/C. For example, during the FGD, one midwife said:

> Some of the community members think that we are new proud and young midwives, if we said we will not perform the circumcision, they will choose to go to the other midwives who will do the circumcision, although we have the knowledge and we have been trained, but this is not the knowledge the community wants, because they believe the community have the alternatives—the old midwives.

Another stated,

> Well, the communities will not force you to do something you don't want to do, but sometimes when the midwife refuses, they will seek for another midwife to perform it and so on.

The harm reduction "dilemma"

Harm reduction, which generally is about measures to improve its (FGM/C's) safety, raises a moral dilemma highlighted by Shell-Duncan (2001), who argues that

> the debate over medicalization of FGM has, up until now, been cast as a moral dilemma: to protect women's health at the expense of legitimating a destructive practice? Or to hasten the elimination of a dangerous practice while allowing women to die from preventable conditions? (p. 1013)

Harm reduction is a new paradigm in public health that aims to minimize the health hazards associated with risky behaviours, such as intravenous drug use and high-risk sexual behaviour, by encouraging safer alternatives, including but not limited to abstinence. Harm reduction considers a wide range of alternatives and promotes the alternative that is culturally acceptable and bears the least amount of harm. A systematic review on understanding why health-care providers perform FGM/C found that a proportion of health-care providers practise FGM/C or re-infibulation to prevent or reduce the risks for girls and women of undergoing the procedure with a traditional practitioner (Doucet et al., 2017). For example, some studies established that some health workers believe that performing FGM/C in hygienic conditions would reduce the harm for girls (Mostafa et al., 2006; Njue & Askew, 2004); and medicalized procedures, particularly administration of anesthetic medication, would reduce pain for girls. Some midwives in FGDs claimed that they choose to practice re-infibulation "because somebody else would and perform it worse than they would" (Berggren et al., 2004, p. 304); for financial gain; and in response to the requests of families and community members (Berggren et al., 2004; Doucet et al., 2017).

These arguments notwithstanding, human rights protagonists argue that promoting harm reduction, as a strategy in response to FGM/C, would entrench medicalization of the practice, which would further complicate efforts to eliminate it entirely. It would also derail advances in promoting abandonment of FGM/C because it violates women's rights, advances illustrated by the adoption of the Protocol to the African Charter on Human and Peoples' Rights on the Rights of Women in Africa (African Commission on Human and Peoples' Rights, 2003), which explicitly recognizes women's right to be free from FGM/C. It would also derail the advances in legislation against FGM/C, given that the law is being used increasingly to combat the practice and legislation criminalizing FGM/C has been adopted in many countries (Center for Reproductive Rights, 2006, p. 1). Similar arguments have been made that health-care providers are generally respected members of the community, and when they practise FGM/C, this can give the impression that the procedure is acceptable and safe, which can further promote the practice (Doucet et al., 2017, p. 2). It is further argued that "since FGM/C is performed for sociocultural reasons rather than for medical reasons, the practice goes against the Hippocratic Oath of 'Do no harm,' and it violates girls' and women's right to physical integrity, health and life" (p. 3).

Perception of FGM/C as a religious obligation

Some midwives and other health professionals have the perception that FGM/C is a religious issue and that they have an obligation to respond positively to requests from families to cut their daughters. Those with this belief feel that they have a religious and cultural obligation to perform FGM/C: "they being midwives is the will of God and their reward for being midwives will come from God" (Participant FGD midwives). Another midwife elaborated further"

> A reward from God, that's the first thing. We don't pay attention to anything else, as long as we put in our mind to do our job perfectly with dedication, we ask God to reconcile us in what we do, in the sake of God, that's all what we want. . . . From this perspective, those who reject requests from families to cut girls would be acting against the will of God.

Human rights activists and the WHO (1996) have argued that this perception runs counter to what the Prophet Mohamed says: "God curses females who alter His creation." This is interpreted to mean that "God created human beings in the best mold and wanted them to keep the nature in which they were created, forbidding them to make any changes in God's creation" (p. 5).

Despite attempts by Islamic scholars to explain the non-authenticity of the hadith related to female circumcision, there are still claims among sections of the Islamic community that FGM/C, particularly the *Sunna* type, is linked to religion (Shell-Duncan, 2001). Similarly, UNICEF (2005) argues that

> FGM/C is not prescribed by any religion. This is not, however, the general perception, especially regarding Islam. Although there is a theological branch of Islam that supports FGM/C of the *sunna* type, the Koran contains no text that requires the cutting of the female external genitalia. . . . Moreover, the majority of Muslims around the world do not practice FGM/C. Sudan is one of the countries that has a theological branch of Islam that supports the Sunna type of FGM/C. (p. 12)

This is therefore still an area of controversy, and it creates doubts among some families in relation to making decisions for their daughters to undergo FGM/C and puts them at risk of succumbing to pressure from the society and imams. This too creates a dilemma for some health workers, who believe the *Sunna* type of FGM/C is linked to the Islamic religion, about how to respond to the requests from families to have their daughters undergo FGM/C. This is happening in the context of limited awareness about the health consequences of FGM/C by some midwives, and belief that circumcised women are clean and do not attract infections. For example, one of the midwives in the FGD believed that "circumcised women are [as] clean as possible, and they don't get the infections like the uncircumcised women."

Understanding of re-infibulation to be different from FGM/C

There is a perception among midwives that when a woman gives birth, re-infibulation (a procedure to recreate an infibulation, for example after childbirth when de-infibulation is done) is necessary because it restores the vagina to its original state and "avoids more complications and helps her to increase her value and maintain her marriage . . . striving for beautification and completion" (Berggren et al., 2004, pp. 299–300). Midwives in the FGDs had a perception that re-infibulation would only refer to "narrowing beyond the initial infibulation." To them, restoring the woman to the status of her original infibulation state was not perceived as re-infibulation. In other words, for the midwives in the FGDs re-infibulation is the norm as long as it does not go beyond the initial infibulation. "We restore as much as we cut for delivery, we stitch it back, nothing more, even if her original vagina was narrow; we get it back the same." Another midwife remarked that

> we only cut what is suitable for the baby's head to come out (de-infibulation), nothing more, and then we stitch this cut itself, only. And if there is a previous scar of episiotomy, I open at the same place with the same measures and then stitch it from inside to outside. . . . We measure it with our digits along with head of the baby avoiding cutting more than it is supposed to be . . . because the cut that is made by the scissors won't be self-returning, and if you don't do the stitches, it will get infected and she may bleed as well, so the stitches to stop bleeding and not to get the area infected.

Therefore, for these midwives, re-infibulation is the normal thing to do. This indicates a lack of training in clinical management of FGM/C complications aligned to the WHO guidelines.

Negotiation between societal norms, values, and policies

One of the issues emerging from interaction with midwives was that they belong to a culture and religion that treasures FGM/C and they had to constantly negotiate and balance between demands from families, their cultural/religious obligations, and professional ethics, especially to do no harm and not violate the rights of people. With respect to social norms, Doucet et al. (2017) in their systematic review found a number of studies in which health-care providers, including those from Sudan, cite cultural reasons to justify their practice of FGM/C (Berggren et al., 2004; Refaat,

2009). In the FGDs with midwives in Khartoum, one of the midwives described how she carefully negotiated between culture and medical ethics in relation to FGM/C:

> Two girls came from Gezira state, to study at university, they felt they are less than their colleagues because they were uncircumcised, and even their aunts gave them a hard time because of that. They actually developed a psychological complexity because they were uncircumcised, so one of them dropped the university for two weeks and she said won't get back till I'll be equal with my colleagues. They brought me to her, I tried to discuss with her the situation and she was insisting to do the Pharaonic circumcision, I said do you know what is it? She said yes and I want it, I actually did for her a very light cutting for her clitoris and stitched her and that was it, then she called her aunts to prove to them that now she became a circumcised girl, her aunts were finally pleased.

This is happening in a context where many midwives are administratively not hired by the Ministry of Health (MOH) and with limited livelihood options. A considerable number of community midwives (trained for nine months) are not employed and perform FGM/C as a financial survival strategy. For these midwives, previous studies have established that re-infibulation represents a considerable source of income, but motives of midwives are more complex than simply economic (Berggren et al., 2004). Therefore, the complexities of entrapment by social norms, religious beliefs, not being employed, and not accountable administratively to MOH to apply existing code of conduct policies make midwives susceptible to engaging in the medicalization of FGM/C.

Conclusions

FGM/C is one of the major forms of gross SRHR abuses in countries where it is still practised. Its medicalization under the guise of harm reduction has exacerbated the vice because it tends to project it as legitimate, although it is a human rights violation for the girls and women. As clearly shown by the results of the MICS (UNICEF, 2016), trained midwives that are part of the health-care system represent the major health-care worker cadre who are carrying out FGM/C. FGM/C medicalization has socio-economic drivers, and it has a social norms dimension that needs to be considered in SRHR policy and programming in prevention and response to FGM/C. Strengthening knowledge on health consequences of FGM/C is very important, but this needs to be coupled with social norm interventions targeting midwives because they also share similar socio-cultural and religious norms and beliefs with the other community members.

These results point to the need for a health-system and multi-sectoral response to FGM/C and for strengthening accountability frameworks for health workers as deterrence to medicalization. They point to the need to develop training tools that, from the onset, conceptualize FGM/C and its medicalization as a violation of human rights. Given the complexity of FGM/C and its social norms, changing workload, and clinical management of complications, multi-sectoral and multi-disciplinary teams involving health workers and social workers need to work together, especially in the context of health and social policies, in the realization of the sustainable development goals that link gender equality and health as well as universal health coverage. The health professionals and social workers, who command respect in communities, can play a key role in providing a supportive social environment, where the consequences of FGM/C and the benefits of abandoning the practice are discussed (WHO, 2010).

Given the purported religious inclinations associated with FGM/C, community-driven approaches involving religious and cultural leaders, including Islamic scholars, as part of multi-disciplinary social norm change interventions are critical to the success of interventions. The literature on FGM/C shows that using an approach that reinforces the human rights values and social support has catalyzed communities to collectively dialogue and agree on better ways to fulfill these values, "and has led to sustainable large-scale abandonment of FGM as well as other harmful practices" (WHO, 2010, p. 3).

This chapter has made reference to evidence that demonstrates that FGM/C of any type, and irrespective of who carries it out, is a violation of the human rights of girls and women, including, as stated by the WHO

(2010, p. 6), "the right to non-discrimination on the grounds of sex; the right to life when the procedure results in death; the right to freedom from torture or cruel, inhuman or degrading treatment or punishment; and the rights of the child." The findings mainly suggest that health-care providers need more information and training in order to refrain from engaging in these harmful practices (Doucet et al., 2017). However, I argue that the training should be rooted within the human rights–based approach. It should also go beyond providing technical tools and knowledge about health consequences of FGM/C to include social norm change, address structural issues like high unemployment, particularly of community midwives, and deal with the power dynamic that motivates midwives and other health professionals to carry out FGM/C. Interventions, though rooted in the human rights approach, should elicit and address specific drivers of medicalization in each of the diverse contexts.

NOTES

1   Jack Donnelly (1984) in his article "Cultural Relativism and Universal Human Rights," noted that cultural relativism is a doctrine that holds that such variations are exempt from legitimate criticism by outsiders, which is mostly supported by the notions of communal autonomy and self-determination. He adds that radical cultural relativism would hold that culture is a sole source of the validity of moral right or rule.

2   "Cosmopolitan localism seeks to amplify the richness of a place while keeping in mind the rights of a multi-faceted world. It cherishes a particular place, yet at the same time knows about the relativity of all places" (Sachs, 2006, p. 224).

REFERENCES

Adam, T., Bathija, H., Bishai, D., Bonnenfant, Y. T., Darwish, M., Huntington, D., & Johansen, E. (2010). Estimating the obstetric costs of female genital mutilation in six African countries. *Bulletin of the World Health Organization*, *88*(4), 281–288. https://doi.org/10.2471/BLT.09.064808

African Commission on Human and Peoples' Rights.. (2003). Protocol to the African Charter on Human and Peoples' Rights on the Rights of Women in Africa. http://www.achpr.org/files/instruments/women-protocol/achpr_instr_proto_women_eng.pdf

Applebaum, J., Hagit, C., Matar, M., Yones, A. R., & Kaplan, Z. (2008). Symptoms of posttraumatic stress disorder after ritual female genital surgery among Bedouin in Israel: Myth or reality? *Prim Care Companion J Clin Psychiatry*, *10*(6), 453–456. https://doi.org/10.4088/pcc.v10n0605Berg, R.C., Denison, E., & Fretheim, A. (2010). *Psychological, social and sexual consequences of female genital mutilation/cutting (FGM/C): A systematic review on quantitative studies*. Report from Kunnskapssenteret nr 13-2010. Oslo, NO: Nasjonalt kunnskapssenter for helsetjenesten.

Berg, R.C., Odgaard-Jensen, J., Fretheim, A., Underland, V., & Vist, G. (2014). An updated systematic review and meta-analysis of the obstetric consequences of female genital mutilation/cutting. *Obstetrics and Gynecology International* (2014), 1–8. https://doi.org/10.1155/2014/542859

Berg, R.C., Underland, V., Odgaard-Jensen, J., Fretheim, A., & Vist, G.E. (2014). Effects of female genital cutting on physical health outcomes: A systematic review and meta-analysis. *BMJ Open, 4*(11), 1–12.

Berggren, V., Abdel Salam. G., Bergström. S., Johansson. E., Edberg. A. K. (2004). An explorative study of Sudanese midwives' motives, perceptions and experiences of re-infibulation after birth. *Midwifery, 20* (4):299–311.

Center for Reproductive Rights. (2006). *Female genital mutilation: A matter of human rights— An advocate's guide to action*. New York, NY: Center for Reproductive Rights. https://www.reproductiverights.org/sites/default/files/documents/FGM_final.pdf

Dahl, R. A. (1968). Power. *International encyclopedia of the social sciences* (Vol. 12). New York, NY: Free Press

Dixon-Woods, M., Agarwal, S., Jones, D., Young, B., & Sutton, A. (2005). Synthesising qualitative and quantitative evidence: A review of possible methods. *Journal of Health Services Research and Policy, 10*(1), 45–53. https://doi.org/10.1177/135581960501000110

Donnelly, J. (1984). Cultural relativism and universal human rights. *Human Rights Quarterly, 6*(4), 400–419.

Doucet, M. H., Pallitto, C., & Groleau, D. (2017). Understanding the motivations of health-care providers in performing female genital mutilation: An integrative review of the literature. *Reproductive Health, 14*(1), 46. https://doi.org/10.1186/s12978-017-0306-5

Elisheva, S. (2004). *Empowerment and community planning: Theory and practice of people-focused social solutions*. Tel Aviv, IL: Hakibbutz Hameuchad. http://scholar.google.com/scholar?q=intitle:Empowerment+and+Community+Planning#7

Finke, E. (2006). Genital Mutilation as an expression of power structures: Ending FGM through education, empowerment of women and removal of taboos. *African Journal of Reproductive Health, 10*(2), 13–17. https://doi.org/10.2307/30032454

Gostin, L. O. (2001). Public health, ethics, and human rights: A tribute to the late Jonathan Mann. *Journal of Law, Medicine & Ethics, 29*, 121–130. http://doi/10.1111/j.1748-720X.2001.tb00330.x

Gruenbaum, E. (2001). *The female circumcision controversy : An anthropological perspective*. Philadelphia: University of Pennsylvania Press.

Iavazzo, C., Sardi, T. A., & Gkegkes, I. D. (2013). Female genital mutilation and infections: A systematic review of the clinical evidence. *Archives of Gynecology & Obstetrtics, 287*(6):1137–1149.

Kaplan, A., Hechavarría, S., Martín, M., & Bonhoure, I. (2011). Health consequences of female genital mutilation/cutting in the Gambia, evidence into action. *Reproductive Health, 8*(1), 26. https://doi.org/10.1186/1742-4755-8-26

Kizilhan, J. I. (2011). Impact of psychological disorders after female genital mutilation among Kurdish girls in Northern Iraq. *European Journal of Psychiatry, 25*(2), 92–100.

Kleinman, A. (1978). Concepts and a model for the comparison of medical systems as cultural systems. *Social Science and Medicine. Part B Medical Anthropology, 12*(1), 85–93. https://doi.org/10.1016/0160-7987(78)90014-5

Mann, J., Gostin, L., Gruwskin, S., Brennan, T., Lazzarini, Z., & Fineberg, H.V. (1994). Health and human rights. *Health and Human Rights: An International Journal, 1*(1), 6–23.

Mostafa, S. R. A., El Zeiny, N. A. M., Tayel, S. E. S., & Moubarak, E. I. (2006). What do medical students in Alexandria know about female genital mutilation? *Eastern Mediterranean Health Journal, 12*(Suppl. 2), 78–92.

Njue, C., & Askew, I. (2004). *Medicalization of female genital cutting among the Abagusii in Nyanza Province, Kenya*. Population Council Frontiers in Reproductive Health Program. http://www.carraguard.org/pdfs/FRONTIERS/FR_FinalReports/Kenya_FGC_Med.pdf

Nyangweso, M. (2016). Negotiating cultural rights to affirm human rights. *Journal of Religion and Violence, 4*(1), 39–57. https://doi.org/10.5840/jrv20165224

Refaat, A. (2009). Medicalization of female genital cutting in Egypt. *Eastern Mediterranean Health Journal, 15*(6), 1379–1388.

Sachs, W. (2006). One world. In W. Dietrich, J. Echavarria, & N. Koppensteiner (Eds.), *Key texts of peace studies* (pp. 209–226). Vienna, AT: LIT Verlag.

Shell-Duncan, B. (2001). The medicalization of female "circumcision": Harm reduction or promotion of a dangerous practice? *Social Science and Medicine, 52*(7), 1013–1028. https://doi.org/10.1016/S0277-9536(00)00208-2

UN. (1948). Universal Declaration of Human Rights. Retrieved March 16, 2019 from http://www.un.org/en/udhrbook/pdf/udhr_booklet_en_web.pdf

UN. (1966). International Covenant on Economic, Social and Cultural Rights. Retrieved February 10, 2019 from https://www.ohchr.org/Documents/ProfessionalInterest/cescr.pdf

UN. (1976). International Covenant on Civil and Political Rights. Retrieved February 10, 2019 from https://www.ohchr.org/Documents/ProfessionalInterest/ccpr.pdf

UN. (1989). Convention on the Rights of the Child. Retrieved February 27, 2019 from https://www.childrensrights.ie/sites/default/files/submissions_reports/files/UNCRCEnglish_0.pdf

UN. (2014). *Joint general recommendation/general comment No. 31 of the Committee on the Elimination of Discrimination against Women and No. 18 of the Committee on the Rights of the Child on harmful practices.* Committee the Elimination of All Forms of Discrimination against Women. Retrieved February 27, 2019 from https://reliefweb.int/sites/reliefweb.int/files/resources/CEDAW_C_GC_31_CRC_C_GC_18_7557_E.pdf

UN. (2015a). *Transforming our world: The 2030 agenda for sustainable development.* Retrieved February 10, 2019 from https://sustainabledevelopment.un.org/post2015/transformingourworld

UN. (2015b). *Global Strategy on Reproductive, Maternal, Newborn, Children's and Adolescents' Health.* https://www.unaids.org/sites/default/files/media_asset/EWECGSMonitoringReport2018_en.pdf

UNICEF. (2005). *Changing a harmful social convention: Female genital mutilation/cutting.* Florence, IT: UNICEF Innocenti Research Center. https://www.unicef-irc.org/publications/396/

UNICEF. (2013). *Female genital mutilation/cutting: A statistical overview and exploration of the dynamics of change.* New York, NY: 'Author. https://doi.org/10.1111/jsm.12655

UNICEF. (2016). *Female genital mutilation/cutting (Fgm/C) and child marriage in Sudan— Are there any changes taking place ? In depth analysis using multiple indicators cluster surveys (MICS) and Sudan health surveys (SHHS).* Khartoum, SD. https://www.unicef.org/sudan/reports/female-genital-mutilationcutting-and-child-marriage-sudan-are-there-any-changes-taking

Vloeberghs, E., van der Kwaak, A., Knipsheer, J., & van den Muijsenbergh, M. (2012). Coping and chronic psychosocial consequences of female genital mutilation in the Netherlands. *Ethn Health, 17*(6), 677–695.

Whitehorn, J., Ayonrinde, O., & Maingay, S. (2002). Female genital mutilation: Cultural and psychological implications. *Sex Relation Therapy, 17*(2), 161–170.

WHO. (1996). *The right path to health-health education through religion: Islamic ruling on female genital circumcision.* Cairo, EG: WHO Regional Office for the Eastern Mediterranean.

WHO. (1998). *Female genital mutilation:An overview.* Geneva, CH: Author. http://apps.who.int/iris/bitstream/10665/42042/1/9241561912_eng.pdf

WHO. (2006). WHO study group on female genital mutilation and obstetric outcome. Female genital mutilation and obstetric outcome: WHO collaborative prospective study in six African countries. *Lancet, 367*(9525), 1835–1841.

WHO. (2008). *Closing the gap in a generation: Health equity through action on the social determinants.* Final Report of the Commission on Social Determinants of Health. Geneva, CH: Author. https://www.who.int/social_determinants/final_report/csdh_finalreport_2008.pdf

WHO. (2010). *Global strategy to stop health-care providers from performing female genital mutilation.* Geneva, CH: WHO, in partnership with FIGO, ICN, & MWIA. http://www.unfpa.org/sites/default/files/pub-pdf/who_rhr_10-9_en.pdf

WHO. (2016). *WHO Guidelines on the management of health complications from female genital mutilation.* Geneva, CH: Author. https://www.who.int/reproductivehealth/topics/fgm/management-health-complications-fgm/en/

WHO. (2019). *Female genital mutilation.* http://www.who.int/mediacentre/factsheets/fs241/en/

World Health Assembly (2008, May 24). *WHA 61.16: Female genital mutilation.* Sixty-first World Health Assembly agenda item 11.8. https://apps.who.int/iris/bitstream/handle/10665/23532/A61_R16-en.pdf;jsessionid=A3C495C283B4E6E74C08301B7BA082EA?sequence=1

Cultural Dimensions of HIV/AIDS and Gender-Based Violence: A Case of Alur and Tieng Adhola Cultural Institutions in Uganda

Paul Bukuluki, Ronard Mukuye, Ronald Luwangula, Aloysious Nnyombi, Juliana Naumo Akoryo, and Eunice Tumwebaze

Culture is a "set of guidelines (both explicit and implicit) that individuals inherit as members of a particular society, and that tell them how to view the world, how to experience it emotionally, how to behave in it in relation to other people, to supernatural forces or gods and to the natural environment" (Helman, 2007, p. 2). It is the "foundation on which behaviour, specifically health behaviour, is 'expressed and through which health must be defined and understood" (Airhihenbuwa & Webster, 2004, p. 5). It is an important determinant of the level of health of the individual, the family, and the community

Several studies have positioned culture as a determinant of HIV and gender-based violence (GBV). Tiruneh (2009) considers cultural variations, especially norms governing sexuality, as influencing the spread of HIV. According to UNESCO (2002), cultural factors that range from beliefs and values regarding courtship, sexual networking, contraceptive use, perspectives on sexual orientation, explanatory models for disease and misfortunes, and norms for gender and marital relations are factors that have an impact on HIV/AIDS in African societies. Moyo and Muller

(2011) conclude that some rites of passage associated with birth, puberty, marriage, and death influence the spread of HIV. UN Women et al. (2016) note that social norms assign "strict gender roles based on stereotypes of men as providers and women as care givers, prizing physical strength, aggression and sexual experience in men, and submissiveness, passivity and chastity in women. This leads to harmful constructions of a dominant masculinity based on power, control and (hetero) sexual entitlement over women, and the socio-cultural acceptance of violence and abuse as a way to assert dominance" (p. 8).

This chapter builds on existing knowledge about the relationship between culture and behaviour. We do propose an understanding that human behaviour is rooted in cultural norms, values, and practices. Situating human behaviour within culture allows us to explore both the negative and positive influences of culture on human behaviour, and on the positive cultural resources that can be tapped into to curb the prevalence of HIV and GBV. Positive cultural resources are increasingly being considered in global health circles as an area of intervention (Bruun, 2006; Sovran, 2013).

Context

HIV/AIDS

Uganda has suffered a severe HIV/AIDS epidemic for over a quarter of a century, since the early 1980s. Since then, there has been a comprehensive and multi-sectoral national response to battle the pandemic. Currently the national prevalence stands at 6.2 percent among adults aged 15–49 years. It is higher among women (7.6 percent) than men (4.7 percent). Among children aged 0–14, the prevalence is 0.5 percent, which corresponds to approximately 95,000 children. Among young adults, there is a disparity in HIV prevalence by sex. HIV prevalence is almost four times higher among females than males aged 15–19 and 20–24 (Ministry of Health [MoH], 2017). Uganda is still classified as a high burden country with high numbers of persons living with HIV, with an increasing incidence. This is a result of the continuing spread of HIV, and increased longevity among persons living with HIV (Uganda AIDS Commission [UAC], 2015). The focus of this study was on the Tieng Adhola and Alur ethnic groups. There are 56 legally recognized ethnic groups in Uganda; the Adhola group that lives mainly in Eastern Uganda makes up about 8 percent of the population, and together with the Acholi, Langi, and other smaller groups, the Alur make up about 15 percent of the population (Uganda Bureau of Statistics, 2020).

Gender-based Violence (GBV)

GBV is an "umbrella term for any harmful act that is perpetrated against a person's will, and that is based on socially ascribed (gender) differences between males and females" (Inter-Agency Standing Committee, 2005 p. 7). It comprises all forms of physical, psychological, and sexual violence linked to the survivor's gender and socially constructed gender roles in a society (Keesbury & Askew, 2010). GBV is contrary to international instruments such as the Charter of the United Nations (UN, 1945), Security Council Resolution 1325 (UN, 2000), the Universal Declaration of Human Rights (UN, 1948), and the African Charter on Human and Peoples' Rights (Organization of African Unity, 1981).

Women and girls make up most of the victims of GBV worldwide and the same is true of Uganda. Women are more than twice as likely to experience sexual violence as men. More than 1 in 5 women aged 15–49 (22 percent) report that they have experienced sexual violence at some point compared with fewer than 1 in 10 (8 percent) men. In Alur Kingdom, 21.2 percent of women reported that they have experienced violence (Uganda Bureau of Statistics, 2016).

Methods

This chapter is based on an exploratory study conducted on cultural norms, values, and practices that have an impact on HIV/AIDS and GBV in Uganda in the Alur and Tieng Adhola cultural institutions. The key objectives of the study were to: (1) document the socio-cultural norms, values, and beliefs that have an impact on HIV/AIDS and GBV; (2) take stock of community-acknowledged good practices in responding to HIV/AIDS and GBV; and (3) synthesize community-proposed recommendations for positive change.

The field sites for Alur Kingdom were in Nebbi and Zombo districts and, for the Tieng Adhola, Tororo and Butaleja districts. In Alur Kingdom, data were collected in Nyaravur Sub County in Nebbi district and Atyak Sub County in Zombo District. In the Tieng Adhola Cultural Institution, data were collected in Rubongi Sub County in Tororo District and Busabi Sub County in Butaleja District. The study was commissioned by the Ministry of Gender, Labour and Social Development (MGLSD) with support from the United Nations Education, Scientific and Cultural Organization (UNESCO). It utilized exploratory and descriptive qualitative approaches of data collection and analysis. The main methods of data collection were key informant interviews and focus group discussions (FGDs) targeting cultural leaders. Validation meetings were organized involving stakeholders drawn from cultural institutions, MGLSD, district local governments, and civil society agencies involved in HIV and GBV prevention. In each cultural institution four focus group discussions, each comprising 8 participants and 10 key informant interviews, were conducted. In addition, one validation meeting was conducted in each cultural institution.

The study generated a qualitative data set. Data were typed, processed, and analyzed, focusing on reducing the data set into manageable proportions and summarizing it in a form that brings out salient issues of investigation. Data were organized under two thematic areas of HIV/AIDS and GBV. For each of these thematic areas, sub-themes were drawn in line with the objectives that guided the study and then subjected to further analysis. From the thematic analysis, data under each theme and sub-theme were synthesized to draw out their implications in relation to the study objectives.

Results

The findings revealed diverse but closely related cultural norms, values, and practices that increase the risk of spread of HIV/AIDS and risk of GBV, but also positive cultural resources and opportunities for preventing the same in both cultural institutions. Some of these cut across both cultural institutions while others were unique to each of them.

Practices and Beliefs Related to Death and Widow Inheritance

There are several beliefs and practices associated with death of a husband and widow inheritance that increase vulnerability to GBV and HIV, which bear some similarities with practices in Ghana described by Baoteng and Sottie in chapter 5 of this book, and in Nigeria as discussed by Olaore, Drolet, and Olaore in chapter 2. These include a lengthy period of mourning and the social norms related to widow inheritance.

Widow inheritance

This practice was found to be entrenched in both the Tieng Adhola and Alur cultures. Following the death of a husband, the deceased's elders and clansmen often preside over a cultural function where the young brother or any other earmarked relative of the deceased would inherit the widow. This was rationalized on several grounds, including protecting the family property from being taken over by a "stranger," ensuring continuity of the family lineage, "rescuing" the bride price paid, enabling continued care for the widow, and preventing a scenario where a widow would leave the children and remarry, or bring a man from another clan into the deceased's house. Unfortunately, widow inheritance is often done before an HIV test, hence predisposing both parties to the risk of HIV infection. Related to widow inheritance is another practice wherein if a man lost his wife, he would be "compensated" with the deceased's sister. This practice was mainly reported in Tieng Adhola culture and not in Alur Kingdom.

Lengthy mourning period

This practice was found only in the Tieng Adhola community, where upon the death of someone, mourning could last for up to five days, a time during which people from diverse backgrounds interact day and night and engage in irrational behaviours, including risky sexual practices. Secondly, as part of the mourning period, one of the cultural practices was shaving off the hair of family members. In most cases, this practice was crudely done using the same razor blade on more than one person, which exposed those involved to the risk of HIV infection. Essentially, there was less sensitivity to the risk of HIV as members fulfilled the traditional practices that defined their culture and identity.

Practices and Beliefs Related to Marriage and Dating

Several beliefs and practices related to marriage and dating exist among the Alur and Tieng Adhola cultures that increase vulnerability to GBV and HIV. The major ones elaborated below include polygamy, non-consensual marriages, dowry payment festivities, and multiple and extramarital sexual relationships.

Polygamy

Men marrying more than one wife is an old practice that is highly esteemed in many African cultures. Among the Alur and Tieng Adhola cultures, polygamy was found to be an acceptable and cherished practice. It was identified as risky since all wives and husbands may not be faithful to their spouses. Besides, it was not necessarily the case that before every successive marriage an HIV test would be done. Polygamy was associated with failure by men to sexually satisfy their wives, which made some wives to look elsewhere for sexual satisfaction.

Although polygamy was reported to be declining in both cultures, it still poses significant risk in the context of HIV/AIDS. Besides exposing partners to HIV infection, polygamy was found to be leading to GBV mainly due to the inability of men to meet the needs of their spouses. Sometimes men reportedly secured money from some wives to cater to the needs of other wives, which causes tensions in the family and contributes to violence.

Non-consensual marriages

Subjection of girls to non-consensual marriages was common among the both Tieng Adhola and Alur communities. Among the Alur, such marriage was referred to as *por*. If a man explicitly showed interest in marrying, but was unsuccessful dating, he would organize his peers to kidnap the girl of his interest. The "kidnapped girl" would be confined at the man's place until she agreed to marry him. While in captivity, the girl would be sexually abused as a bondage tool, leading to her eventual acceptance of the marriage. Given the circumstances that surround the marriage, there is hardly any chance for the couple to first test for HIV, hence exposing the parties to risk of infection.

Among the Tieng Adhola, young girls below the age of 18 years were commonly married off due to disregard for the education of the girl-child, and the need for bride price. Marrying off underage girls often leads to early sexual debut in which girls have difficulty negotiating safe sex. Besides, since such marriages are culturally arranged, testing for HIV is not a priority.

Furthermore, parents among the Tieng Adhola community traditionally practised marriage "bookings" for their children. A boy's family could identify his future partner at the age of about eight years. Parents of both children informed the children about this arrangement and allowed them to be friends without getting involved in sexual practices until they reached the age of 14 years. The practice constrained children's choices of marriage partners and subjected them to the wishes of the parents.

Dowry payment festivities

Among the Alur community, payment of dowry involves festivities traditionally known as *keny*. Traditionally, older men and women from the groom's side visited and interacted with older men and women in the family of the bride. Over time, the *keny* ceremony evolved and started involving young men from the visiting team. Eventually, it became an opportunity for young boys and young girls to meet and identify their future partners. However, the festivities, which often last several days, predispose young people to HIV by engagement in unprotected casual sex.

Closely related to the above, the payment of bride price in Tieng Adhola culture was a key driver of gender-based violence. The reason for this is twofold; first, payment of dowry implies the "purchase" of a woman, who becomes the man's property for him to manage "it" the way he wishes. Secondly, women endure violence at the hands of husbands because escaping to their families often prompts men to demand the return of the bride price. Families do not willingly welcome back their daughters for fear of the bride-price repayment. It is for this reason that debates on addressing GBV in the Tieng Adhola culture have centred much on the need to adjust the bride-price requirements.

Multiple and extramarital sexual relationships

Traditionally, there was preference for a boy child among the Alur community. If a couple only bore female children, the husband's family pestered him to look for other women until he produced a boy child. This gave men the "legitimacy" to engage in extramarital relationships. There was also a belief that a woman does not belong to one man. This drove some unfaithful partners into extramarital relationships, at times with already married women.

Practices Related to Healing and Body Beautification

Several beliefs and practices related to healing and beautification exist among the Alur and Tieng Adhola cultures that increase vulnerability to GBV and HIV. These include body incision and traditional healing practices and tooth extraction.

Body incision and traditional healing practices

Body incision among the Tieng Adhola and Alur communities was a common cultural practice, undertaken as part of the traditional healing process involving application of local herbs for purposes of curing some ailments. Among the Adhola community, the practice is common particularly for purposes of beautifying women's bodies. For instance, the women created lines with a resemblance to terraces on their stomachs. Regardless of the purpose, body incision is often done in a crude manner involving use of unhygienic and unsterilized sharp objects such as razor blades and knives on more than one person, thus exposing them to HIV infection.

Tooth extraction

The practice of tooth extraction was found to be mainly among the Tieng Adhola Cultural Institution. Particularly, the lower front teeth of girls were extracted by a local dental surgeon. Among the custodians of the Tieng

Adhola culture, extraction of these teeth was synonymous with beauty. However, the removal of the teeth followed a crude process undertaken using a single shared sharp object, often a knife. The practice thus exposes the girls to the risk of HIV infection. Though the practice was said to be rare of late, it is not yet extinct. Moreover, in the guise of beautification, the practice is a manifestation of gender-based violence against the girls.

Practices Related to Sexuality

Results revealed a number of beliefs and practices related to sexuality among the Alur and Tieng Adhola cultures that increase vulnerability to GBV and HIV. These include sex a few days after delivery, forced abortion, and preference of boy child over the girl child.

Sex a few days after delivery

Among the Tieng Adhola culture, having sex with a woman a few days after delivery was found to be cherished by men. The practice, termed "*kala adila*," involves having sex with a woman three to five days after delivery, based on the belief that it would make the child put on weight and increase the availability of breast milk. Although this practice is declining, men practice it without due regard for the emotional and physical state of the mother and her needs. While there is no mandatory abstention period, health care professionals generally recommend a waiting period of four to six weeks following the birth of a baby (Mayo Clinic, 2018).

Forced abortion

Among the Tieng Adhola, unmarried teenage pregnancy was not tolerated. Girls were expected to conceive only after marriage. Teenage girls who became pregnant out of wedlock normally had to endure untold suffering involving painful forced abortions, locally known as "*yath dero*." This was mainly done to deter other girls from getting pregnant before marriage and to protect the family's honour. Currently, the practice is less prevalent. Despite the good intentions of the practice in attempting to prevent early sexual debut and pregnancy, the punishment meted out to those who deviated from the norm was an extreme case of GBV, with potentially fatal effects.

Preference of boy child over the girl child

In Tieng Adhola culture, boys are generally liked because of the belief that they ensure continuity of the family lineage compared with girls, who are eventually taken away by their husbands. Girls are perceived to be valuable only in relation to what they can bring in terms of bride price. As a result, girls are often excluded from attending good schools, and when they make mistakes they are harshly treated compared to boys. The parental preference of boys over girls leads to several issues that affect not only the girls but their mothers and the general domestic relationships. Men engage in extramarital affairs to get boy children, girls are overworked, their education is compromised, and there is gender-based discrimination of opportunities between girls and boys.

Positive cultural practices

In contrast with the above, the results revealed several positive cultural resources among the Alur and Tieng Adhola that, if reconceptualized and practised within gender-transformative and human rights frameworks, can be harnessed to promote HIV and GBV prevention. These include: parenting and preparing children for marriage; self-discipline and respect; willingness of cultural leaders to promote sensitization against HIV & AIDS: the value and role of traditional aunties and uncles; the use of evening fire places as spaces for socialization of young people; and prolonged courtship.

Parenting and preparing children for marriage

In the Alur culture, it was a common practice for boys and girls intending to marry to fully involve their parents or relatives from the paternal and maternal sides. Such involvement by both families helped in preventing sex before marriage to the extent that by the time of marriage, the couple was well prepared and equipped with the virtues of marriage. The findings show that this practice is changing, and young men and women only inform their families, without involving them in marriage arrangements.

Similar practices were found in Tieng Adhola culture. Virginity was highly valued as it was considered critical in helping families fetch more cows as bride price from their girls. In some communities, with a distorted sense of family honour, girls who lost their virginity would be killed. Unfortunately, such excessive punishment shows how a well-intended practice inherently embeds GBV.

Culture-led sensitization against HIV/AIDS

Acknowledging the power and authority over its subjects, the Alur Cultural Institution considered using its position to contribute to the prevention of HIV in its area of jurisdiction. It is not unusual for cultural leaders to meet and talk to their subjects about HIV/AIDS. Some use platforms such as burial ceremonies to sensitize the masses against cultural practices such as '*keny*' that expose people to HIV infection. When cultural leaders make pronouncements, their subjects listen.

Self-discipline and respect

This core cultural value particularly prevented women from engaging in extramarital affairs; it ensured family stability and supported the appropriate nurturing of children so that they internalized socially acceptable values. Discipline and self-control prevented the spread of sexually transmitted diseases such as gonorrhea, syphilis, and HIV. Culturally, the Tieng Adhola and Alur valued dignity, and boys, girls, and women whose economy revolved around the household would not leave their homes without a serious reason. The impression was that where such practices are upheld today, they can have a positive effect in the struggle against HIV/AIDS.

The value of traditional aunties

Traditional aunties particularly guided girls to develop into responsible adults with acceptable behaviours essential in marriage. They guided girls through a set of values and virtues including hard work, respect for the husband, faithfulness in marriage, and being welcoming to visitors, and taught that adultery is the biggest sin a woman can ever commit against her husband. Boys went through similar orientation at the hands of uncles. Sex education of young girls and boys largely defined the roles of aunties and uncles. Such moral imperatives nurtured and prepared girls for marriage, with implications for domestic stability and prevention of HIV/AIDS. This checked early sex debut, which in current times exposes girls and boys to risky sexual practices and HIV infection. However, these must be understood in changing socio-cultural and historical contexts. This is because they can also serve to reinforce patriarchal social norms that sustain unequal gender roles, power relations, and access to and control of resources between males and females. In the long run, these may not protect females and males against HIV. What must be considered is a recommitment to fundamental human values of respect, regard, and restraint for self and for other boys and girls, and for women and men alike. For example, as much as it is important to educate young women about the virtues of hard work, maintaining a good household and being faithful in marriages, young men must also be socialized into the same values. Young men must also be taught that adultery is the greatest sin that they can commit against their wives! For this to happen, the traditional aunts and uncles need reorientation to embrace gender equality and core human rights values.

The practice of evening fire

The Adhola community has a tradition of evening fire places in a homestead where elders meet and interact with boys and girls over several topical issues, such as the importance of virginity until marriage for both girls and boys. Parents and grandparents pass on generational messages to boys and girls through open discussion, folk songs, stories, and riddles. Such messages help greatly to check premarital sex and other forms of irresponsible sex and reduce chances of contracting HIV. In terms of social control, children spend their evenings within the vicinity of adults/parents. Children and youth spent their evenings with adults at the evening fire places, or in the kitchen in the case of girls with their mothers. This kept them from the so-called "evening walks," video cinemas, bars, and night clubs. It cannot be overemphasized that today, these are key drivers of susceptibility to HIV infection.

Prolonged courtship

Long courtships were an integral practice in the Adhola culture. As boys and girls were prepared for marriage, they were advised by their parents, aunties, uncles, and elders to take their time after a marriage partner was identified for them. Thus, boys and girls were encouraged to get to know their respective families before marriage. Even where the boy and the girl met each other with limited influence from their families, the two were encouraged to understand themselves adequately before making a commitment to marry. This served multiple purposes; for instance, it ensured that boys and girls made the right marriage choices but also checked on the problem of early pregnancy and GBV.

Positive Cultural Norms, Values, and Practices in Relation to GBV

The study unraveled several positive cultural resources among the Alur and Tieng Adhola cultures that can be harnessed to complement efforts geared toward prevention and responses to GBV. These include: clear separation of men and women's roles and holding men responsible for fulfilling their roles; cultural context–specific methods of conflict resolution; succession planning particularly writing of wills; and values of mutual respect.

Clear separation of men's and women's roles

In the past, there were clearly defined roles of men and women. Men mainly took care of the livestock and fulfilled the provider role to support the family. Women, on the other hand, have been traditionally involved in farm activities and household chores such as cooking, although this has been changing over time. Men have tended to increasingly abdicate their provider roles, and this has increased the burden of care for the girls and women. This, coupled with alcohol abuse, has been blamed for the increasing intimate partner violence.

Traditional methods of conflict resolution

Traditionally, the Alur and Tieng Adhola communities devised ways of handling conflicts at individual, family, and community levels. It was found that clan structures were crucial in conflict resolution. In some cases, men who beat their wives would be publicly caned as a deterrent to such practices. When there were any disagreements, conflicts, or violence in a home, elders and relatives would come together to ensure that these were resolved or managed.

However, the drawback is that these social norms are not necessarily gender transformative; they tend to maintain the status quo of the subordinate position of women relative to men. Therefore, unequal gender relations as a structural driver of intimate partner violence tend to remain unchecked. These cultural resources have not been adequately engaged and used to transform gender relations.

Succession planning, including writing of wills

Another practice that should be promoted is preparing of wills before death. This used to be done by men in the past and it helped in ensuring appropriate apportioning of the deceased property. It is the lack of wills that is causing problems, especially for widows and children after the' death of the husband/father. It is important to seriously revive and support asset distribution following death as a strategy for preventing the suffering of widows, which is evident in property grabbing by the relatives of the deceased man.

This is a constructive tool for protecting widows and orphans and vulnerable children. However, this cultural resource exists in the context of patriarchal gender relations and the will itself may tend to favour the male children over the females. Although it is a building block supporting child protection and social protection of widows, it lacks the gender-transformative dynamic that would make it work to effectively protect women and girls. The written wills tend to reinforce existing unequal gender relations.

Values of mutual respect

Traditionally, the Alur were supposed to be respectful people. Although women were particularly expected to be submissive and humble, men were also expected to be respectful. Married women were respected in the community. With this respect, one would expect that there would be little room for violence.

This notwithstanding, men are the gate keepers who control resources and maintain power relations, and they tend to make decisions that favour males. In this case demonstrating respect, within dominant patriarchal expectations, may favour women who play along with the unequal power relations to access resources. Those who attempt to challenge this inequality are perceived as outliers who are not well socialized. There are therefore inherent contradictions in the notions of mutual respect in the context of the Alur and Tieng Adhola social norms.

Conclusion

In this chapter we have presented norms, values, and practices that have the potential to positively contribute to the fight against HIV and GBV. However, it was a challenge to identify and interpret norms, values, and practices that positively contribute to prevention of HIV and GBV. This is partly because of the inherent contradictions in some of the norms, values, and practices, which on the one hand had potential to reduce vulnerability to HIV and GBV, but when analyzed further, are likely to maintain structural gender inequality and subordination of women and girls. This implies that for cultural norms, values, or practices to be utilized in the prevention and response efforts for HIV and GBV, they need to be conceptualized in the context of human rights and gender equality to qualify as resources in prevention and response efforts for HIV and GBV (Sengendo & Sekatawa, 1999).

As Mofolo (2010) observed, the relationship between culture and HIV/AIDS is complex and has been perceived in terms of gender inequalities and the patriarchal society that culture entrenches. Culture also perpetuates risky practices such as widow inheritance, polygamy, non-consensual marriages, and multiple and extramarital relationships, among others, that predispose individuals to the risk of sexually transmitted infections.

Cultural structures, including cultural leaders, clan leaders, and their representatives at different levels, have potential to contribute to HIV and GBV prevention, but their roles must be entwined with human rights and gender-transformative programming. For example, in Uganda, the Tieng Adhola and Alur cultural institutions have been engaged by the Ministry of Gender, Labour and Social Development (MGLSD) and the Uganda AIDS Commission. Staff have been trained in human rights and gender equality, and these institutions are being used in HIV and GBV prevention work. Cultural institutions have also been engaged by MGLSD and the Uganda AIDS Commission to declare some cultural norms and practices "not part of their culture any more" through developing policy briefs and making public statements against social norms that perpetuate GBV or increase vulnerability to HIV infection (MGLSD, 2013).

GBV within the Tieng Adhola and Alur communities is strengthened and driven by patriarchy and distorted notions of family honour. The patriarchal beliefs, norms, and practices in both communities support power relations among men and women that render women vulnerable to abuse. It should, however, be noted that often men abuse and distort given cultural norms, values, and practices (Robins, 2008; Palitza, 2006). Practices like payment of bride price are intended to symbolize respect for the family of the girl, but often are taken to signify "purchasing of the bride," an assumption that might be used to legitimize violence against women (MGLSD, 2013).

Overall, although the positive cultural resources have potential to contribute to prevention of HIV and GBV, their full potential can only be realized by adopting a gender-transformative and human rights lens. The major drawback is that these norms, values, and practices are not necessarily gender transformative. They tend to maintain the status quo of the subordinate position of women relative to men. Therefore, unequal gender relations, as a structural driver of intimate partner violence, tend to remain in place. These cultural resources need to be adequately engaged as building blocks to transform gender relations that continue to promote and sustain GBV and make women and girls, and men and boys, vulnerable to HIV infection (Sengendo & Sekatawa, 1999; UNESCO, 2002).

Cultural dynamism, emphasized by social anthropologists and social workers, provides a useful resource. For example, Norval (1999, pp. 7–8) argues that culture cannot be seen as closed and positive but it "exists as fragile and vulnerable—as a hybrid and non-pure" (Norval 1999, p. 7). It is therefore amenable to change through deliberate but culturally sensitive social norm change programs that build on cultural resources and assets while they engage with relevant stakeholders to change social norms that are inimical to human rights (Sengendo et al., 2001) and the core values of social work.

REFERENCES

Airhihenbuwa, C. O., & Webster, J. D. (2004). Culture and African contexts of HIV/AIDS prevention, care and support. *SAHARA-J: Journal of Social Aspects of HIV/ AIDS*, *1*(1), 4–13.

Bruun, B. (2006). *Questioning the role of culture and traditional practices in HIV transmission: NGOs" involvement in changing unsafe local practices*. Copenhagen: DK: AIDSnet Children and Youth Network.

Helman, C. G. (2007). *Culture, health, and illness* (5th ed.). London, UK: Hodder Arnold.

Inter-Agency Standing Committee. (2005). *Guidelines for gender-based violence interventions in humanitarian settings: Focusing on prevention of and response to sexual violence in emergencies* (Field test Version). Geneva, CH: Inter-Agency Standing Committee. www.unhcr.org/453492294.pdf

Keesbury, J., & Askew, I. (2010). *Comprehensive responses to gender-based violence in low resource settings: Lessons learned from implementation*. Lusaka, ZM: Population Council. http://www.genderhub.org/get-in-the-know/resource-library/comprehensive-responses-to-gender-based-violence-in-low-resource-settings-lessons-learned-from-implementation

Mayo Clinic. (2018). *Sex after pregnancy: Set your own timeline*. https://www.mayoclinic.org/healthy-lifestyle/labor-and-delivery/in-depth/sex-after-pregnancy/art-20045669

Ministry of Gender, Labour and Social Development (MGLSD). (2013). *Tieng Adola cultural institution policy brief on HIV, GBV, and maternal health*.Kampala, UG: Author.

Ministry of Health. (2017). *The Uganda population-based HIV impact assessment 2016*. Kampala, UG: Author. http://www.afro.who.int/sites/default/files/2017-08/UPHIA%20Uganda%20factsheet.pdf

Mofolo, T. (2010). *The role of culture in contributing to the spread of HIV/AIDS: Understanding how cultural norms and practices, specifically female genital mutilation facilitate the spread of HIV/AIDS* Africa Institute of South Africa Policy Brief No. 29.

Moyo, N., & Müller, J. C. (2011). The influence of cultural practices on the HIV and AIDS pandemic in Zambia. *HTS Teologiese Studies/Theological Studies*, *67*(3), 1–5.

Norval A. (1999). "Hybridization": The im/purity of the political. In J. Edkins, N. Persram, & V. Pin-Fat (Eds.), *Sovereignty and Subjectivity* (pp. 99–116). London, UK: Leine Reiner.

Organization of African Unity. (1981). African Charter on Human and Peoples' Rights. Addis Ababa, ET: Author.

Palitza, K. (2006). Culture (ab)used to dodge women rights. *Agenda*, *68*, 108–111.

Robins, S. (2008). Rights. In N. Shepherd & S. Robins (Eds.), *New South African keywords*. Sunnyside, ZA: Jacana Media.

Sengendo, J., Bukuluki, P., & Walakira, E. J. (2001). *A cultural approach to HIV/AIDS prevention and care*. UNESCO/UNAIDS Research Project, Kampala Pilot Project Phase One Scientific Report (Studies and Reports, Special Series of the Cultural Policies for Development Unit, Issue No. 15). Paris, FR: UNESCO. http://unesdoc.unesco.org/images/0012/001255/125587e.pdf accessed 3/05/2018.

Sengendo, J., & Sekatawa, E. A. (1999). *A cultural approach to HIV/AIDS prevention and care: Uganda's experience country report*. UNESCO/UNAIDS Research Project (Studies and Reports, Special Series of the Cultural Policies for Development Unit, Issue No. 1). Paris, FR: UNESCO. http://unesdoc.unesco.org/images/0012/001206/120611e.pdf

Sovran, S. (2013) Understanding culture and HIV/AIDS in sub-Saharan Africa. *SAHARA-J: Journal of Social Aspects of HIV/AIDS, 10*(1), 32–41.

Tiruneh, G. (2009). Determinants of adult HIV/AIDS prevalence in Africa: Do cultural variations matter? *Mid-South Political Science Review, 10*, 103–124.

Uganda AIDS Commission. (2015). *2014 Uganda HIV and AIDS country progress report*. Kampala, UG: Author.

Uganda Bureau of Statistics. (2016). *Uganda demographic and health survey (2016)*. Kampala, UG: Author.

Uganda Bureau of Statistics. (2020). https://www.ubos.org

UN. (1945). Charter of the United Nations. Geneva, CH: Author.

UN. (1948). Universal Declaration of Human Rights. Geneva, CH: Author

UN. (2000). Security Council Resolution 1325. New York, NY: Author

UNESCO. (2002). *A cultural approach to HIV/AIDS prevention and care: Summary of country assessments*. Division of Cultural Policies. Paris, FR: UNESCO.

UN Women. (2016, December 1–2). *Preventing violence against women and girls through social norms change*. Learning paper from the Asia-Pacific forum on preventing violence against women and girls: Evidence and tools for social norm change. Bangkok, TH.

When National Law and Culture Coalesce: Challenges for Children's Rights in Botswana with Specific Reference to Corporal Punishment

Poloko Nuggert Ntshwarang and Vishanthie Sewpaul

Botswana has made several strides in its attempt to adhere to human rights standards, especially in relation to children' rights. The country is a signatory to the Universal Declaration of Human Rights (UDHR) (UN, 1948); the United Nations Convention on the Rights of the Child (CRC) (UN, 1989), the African Charter on the Rights and Welfare of the Child (ACRWC) (African Commission on Human and People's Rights [ACHPR], 1990), and the UN World Declaration on the Survival, Protection and Development of Children (UNDSPDC) (UN, 1990). The CRC (UN, 1989) requires states to take

> all appropriate legislative, administrative, social and educational measures to protect the child from all forms of physical or mental violence, injury or abuse, neglect or negligent treatment, maltreatment or exploitation, including sexual abuse, while in the care of parent(s), legal guardian(s) or any other person who has the care of the child. (Article 19)

The CRC and the ACRWC emphasize the right to be treated with dignity, protection, and integrity, with the CRC calling for children to be protected from "torture or other cruel, inhuman or degrading treatment or punishment" (Article 37), a right also enshrined in the UDHR.

Botswana promulgated the Children's Act of 2009 (Government of Botswana, 2009), which is largely (but not entirely) aligned with the CRC and the ACRWC. Nonetheless, the use of corporal punishment (hereafter referred to as CP) in Botswana at family and state levels indicates that disciplinary practices that are normalized in law and culture are unlikely to be perceived as a threat to children's rights and well-being. It is an anomaly that while adults are protected in law against assaults, children—who because of their age and size are more vulnerable—are not granted such protection.

The UNDSPDC (UN, 1990) asserts that "all children must be given the chance to find their identity and realize their worth in a safe and supportive environment, through families and other care-givers committed to their welfare" (Article 15). However, not every society conforms to established rights, largely because of entrenched and enduring cultural practices. The majority of countries do not prohibit CP in the home, even where it is prohibited in other spheres, and CP affects 80 percent of the world's 1.7 billion children who experience violence (Global Initiative to End All Corporal Punishment of Children [GIEACPC], 2017). Despite progress, with 53 states across the world now banning all forms of CP in all settings, 9 out of 10 children worldwide live in states where the law does not recognize their rights to protection from CP (GIEACPC, 2017).

Botswana is one of the few countries where CP is not prohibited in *any* setting and is one of six African countries with non-prohibition in *all* settings, with others being Mauritania, Nigeria, Somalia, Tanzania, and Zimbabwe (GIEACPC, 2017). Botswana's Penal Code (Government of Botswana, 1964, Section 28); the Botswana Education Act (Government of Botswana, 1967, Sections 23 and 24); the Botswana Customary Law Act (Government of Botswana, 1969, Sections 21 (2)), and the Botswana Children's Act (Government of Botswana, 2009) all condone CP of children. The Children's Act (Government of Botswana, 2009) prohibits only "unreasonable" correction of a child by parents, thus allowing "reasonable" correction. The Children's Act also expressly states that the legal provisions protecting a child's dignity and prohibiting cruel, inhumane, and degrading treatment or punishment do not preclude the use of CP (Articles 27 and 61).

CP is performed with the deliberate intention to cause pain on other persons to correct undesirable behaviours without causing injuries (Lansford, 2010). While Lansford emphasizes not causing injuries, the GIEACPC (2018) asserts that CP "includes any punishment in which physical force is used and intended to cause some degree of pain or discomfort, however light, as well as *non-physical forms of punishment that are cruel and degrading*" (emphasis added, para. 1). CP is an assault not only on the bodies of children, but their spirits; it is degrading and inhumane and produces enduring effects. The Government of Botswana rejected the recommendations of the international community to ban CP, arguing that "it is a legitimate and acceptable form of punishment, as informed by the norms of society" (GIEACPC, 2018, p. 5).

The norms of society and the legal sanction of CP in all spheres in Botswana enable its pervasive use. The state, as custodian of children's rights, has an obligation to protect children, educate its citizens about the harmful consequences of CP, and foster positive parenting practices. The justification of the law being informed by "the norms of society" is akin to the tail wagging the dog, and the state abrogating its responsibilities. Legal reform is no guarantee of the protection and promotion of human rights, but it does play a huge role in enabling the achievement and protection of rights. At the very least, it makes the roles of advocates against the use of CP easier. It is harder to confront, challenge, and change harmful cultural practices when there is legal sanction for them.

Brief Literature Review

The use of CP in the home is not distinctive to African countries; it is practised in both Western and non-Western societies. With international pressure, advocacy, and public education campaigns, seven African countries have achieved prohibition of CP in all settings, while a further 18 countries have expressed commitment to banning CP in all settings (GIEACPC, 2017). The persistent use of CP across the world represents a major challenge in penetrating culturally entrenched parenting practices.

The GIEACPC (2017) points to the double standards adopted by states, asserting that "too many governments claim to support ending all forms of violence against children while failing to prohibit violence disguised as discipline or punishment" (p. 4).

The normalization of CP to discipline children is endorsed by supportive societal attitudes and norms, even where CP is not condoned in law (Ellison & Bradshaw, 2009; Lansford, 2010). Renzaho et al. (2011), for example, found that parents used CP when the children failed to comply with their demands, and Weis and Toolis (2010) found that parents of African descent used parenting practices that valued respect for authority figures and unquestioning obedience to adults' expectations. This coheres with the finding of Julius (2013) in the Kenyan context, where the majority (78 percent) of guidance counsellors expressed the view that CP was very effective or effective in disciplining children, yet paradoxically the majority of the 300 male and female learners, from day and boarding schools included in the study, believed that they should be referred to guidance counsellors, for assistance, rather than be subject to CP. However, Durrant (2000), a strong advocate against CP, discussed attitudinal changes following the legal banning of CP in Sweden.

There are several factors that contribute to the use of CP. These include: (1) the belief that it is the right and duty of parents to discipline children via the use of CP, as enshrined in the Biblical injunction "He who spares the rod hates his son, but he who loves him disciplines him promptly" (Proverbs 13:24, New King James Version); (2) in African traditional practices there is a pre-eminent respect for authority, elders, and customs, and there is a tendency to conflate fear with respect—and thus the misuse of values like *Ubuntu* and *Botho*, as discussed in chapter 1 (Weis & Toolis, 2010); (3) CP allows parents to feel in control and to ensure children's compliance (Renzaho et al., 2011); (4) fear that children will become uncontrollable in the absence of the use of CP; (5) belief that CP shapes character and strengthens children's moral development; and that (6) CP serves as a deterrent to undesirable behaviours (Gudyanga et al., 2014).

While CP gives parents immediate gratification, with children's conformity and obedience (Bitensky, 1997; Gershoff & Bitensky, 2007), there is evidence that it has physical, psychological, and emotional consequences that impede healthy functioning. The negative consequences of CP have been documented in relation to decreased cognitive ability, poor academic performance, and school dropout (Ahmad et al., 2013; Gershoff, 2010; Tafa, 2002; UNICEF, 2014); manifestations of depression and anxiety in later life; reproduction of violence and aggression (Gershoff, 2010; Smith et al., 2004); inability to contribute to the internalization of ethics and desired societal values (Shumba, 2004); and poorer problem-solving skills (Smith et al., 2004).

Apart from its consequences, there are arguments that the use of CP is intrinsically unacceptable, as it violates the dignity of children; children are not property for parents to act upon as they please (Shumba, 2004). The distinction between CP and physical abuse is thin, thus the call for its total abolishment (Durrant, 2016; Gershoff, 2010; Lansford, 2010). However, Gudyanga et al. (2014), who approve of the use of CP under specific circumstances, argue that "the absence of corporal punishment is not a guarantee to achieving zero physical abuse of children" (p. 495). Given the size and age of parents compared with children, and the power differential between them, and the harmful effects of CP on a child's sense of self (Bradshaw, 1996), its potential for physical injuries cannot be refuted (Gershoff, 2010). Parents might not intend to harm children, but the use of CP does cause emotional and physical harm (Gershoff, 2010; Lansford, 2010).

CP is abuse, but it also opens doors to other forms of child abuse. The frequent use of CP is associated with poor parent-child relations and poor attachment, as parents who use CP fail to build emotional bonds with their children (Gershoff, 2010). Parents are the primary caregivers who are supposed to ensure that children feel safe, secure, and protected, factors that are prized from an Afrocentric perspective. When children are exposed to pain by the very persons who are supposed to protect them, it contributes to mistrust and internalized shame, which may in later life manifest in codependent or survival personalities that typify a range of mental health problems, including addictive disorders (Bradshaw, 1996). It is against this background that this study sought to understand the parenting practices adopted by women across three different family structures.

Methodology

Guided by critical, structural social work theory (Mullaly & Mullaly, 2014), a cross-sectional qualitative, phenomenological research was conducted with 24 women, parenting children under 19 years of age from Selebi Phikwe town in Botswana. The main aim of the study was to understand the parenting practices of women with children in the following family structures: (a) female-headed families where the head of the family was employed; (b) two-parent families where both parents were employed; and (c) a two-parent family where the woman was unemployed and her partner was employed.

Snowball and purposive sampling strategies were used to select eight women in each category for inclusion in this study. Although these sampling strategies are haphazard and prone to researcher bias (Neuman, 2007), they were useful as they offered control over sample selection in relation to the required characteristics of the participants.

Data were collected using face-to-face interviews with the help of genograms and eco-maps to elicit data on the composition and structure of families, and on personal and family relationships (Rempel et al., 2007), and were primarily collected via home visits. Data were audio-recorded and transcribed, and thematic qualitative analysis was used (Babbie, 2016), with thick descriptions helping to retain the participants' voices in the presentation of the data. All ethical research requisites in relation to doing no harm, maintaining confidentiality, informed consent (forms were translated into Setswana and the interviews were conducted in the local language, when necessary), assurance that participants could withdraw participation at any time, and ensuring anonymity in the reporting of the data, were assured. Ethical approval was granted from the University of KwaZulu-Natal Research Ethics Committee.

Key Research Results

One of the main objectives of the study was to understand whether family structure played a role in the types of parenting practices that the women adopted. The ages of the participants ranged from 31 to 52 years, with the average age being 42 years. The relatively mature age of the participants is linked to one of the inclusion criteria: that the participants must have parented at least one child who had reached adolescence or adulthood. As per the national norm, most women identified as belonging to the Christian faith. One woman had no formal education. Of those who had been to school, one-third acquired tertiary education, followed by 25 percent who had completed primary school, and 20.8 percent who had completed secondary school.

It was interesting to note that five of the eight women who held tertiary qualifications were from female-headed households, perhaps supporting the notion that women with higher educational qualifications are more financially independent, and three were from families where both partners were working. None of the unemployed women held any post-school qualification. Regarding CP, family structure seemed to make no difference.

The results of the study indicated that the entrenchment of CP in Botswana is deep, and it cuts across different family structures and socio-economic status, with most women (21) having used CP as a form of discipline. This resonates with Sebonego's (1994) findings that CP was a universal form of discipline in Botswana, embedded in Tswana traditions. The results are presented under two key interrelated themes: (1) parental versus children's rights and responsibilities; and (2) the normalization of the use of CP.

Parental versus Children's Rights and Responsibilities

The findings of the study showed that there was limited awareness and understanding of the law pertaining to children's rights in Botswana. All 24 women indicated that they had heard of children's rights in the abstract, but the majority (18) were unaware of the Botswana Children's Act (Government of Botswana, 2009). The results indicated that women who held higher educational qualifications, and who worked in specific sectors such as education and health, had an advantage in terms of access to the Children's Act. Gorata, who was a 42-year-old single parent and a teacher, and had worked as a school guidance counsellor said:

I am aware of that. I have read it. It is helpful because it sends a reminder to the parent that one has to act in the best interest of the child. . . . It is helpful in curbing abuse of children. . . . Children sometimes misuse their rights, but they have to know them. A parent should teach her children about their rights. . . . I tell her [her daughter] that she should not use her rights to abuse me or to abuse others, because if one is not aware of his or her rights the child could take advantage of a parent's lack of knowledge and abuse him or her. Sometimes when I tell her that I am going to beat her, she tells me that "this time when you beat me, I am going to the social workers to report you that you abuse my rights," I tell her that "this house is mine, as long as you live with me and under my care, you have to listen to me, whether you have rights or not, we both have rights so we need to meet somewhere."

Gorata's narrative emphasizes both children's and parental rights and responsibilities. Even with her background and knowledge, there was an overriding narrative of parental power over children. The discourse speaks to the lesser status of children, with the child's dependent status translating into "you have to listen to me," and to fear of parental abuse by children. Gorata's knowledge of children's rights did not prevent her from using CP. This coheres with the finding of Julius (2013) in the Kenyan context, which is discussed earlier.

The fear of giving up parental authority, and the possibility of the emphasis on children's rights paving the way for parental abuse by children, was reiterated by Maano, who held a college diploma and worked as a nurse:

Yes, children abuse us. When you talk to today's children, they talk about Childline, and children's rights. . . . When you attempt to discipline a child, the child tells you "I will report you." . . . I think children should also be taught about their parents' rights, they should not only emphasize their own rights.

In desperation Maano said, "The law only pays attention to child abuse but overlooks parent abuse. Children abuse us, yes," and she was of the view that the issue of parental abuse required urgent attention. Maano's concerns bear some legitimacy, particularly in the face of lack of public education campaigns for children and adults on their reciprocal rights and responsibilities (which the ACRWC does pay attention to), and on the use of alternative, conscious positive parenting practices in the home, in schools, and in alternative care settings for children. While Mweru (2010) found higher levels of indiscipline among learners following the banning of CP in Kenyan schools, the author did not recommend its reinstatement, but called for education and sensitization about alternative forms of discipline.

Normalization of the Use of CP

The women's knowledge about children's rights did not translate into ensuring that those rights were respected. Sharon, who was a 43-year-old stay-at-home mum, adopted primarily authoritarian parental practices. She said:

> I think I should discipline the child, I am not afraid to beat my child on the basis that my child has rights. My child cannot threaten me by telling me that he or she has rights and therefore she or he is going to report me for beating him or her . . . Sometimes when I listen to radio discussions about children's deviant behaviours, I have heard parents complaining that we fail to discipline our children because of children's rights.

Naledi, a 40-year-old unemployed woman, said: "I only heard about children's rights but not that much. I know that we are not supposed to abuse children such as beating them too much." Naledi's view resonates with the Children's Act (Government of Botswana, 2009), which approves *reasonable* use of CP. Regina, a 34-year-old unemployed woman with primary school education, who said she knew about children's rights, indicated that they played no role in her disciplining her children. She said: "I beat them and when a person comes by and says, 'their rights,' I tell them to go away with them [rights] because I am disciplining my child." She said, "I beat a child just right," adding, "I never play with a child" (meaning she was hard on children when disciplining them).

Regina, as with the other participants, said she knew that the child had a right not to be beaten, but believed it was wholly okay for her to do so. The women expressed the view that they had to exercise control, and that it was their duty to discipline their children. Baboloki, who was from a female-headed family, and worked as a cleaner, said: "I like to talk to them before I introduce the whip, but when they do not listen or do as I want, I really discipline them," while Lesedi asserted, "If one doesn't beat them a bit one may find that one song is sung on a daily basis. Once you introduce a whip to beat them they will do as you want quickly." The voices of the women support the notion of parents getting gratification from children's immediate compliance and obedience, while failing to consider the long-term consequences of their actions.

As they did not know of the specific provisions of the Children's Act (Government of Botswana, 2009) allowing for *reasonable* CP, the participants erroneously believed that all forms of CP were illegal. Their responses suggest that even if national law prohibited CP, they would most likely continue to use it. Disciplining of children was clearly not seen to be within the purview of the state, but as a private matter with the state having no right to intrude into the private space of the family. Given the extent of the normalization of the use of CP, this is not unusual. Julius (2013) reported that over 90 percent of the 300 learners in his study, in Kenya, reported the continued use of CP despite its banning, a finding reported by others such as Mweru (2010). The views of the participants were contrary to that expressed by the GIEACPC (2017), which proclaimed, "Violence is not a private matter that should be left to families to resolve, but a matter of human rights that states have a duty to uphold" (p. 11).

Kaone, a stay-at-home mum, who also believed that the law prohibited CP, had this to say: "Yes, . . . it is very difficult for me, when it comes to rights. . . . I just talk on the side saying, 'Hey, these rights I think they have spoiled our children.'" Kaone went on to say:

If one gives her a few lashes she would go to the police. When you get there, they will tell you, "this child has rights." When she is 19 years old! And then you ask yourself, they say she has rights, but she is 19 years old and I feed her and clothe her, but they say she has rights!

Kaone described how "I lashed them with everything I find near me. . . . And honestly speaking I lashed them too hard. . . . I beat children with anything" and talked about the intervention of the pastor at church in getting her to desist from extreme assaults on her children.

Koane's utterances reflect the refrain of those who support CP about children's rights "spoiling children," and parental entitlement to discipline via the use of CP, as they are the primary providers for their children. Mareledi's use of force is reflected in the following: "I would just look at them while they fight. . . . I would silently go to get a rod and whip them . . . and whip, whip, whip!"

Maipelo chuckled as she emphasized the severity of her use of CP: "I don't really talk to a child many times. . . . I lash them, and I do it soundly." Another participant asserted, "I used to beat him when he was young, he was naughty. He would go and play the whole day, he would come late. . . . When he comes I'll whip him" (MmaThobo). While MmaThobo stopped beating her son as he grew older, Kaone felt entitled to beat up her 19-year-old daughter, as "I feed and clothe her."

Of salience is that CP is often accompanied by negative verbal communication that is intended to belittle, humiliate, and emotionally blackmail children. In an extreme pronouncement, loaded with emotional blackmail with the injunction that the children owed her gratitude for being born, Sarah, a 52-year-old single parent with no formal schooling, said:

> I also threaten to beat them or kill them. I also tell them that if I did not like them, I could have aborted them but the fact that I carried them in my tummy for nine months and bore them shows that I love them. They listen!

There was no reason to doubt Sarah's love for her children, and she was unaware of the potentially destructive nature of her communication (see Bradshaw, 1996). The fact that parents do not intend harm, but inadvertently inflict harm in their day-to-day practice, calls for conscious, positive parenting educational programs.

Discussion of Results

The women's accounts of the use of CP indicate that children are exposed to physical discipline from an early age, and for some it continues into adolescence. The women spoke of using CP not to hurt, but to "bring children in line," with many of them being careful to differentiate between child abuse and discipline. However, the non-physical manifestations of CP in relation to a child's poor sense of self and negative childhood life experiences can contribute to survival/codependent personalities (Bradshaw, 1996). Research evidence of CP being linked to school dropout, anxiety, depression, aggression, and anti-social behaviours, and reproduction of violence, are all ignored. The participants saw their actions as legitimate, and they disregarded children's rights to be free from pain and suffering, and from inhumane and degrading conduct.

While the Education Act (Government of Botswana, 1967) specifies under what conditions and how CP is to be administered, and the Children's Act speaks of "reasonable" use of CP, what constitutes "reasonableness" is open to interpretation. The findings of the study support Donnelly's (1984) assertion that, in a cultural context where CP is a deep-rooted parenting practice, its potential for harm is often overlooked. Almost all the 21 women who used CP used the whip, and some talked about hitting children in anger. Therein lies one of the dangers in the use of CP; it is generally associated with hostile parenting, which Smith et al. (2004), in their longitudinal study in Australia, found produced adverse social and psychological consequences.

CP in Botswana is a normalized part of day-to-day practice that is replicated in the school setting. Some women indicated that when children complained about being beaten at school, they responded that teachers were doing it for the children's own good. There is a paradox in teaching children non-violence by inflicting violence upon them. The use of

CP denies children control, relegates them to subordinate positions, and contributes to intergenerational patterns of its use (GIEACPC, 2017). CP undermines the democratic ideals of society (Jotia & Boikhutso, 2012), and its immediate and long-term effects on children compromise the achievement of the 2030 sustainable development goals (GIEACPC, 2017).

An interesting finding is that the women had heard about children's rights in the abstract, and expressed concerns that the focus on children's rights, and the inability to discipline as they saw fit, would threaten parental authority. None of them were aware of the specific legal provisions in Botswana that allow for CP. Although they believed that the use of CP was illegal, they commonly used it as a disciplinary practice. The question that this raises is: If they knew that CP is sanctioned in law might it contribute to its greater use? At the very least for the women, such knowledge would have served to legitimate their choice of CP.

Child rights advocates, who support a child's right to be treated with dignity, and with freedom from torture and inhumane and degrading treatment, experience greater challenges when structural conditions, rooted in legal frameworks, support CP. Given the ideological hegemony of deeply entrenched cultural beliefs and practices, it becomes more difficult when the law supports the violation of child rights. As ideology constitutes "socially, culturally and politically constructed" taken-for-granted assumptions (Sewpaul, 2013, p. 119), there is a need for counter-hegemonic discourses and practices. Such counter-hegemony can be provided through legal and policy reform and broad-based societal education that challenge cultural constructions of children as property to do as adults wish with them, and the way children are treated. Such reforms and education must be directed toward child-centred family policies, programs and laws where conscious, positive parenting practices are advocated for and supported.

Conclusions and Recommendations

Tearing up the roots of such an authoritarian and degrading parenting practice as CP is challenging, as it is normalized in law and in culture in Botswana. The results of this study show that CP is used by parents regardless of family structure and socio-economic background. The structural dimensions of law and culture intersect to play a critical role in maintaining and reproducing parenting practices that hinder children's rights, particularly their right to protection.

Legal reform is central to challenging and deconstructing dominant constructions of children and the ways in which adults relate with them. The laws supporting the use of CP in Botswana must be amended to ban the use of CP. But beyond the law is the role of social workers as cultural mediators, as evidence suggests that banning of CP is insufficient to produce desired changes. Social workers need to engage communities in dialogue to challenge some of the taken-for-granted assumptions underlying CP by providing evidence-based research that documents the negative consequences of CP, and engage in public education about alternatives, embracing conscious, positive parenting practices.

The banning of CP, combined with public education, holds the potential for disrupting intergenerational cycle of abuse, and for reducing the long-term negative impact of CP on children, families, and society at large (GIEACPC, 2017). Such education must be underscored by emancipatory forms of praxis and consciousness raising, designed to disrupt deeply held myths and misconceptions. Harmful cultural practices endure, often from one generation into the next, as ideology constitutes false consciousness that one is generally not aware of (Althusser, 2006; Sewpaul, 2013). But this does not mean that ideology cannot be disrupted. Sewpaul (2013) argued that "if people are provided with alternative learning experiences whether formal or informal they have the ability to disrupt dominant thinking" (p. 119). The UN Committee on the Rights of the Child (2006) advises:

> The first purpose of law reform to prohibit corporal punishment of children within the family is prevention: to prevent violence against children by changing attitudes and practice, underlining children's right to equal protection and providing an unambiguous foundation for child protection and for the promotion of positive, non-violent and participatory forms of child-rearing. . . . The aim should be to stop parents from using violent or other cruel or degrading punishments through supportive and educational, not punitive, interventions. (Article 1)

Prevention includes having resources available to support families in changing their practices concerning CP.

Parenting is challenging and daunting, and parents need support with child rearing and positive parenting, which include the following key components: long-term solutions directed at children's self-regulation; clear communication of expectations, rules, and limits; building mutually respectful relationships; teaching children skills for life; increasing children's confidence and ability to deal with challenging life circumstances; and teaching courtesy, non-violence, empathy, human rights, self-respect, and respect for others (Durrant, 2016, p. 6). Activities such as public meetings, workshops, and media programs to educate families and the public about the effects of CP are needed to enhance positive parenting practices.

Educational programs, based on dialogue and the development of critical consciousness (Parsons, 1991) rather than didactic pedagogical strategies, have the potential to empower people. For example, in Botswana, issues concerning CP can be dialogued in "*kgotla*" and Parent Teachers Association (PTA) meetings. The "*kgotla*," which is based on Afrocentric communitarian values, is a community-centred gathering place where members of a particular community meet to discuss various issues (Maundeni & Jacques, 2012). Education and sensitization about alternative forms of discipline can help community leaders, parents, professionals, and the community at large to rethink their stance on CP.

As professionals in Botswana, including social workers, are part of their socio-cultural and legal contexts, they are subject to the same dominant discourses and practices, and might have themselves normalized the use of CP (see IASSW, 2018). Research into the views of social workers, as was done by Julius (2013) with school principals, guidance counsellors, and teachers in Kenya, will be useful. Julius (2013) stated that over 90 percent of the 300 learners in his study, in Kenya, reported the continued use of CP, despite its banning, a finding reported by others such as Mweru (2010).

Social workers must engage in processes of ongoing self-reflexivity in order to be aware of the values and assumptions that they bring into their relationships in working with people, and they must work toward social justice by challenging all forms of discrimination, oppression, and transgression of human rights (Sewpaul, 2013; IASSW, 2018). Social work researchers, educators, and practitioners, in collaboration with other stakeholders nationally and internationally, must advocate for laws and policies that prohibit CP in all settings.

Parents in this study had no awareness of the long-term repercussions of CP on their children, and of their violation of children's rights. Some of them were also concerned that the dominant discourse on children's rights might hinder parental rights and contribute to the abuse of parents. While there are huge power imbalances between children and parents, and CP cannot be condoned, the concerns of parents must be addressed. Parental abuse by children is equally unacceptable. There is a need for broad-based community education that deals with parents' and children's rights and responsibilities, combined, when necessary, with individual, family, and small-group based interventions to deal with family conflicts and violence, and to enhance parent-child relationships.

REFERENCES

African Commission on Human and People's Rights (ACHPR). (1990). African Charter on the Rights and Welfare of the Child. Banjul, GM: Author.

Ahmad, I., Said, H., & Khan, F. (2013). Effect of corporal punishment on students' motivation and classroom learning. *Review of European Studies, 5*(4): 130–134.

Althusser, L. (2006). Ideology and ideological state apparatuses (Notes towards an investigation). *The anthropology of the state: A reader, 9*(1), 86–98.

Babbie, E. R. (2016). *The practice of social research* (14th ed.). Scarborough, ON: Nelson Education.

Bitensky, S. H. (1997). Spare the rod, embrace our humanity: Toward a new legal regime prohibiting corporal punishment of children. *University of Michigan Journal of Law Reform, 31,* 353.

Bradshaw, J. (1996). *Bradshaw on the family: A new way of creating solid self-esteem.* Deerfield Beach, FL: Health Communications.

Donnelly, J. (1984). Cultural relativism and universal human rights. *Human Rights, 6,* 400.

Durrant, J. E. (2000). *A generation without smacking: The impact of Sweden's ban on physical punishment.* London, UK: Save the Children.

Durrant, J. E. (2016). *Positive parenting in everyday parenting.* London, UK: Save the Children.

Ellison, C. G., & Bradshaw, M. (2009). Religious beliefs, sociopolitical ideology, and attitudes toward corporal punishment. *Journal of Family Issues, 30*(3), 320–340.

Gershoff, E. T. (2010). More harm than good: A summary of scientific research on the intended and unintended effects of corporal punishment on children. *Law and Contemporary Problems, 73*(2), 31–56.

Gershoff, E. T., & Bitensky, S. H. (2007). The case against corporal punishment of children: Converging evidence from social science research and international human rights law and implications for US public policy. *Psychology, Public Policy, and Law, 13*(4), 231.

Global Initiative to End All Corporal Punishment of Children (GIEACPC). (2017). *Prohibiting all corporal punishment of children in Africa: An essential step towards fullfilling the 2030 agenda for sustainable development.* Retrieved August 2018 from http://endcorporalpunishment.org/wp-content/uploads/regional/DAC-briefing-2017-EN.pdf

Global Initiative to End All Corporal Punishment of Children (GIEACPC). (2018). *Corporal punishment of children in Botswana.* Retrieved August 2018 from https://endcorporalpunishment.org/wpcontent/uploads/global/Global-report-2017-spreads.pdf

Gudyanga, E., Mbengo, F., & Wadesango, N. (2014). Corporal punishment in schools: Issues and challenges. *Mediterranean Journal of Social Sciences, 5*(9), 493.

Government of Botswana. (1964). Penal Code. Gaborone, BW: Government Printing & Publishing.

Government of Botswana. (1967). Education Act. Gaborone, BW: Government Printing & Publishing.

Government of Botswana. (1969). Customary Law Act. Gaborone, BW: Government Printing & Publishing.

Government of Botswana. (2009). Children's Act. Gaborone, BW: Government Printing & Publishing.

IASSW. (2018). *Global social work statement of ethical principles.* Retrieved November 2018 from https://www.iassw-aiets.org/wp-content/uploads/2018/04/Global-Social-Work-Statement-of-Ethical-Principles-IASSW-27-April-2018.pdf

Jotia, L., & Boikhutso, K. (2012). How corporal punishment undermines a democratic society: Is it necessary in Botswana schools? *Journal of Sociology and Social Anthropology, 3*(2): 119–126.

Julius, M. M. (2013). *An Assessment of the extent of use of corporal punishment in secondary schools in Muthambi Divison in Maara District, Tharaka Nithi County, Kenya.* (Unpublished master's thesis).: Kenyatta University, Nairobi, KE.

Lansford, J. E. (2010). The special problem of cultural differences in effects of corporal punishment. *Law and Contemporary Problems, 73*(2), 89–106.

Maundeni, T., & Jacques, G. (2012). "… and a little child shall lead them": Utilising Kgotla meetings to empower children and the communities that nurture them. In T. Maundeni and M. Nnyepi (Eds.), *Thari ya bana: Reflections on children in Botswana* (pp. 74–80). Gaborone, BW: UNICEF and University of Botswana.

Mullaly, B., & Mullaly, R. P. (2014). *Challenging oppression and confronting privilege: A critical social work approach.* New York, NY: Oxford University Press.

Mweru, M. (2010). Why are Kenyan teachers still using corporal punishment eight years after a ban on corporal punishment? *Child Abuse Review, 19*(4), 248–258.

Neuman, W. L. (2007). *The basics of social research: Qualitative and quantitative approaches.* New York, NY: Pearson Education.

Parsons, R. J. (1991). Empowerment: Purpose and practice principle in social work. *Social Work with Groups, 14*(2), 7–21.

Rempel, G. R., Neufeld, A., & Kushner, K. E. (2007). Interactive use of genograms and ecomaps in family caregiving research. *Journal of Family Nursing, 13*(4), 403–419.

Renzaho, A., Green, J., Mellor, D., & Swinburn, B. (2011). Parenting, family functioning and lifestyle in a new culture: The case of African migrants in Melbourne, Victoria, Australia. *Child & Family Social Work, 16*(2), 228–240.

Sebonego, M. M. (1994). *Report of a case study: Child abuse and neglect* (Unpublished doctoral dissertation). University of Botswana, Gaborone, Botswana.

Sewpaul, V. (2013). Inscribed in our blood: Confronting and challenging the ideology of sexism and racism. *Affilia: Journal of Women and Social Work, 28*(2), 116–125.

Shumba, A. (2004). Pupil physical abuse by teachers: A child-rearing practice or a cultural dilemma? *Journal of Aggression, Maltreatment & Trauma, 8*(4), 143–159.

Smith, A., Gollop, M., Taylor, N., & Marshall, K. (2004). *The discipline and guidance of children: A summary of research.* Otago, NZ: Children's Issues Centre, University of Otago, and Office of the Children's Commissioner.

Tafa, E. M. (2002). Corporal punishment: The brutal face of Botswana's authoritarian schools. *Education Review, 54*(1), 17–26. http://dx.doi.org/10.1080/00131910120110848

UN. (1989). Convention on the Rights of the Child. Geneva, CH: Author.

UN. (1948). Universal Declaration of Human Rights. Geneva, CH: Author.

UN. (1990). World Declaration on the Survival, Protection and Development of Children. Retrieved July 2018, from http://www.un-documents.net/wsc-dec.htm

UN Committee on the Rights of the Child. (2006). *CRC General Comment No. 8: The right of the child to protection from corporal punishment and other cruel or degrading forms of punishment.* Geneva, CH: UN. Retrieved November 2020 from http://endcorporalpunishment.org/wp-content/uploads/key-docs/CRC-general-comment-8.pdf

UNICEF. (2014). *Hidden in plain sight: A statistical analysis of violence against children.* New York: Author.

Weis, R., & Toolis, E. E. (2010). Parenting across cultural contexts in the USA: Assessing parenting behaviour in an ethnically and socioeconomically diverse sample. *Early Child Development and Care, 180*(7), 849–867.

Emancipatory Social Work, *Ubuntu*, and Afrocentricity: Antidotes to Human Rights Violations

Vishanthie Sewpaul and Linda Kreitzer

Social work's commitment to respect for cultural diversity must be balanced against adherence to universal human rights values and practices. There are core global social work documents that conceptualize social work as a human rights profession and that highlight the centrality of human rights and social justice in social work. The Global Social Work Statement of Ethical Principles (GSWSEP) (IASSW, 2018), the Global Definition of Social Work (IASSW/IFSW, 2014), the Global Standards on Social Work Education and Training (Sewpaul and Jones, 2004), and the Global Agenda (IASSW/ICSW/IFSW, 2012) resonate with the provisions of various international conventions and declarations on human rights. Dealing with the complex individual and structural, socio-economic and political issues around culture and human rights, as discussed by the various authors in this book, demands that social workers adopt multiple approaches at multi-systemic levels, a view that is entrenched in the key global social work documents.

The Global Definition of Social Work (IASSW/IFSW, 2014) reads as follows:

> Social work is a practice-based profession and an academic discipline that promotes social change and development,

social cohesion, and the empowerment and liberation of people. Principles of social justice, human rights, collective responsibility and respect for diversities are central to social work. Underpinned by theories of social work, social sciences, humanities and indigenous knowledges, social work engages people and structures to address life challenges and enhance well-being. (para. 1)

Given the understanding that social work is a contextual profession that must be responsive to local contexts, the following: "The above definition may be amplified at national and/or regional levels" (para. 1) was added as part of the definition. The definition is followed by a six-page commentary unpacking key concepts that are informed by critical, post-colonial theorizing, and structural, emancipatory approaches to social work education, research, policy, and practice.

There is detailed commentary on social work's core mandates, principles, knowledge, and practice. In terms of social work's core mandates, the emphasis is on: working toward social change as well as promoting social stability, continuity, and harmony; promoting social development, which is conceptualized as desired end states, strategies for intervention, and as a policy framework; and the empowerment and liberation of people. The core principles are: respect for the inherent worth and dignity of human beings; doing no harm; respect for diversity; upholding human rights and social justice; co-existence of human rights and collective responsibility; and interdependence. In relation to knowledge, the commentary deals with the meaning of science, with emphases on critical, post-colonial social work theories that are applied and emancipatory; the co-construction of knowledge; and on indigenous knowledges. Regarding practice, the commentary details the importance of working *with*, rather than for people, and also the system-stabilizing and system-destabilizing functions of social work, emphasizing that social workers engage on a continuum from direct work with individuals to political level interventions, and that social work challenges personal-political and micro-macro dichotomies.

The Global Standards for Social Work Education and Training (Sewpaul & Jones, 2004), in several of their core purposes, reiterate a human rights and social justice approach. The core purposes elucidate both the system-stabilizing and system-destabilizing functions of social work. Recognizing that the cultural emphasis on stability, harmony, and continuity might be used to oppress some groups of persons, the GSWSEP (as does the Global Standards) adds the qualifier, "insofar as these do not conflict with the fundamental rights of people" (IASSW, 2018), Section 2). The qualifier is reiterated in the 2014 Global Definition (IASSW/IFSW, 2014)).

In this chapter we discuss the tensions between universal and relativist discourses in social work, and we call for the reclaiming of Afrocentric values, with *Ubuntu* as their core, in challenging neoliberal capitalism and violations that occur in the name of culture. Each chapter in this book gives examples of human rights violations and the social worker's roles in addressing these violations. In this chapter, we challenge social workers to be informed by an emancipatory framework that embraces the values of Afrocentricity and human rights.

Culture and Social Work: The Universal–Relativist Debates

The juxtapositioning of respect for diversity and the promotion of human rights might at times seem paradoxical, as specific cultural traditions threaten people's rights to dignity, well-being, bodily integrity, security, and life itself. But respect for peoples in all their diversity with regard to, for example, religious affiliation; music, dance, dress, and food preferences; the ways people eat and sleep; language; modes of speech; and non-discriminatory marriage, death, and coming-of-age rituals, must not be confused with acceptance of beliefs, values, and practices that are malicious. Hallen (2002) characterizes the tension between the universal and the relative in two chapters titled "Rationality as culturally universal" (p. 19) and "Rationality as culturally relative" (p. 35).

Logical-positivist rationality, which originated in the West and has come to be universalized, has significant impact on social work's ontologies, epistemologies, and practices, including its formulations of codes of ethics and codes of practices. Thus, we have the taken-for-granted education, research, and practice frameworks, rooted in the natural sciences and transposed into the social sciences, that support researcher/practitioner non-involvement, detachment, neutrality, generalization, replication, separation of the professional from the personal, technical-bureaucratic models in social work, and the demand to prove one's truth according to positivist empiricism's all too often linear reductionist reasoning (Dominelli, 1996; Henrickson & Fouché, 2017; Metz, 2014; Sewpaul, 2010; Sewpaul & Hölscher, 2004). Such emphases have derided alternative and different ways of knowing and doing that are embedded in emancipatory and indigenous epistemologies (Sewpaul & Henrickson, 2019).

A critique of logical-positivist rationality, that presupposes the Kantian autonomous, rational being, and which minimizes the centring of people as social beings in an interdependent world, does not mean an eschewing of the importance of reason. Hallen (2002) discusses the West's characterization of the indigenous African intellect as "a-critical, non-reflective, and therefore . . . non-rational" (p. 47). Reason is not exclusively the purview of the West. Countering Eurocentric representations of African thought, Sogolo (1993) contended that "there are certain universals which cut across all human cultures. . . . Pre-eminent among these . . . is the ability for self-reflection and rational thought" (p. xv), but cautions that such reasoning "has its own local colour and particular mode of manifestation depending on the contingencies of the intervening culture" (p. xv). In response to the illogicality of Eurocentric assumptions of African (ir)rationality, Makinde (1988) asserted that "logic is either universal in all thought or it is relative to different thought systems. So, in neither case can we deny logic in the thought systems of others" (p. 43). Rationality is thus both universal, cutting across all cultures, and relative within cultures.

Adopting a postmodern lens in understanding the relationship between the universal and the particular, Williams and Sewpaul (2004) concluded that "the presence of a multiplicity of incommensurable contexts and identities does not render reference to universal values obsolete, ethnocentric and totalitarian" (p. 559). Even within cultures there are competing and conflicting discourses, for example reconciling religious and scientific discourses, and questions around God, the supernatural, destiny, causality, free will, science, ethics, and morality (Hallen, 2002; Sogolo, 1993), so no culture must be reduced to an essentialized, monolithic construction. Appiah (1992) balances the culturally universal and the culturally relative debate thusly: "We will only solve our problems if we see them *as human problems* arising out of a *special situation*, and we shall not solve them as African problems, generated somehow by *our being unlike others*" (pp. 135–136, emphasis added).

Such arguments bear salience in an intensely globalizing, interdependent world, where solutions for the particular must be sought in the universal, and where local solutions feed into global discourses and practices. The relationship between the universal and the particular must be thought of in dialectical terms, to "prevent the reduction of the particular to the universal as well as the reduction of the universal to the particular" (Torfing, as cited in Williams & Sewpaul, p. 560). On the universal-particular culture debate, Donnelly (2006) concluded:

> If cultural relativism is to function as a guarantee of local self-determination, rather than a cloak for despotism, we must insist on a strong, authentic cultural basis, as well as the presence of alternative mechanisms guaranteeing basic human dignity, before we justify derogations from 'universal' human rights. (p. 103)

Afrocentricity, inscribed with *Ubuntu* and *being for the other* (Bauman, 1993; Levinas, 1985; IASSW, 2018; Sewpaul, 2015a), we argue, is that *authentic cultural basis* that has universal appeal. Levinas (1985) and Bauman (1993) assert that the moral self accords the unique *Other* that priority assigned to the self. For Levinas (1985), to be responsible means to make oneself available for service of the *Other* in such a way that one's own life is intrinsically linked with that of others.

The latest GSWSEP (IASSW, 2018) attempts a balance between culture and human rights, and thus the tensions between universal and the relative, by calling on social workers to not stretch the boundaries of moral relativism to the point where the rights of some groups of persons are violated (Principle 3.2b) and for social workers to adopt the role of cultural mediators (Principle 2.3). Managing the tensions between the universal and the particular does not depend on formulaic answers. In recognition of the fact that no code can *make* social workers ethical, the IASSW (2018) calls for social workers to uphold ethical practices through "processes of constant debate, self-reflection, willingness to deal with ambiguities, and to engage in ethically acceptable processes of decision-making" (p. 1). In making explicit social workers" commitment to the core values and principles of the profession, the GSWSEP is designed to ensure multiple levels of accountability—most importantly accountability toward the people social workers engage with.

Reclaiming Ubuntu and Afrocentric ideals: Toward Alternative Socio-Political and Economic Governance

Cultural norms and traditions do not occur in a vacuum. They have antecedents, rooted in Africa's devastating colonial history. Serequebehan (2000) asserted that "we are . . . at a point in time when the dominance of the *univ*erse of European singularity is being encompassed or engulfed by the *multiv*erse of our shared humanity. The colonizer, self-deified imperial Europe, is dead!" (pp. 52–53, emphasis in original). There is cogency in the former part of this assertion but, unfortunately, colonial Europe is not dead! Neocolonial imperialism, with other colonial powers such as the United States and China, continues to keep people in the Global South in poor, marginalized, and excluded positions, and there are contemporary socio-political and neoliberal economic factors that violate human dignity and human rights (Annan, 2006; Dominelli, 2008; Hahn, 2008; Sewpaul, 2014, 2015a; Shai, 2018).

In contrast with neoliberalism, which has exacerbated poverty and inequality and has disproportionately disadvantaged women and children (Bond, 2005; Hahn, 2008; Sewpaul, 2005; 2015b; Shai, 2018), Afrocentric ideals embrace non-discrimination, communitarian values, cooperation, generosity, interdependence, equality, respect, and the recognition of the inherent dignity of all of persons. Aligned with the views of Sewpaul and Henrickson (2019), our conceptualization of the person is not limited to Kantian, liberal notions of individual persons; it includes families, tribes, and communities, and ultimately the unity of self with that of the universe—the interdependence of the self with the whole. Thus, acknowledging the dignity of humanity means opposing the legal and cultural subjugation of women and girls, as individuals and as groups, as much as it means opposing colonialism, capital punishment, mob lynching, genocide, and working toward environmental and climate justice.

Race and location constitute the centres of identity in Afrocentric theorizing and methodology. If Afrocentricity is to make meaningful contributions to policy developments, it must integrate into its framework, far more than it currently does, key social criteria such as class, (dis)ability, sexuality, gender, and distributive justice, as emancipatory social work does. Many cultural traditions that constitute sources of human rights violations, such as child marriages, harmful traditional practices in the face of physical and mental ill-health, female genital mutilation/cutting, and bride wealth, have as much to do with values and beliefs of groups of persons as they do with socio-economic exigencies. These are brought out in the various chapters of this book, with Abukari, for example, paying particular attention to how socio-cultural constructions of childhood intersect with socio-economic realities to render children vulnerable to child labour. Women who perform the acts of female genital mutilation/ cutting (FGM/C), as discussed in Bukuluki's and Boateng and Sottie's chapters, are indicted for being the torchbearers (Opoku, 2017) of such practices, and they are, indeed, complicit in reproducing harm, within patriarchal societies that condone harm. But patriarchy, and stereotypical gender roles, manifest differently in different contexts, with both women and men being involved in their disruption and/or continuity (Sewpaul, 2013), are often linked to socio-economic circumstances.

What must be examined are the socio-economic and political structural constraints within which women operate, particularly the constraints of alternative forms of gainful employment. For example, educating women about how FGM/C violates female rights to dignity and bodily integrity, and on the dangers and consequences of FGM/C, is likely to produce small gains if participation in this is the only viable source of income for those women. Similarly, the problem of child marriages is unlikely to dissipate without expanding socio-economic opportunities and civil liberties of families. Under conditions of extreme deprivation, marrying one's child early means having one less person to feed, clothe, and educate, and perhaps reflects the hope that by being married, one's child would be better provided for. In this text, Muchacha, Matsika, and Nhapi discuss how child marriages are significantly shaped by poverty in the Global South, and they call for, in addition to other measures, prioritizing the eradication of poverty. Likewise, if we are to prevent or minimize the consequences of harmful traditional practices related to health, as Mugumbate and Gray examine in relation to how poverty, stigma, and misrecognition contribute to the gross violation of the rights of persons with epilepsy, people must have access to education, employment, and free or affordable quality health services.

We look to Africa's history for some lessons that might be carried into contemporary Africa and draw on Nyerere's (1967) conceptualization of African socialism—*Ujamaa*, which embraces the principles of Kwanzaa discussed in the Introduction. Nyerere's dictatorship (constructed by some as authoritarian and by others as benevolent [see, e.g., Fouéré, 2014]), his failed policy choices, the demoralizing consequences of his enforced villagization program, and the extraneous influences of the West on Tanzania and other African countries' post-colonial statuses, do "not deny the legitimate intentions and aspirations that informed *Ujamaa* as a developmental strategy" (Ibhawoh & Dibua, 2003, p. 60). *Ujamaa* emphasized people participation, communitarianism, non-exploitative development, national self-reliance, freedom, equality, and national unity. Nyerere (1967) was intensely opposed to foreign aid and the neoliberal impositions of the IMF and the World Bank, and while he encouraged and supported national self-sufficiency, he rejected isolationism.

Nyrere's ideas cohere with those of Keynesian economics, which played a key role in establishing the welfare states of the West (Leonard, 1997). Keynesian egalitarianism involved state intervention, regulation of the market, the involvement of organized labour to promote full employment and economic growth, and some state ownership of crucial national enterprises like railroads, public utilities, and energy (Keynes, 1933). Keynes (1933) argued that

> ideas, knowledge, science, hospitality, travel . . . should of their nature be international. But let goods be homespun whenever it is reasonably and conveniently possible, and above all, let finance be primarily national. . . . National self-sufficiency . . . though it costs something, may be a luxury, which we can afford, if we happen to want it. (unpaged)

Therein lay the crunch—*if we happen to want it*—as states, across Africa and the world submit to neoliberal free markets, trade liberalization, privatization, and deregulation (Hahn, 2008; Sewpaul, 2015a; Shai, 2018). Despite the vast body of research that reflects its pernicious consequences, "capitalism succeeds through ideological control of consciousness, designed to make us believe that neoliberalism is in our interests and is inevitable" (Sewpaul, 2015b, p. 463).

Sadly, Nyerere's ideals gave way to "state bureaucratic capitalism—the use of state capital by a managerial elite" (Shijvi, cited in Ibhawoh & Dibua, 2003, p. 85). Nyerere's single-party state leadership reflected the dangers of post-colonialism, commanded by the new emergent national elite, that Fanon (1963) so strongly warned about. These patterns have seen replication across post-independent African states, including post-apartheid South Africa (Bond, 2005). Fanon (1963), in his theses on colonialism, post-colonialism, capitalism, and culture, concluded that "the poverty of the people, national oppression and the inhibition of culture are one and the same thing" (p. 191).

If African states have to live up to Afrocentric ideals they must make policy choices that counter neoliberal capitalism. Within the Afrocentric paradigm, the well-being of the individual is aligned with the well-being of the society, with an attempt to maintain a "delicate balance between the concepts of community and individuality" (Gyekye, 1995, p. 132), and it is humanistic ethics—not ethics founded on capitalism—that must underpin approaches to dealing with the various contemporary problems confronting Africa. Gaining economic freedom and expanding opportunities and choices are just as important as civil and political freedoms (Sen, 1999), with social solidarity and deepened democracies being the essence of societies. There are arguments that Afrocentricity is a poor fit with neoliberal capitalism, which places primacy on the individual, and profit above people. Hallen (2002) contended that socialism "in its democratic forms appear[s] to be more compatible with the humanitarian values definitive of Africa's 'communitarian' societies" (p. 34). Nyerere's (1967) rejection of neoliberal austerity measures imposed by the IMF and World Bank, and his bringing together development, empowerment, freedom, and people participation, bear much relevance for contemporary Africa.

Ibhawoh and Dibua (2003) point out that *Ujamaa* failed as an economic project, as measured by GDP, which should not be the sole criterion of its success. The role of the West, particularly Europe and the United States, in undermining socialism in Africa and other parts of the world must not be underestimated. Indeed, to ensure that other African countries did not follow suit, Western countries and international financial institutions did everything possible to ensure the failure of the pursuit of any socialist forms of governance (Hahn, 2008; Ibhawoh & Dibua, 2003; Shai, 2018; Sewpaul, 2014). According to Annan (2006), "across Africa, undemocratic and oppressive regimes were supported and sustained by the competing super-powers in the name of their broader goals" (p. 241)—the broader goals being primarily the disavowal of socialism, the propagation of neoliberal ideology and securing domestic trade and profit. The *Ujamma* experiment produced greater national unity and literacy (Ibhawoh & Dibua, 2003; Parmar, 1975; Samoff, 1990), and it was the "harbinger of social welfare development" (Ibhawoh & Dibua, 2003. p. 71). For social justice and human rights to flourish, a pursuit of socialist forms of democracy that encourage social solidarity and distributive justice, rather than the forms of liberalism that characterize capitalistic democracies, or autocracies disguised as democracies, must be supported.

Afrocentricity and Emancipatory Social Work

Afrocentricity places, in its centre, the location, cultures, histories, knowledges, and experiences of African peoples, both within Africa and across the Diaspora, without the reduction of Africans to a single, fossilized identity (Asante, 2014; Sewpaul, 2007). Such centring in Afrocentricity is grounded on awareness of the annihilation of African heritages and ways of being through the long histories of slavery and colonialism, contemporary forms of neocolonialism, and the archetypical representations of Africa and Africans. For the colonizer the logic of colonizing peoples—controlling their bodies, minds, and spirits; dispossessing them of their lands; and extracting their labour—rested on benevolence through their civilization and the Christianization missions. In many ways it was relegating Africans to a subhuman species that granted the colonizer justification for the atrocious treatment of Africans, as so cogently described by Fanon (1963; 1967) and Cesaire (1972). Cesaire (1972, p. 43) wrote of "societies drained of their essence, cultures trampled underfoot, institutions undermined, lands confiscated, religions smashed, magnificent artistic creations destroyed, extraordinary possibilities wiped out" and about "millions of men in whom fear has been cunningly instilled, who have been taught to have an inferiority complex, to tremble, kneel, despair, and behave like flunkeys."

At the heart of Afrocentricity is the transformative agenda, and the goal of liberating African peoples from the constraints of their own thinking—a goal that emancipatory social work shares. While it is constructed as a non-hegemonic alternative to Eurocentrism, as we caution in the Introduction, some African scholars do construct Afrocentricity as superior to Eurocentricity and call for a replacement of the Eurocentric with the Afrocentric. This, we argue, is to fall into the same trap as the colonizers and neocolonizers and is a negation of the more unifying goals of emancipatory social work. Sewpaul (2007, 2016) challenged the views of authors such as Cobbah (1987) and Makgoba and Seepe (2004) who saw respect, restraint, responsibility, reciprocity, and emancipatory ideals as distinguishing features of African society, and thus antithetical to the values of Western societies. Rejecting dichotomous depictions of the West and the Rest, she called for unity in diversity and "dialogue; tuning into the life worlds of people; responsiveness; reasoned debate; recognizing the power of care, interdependence, reciprocity and validation" (Sewpaul, 2016, p. 37). Furthermore, while Afrocentricity calls for the cognitive independence and the redefinition of African identities (Asante, 2014; Kumah-Abiwa, 2016), we, like emancipatory thinkers such as Biko (1978), Fanon (1963), and Mandela (1995), argue that both the oppressor and the oppressed need to be liberated from colonial and racist forms of thinking for true transformation to occur at individual and societal levels—thus the emancipatory social work goal to critically interrogate and undo sources of both oppression and privilege (Sewpaul, 2013, 2016).

Deconstructing Archetypes: The Classroom as Context

We concur with Mazama (2001) that the appeal of Afrocentricity "lies both in the disturbing conditions of African people and the remedy that Afrocentricity suggests" (p. 387). Afrocentricity is an antidote to the devastating archetypes induced by colonialism. But the danger is not just the construction of Africans by the West; the real dangers lie in the naturalization and internalization of these archetypes by Africans (Asante, 2014; Fanon, 1963, 1967; Sewpaul, 2007, 2013). Sewpaul (2007) wrote about the incongruous worlds of students who associate Africa and African with all that is negative, reflecting the debilitating and shameful effects of colonization, racism, and race thinking. Ongoing exercises with both Western and non-Western students, within and outside of Africa, reflect a continuous reproduction of such representations, which are reinforced by the media and some political figures, the most recent being Donald Trump, who despite his geographic ineptitude, referred to Africans belonging to "shithole" countries (Vitali et al., 2018).

Students who are African *live* in a world of denim jeans (often designer ones), cellphones, TVs, computers, and concrete buildings in developed urban settings, yet *carry* an archetypical Africa in all its negativity, with dominant images of poverty, disease, underdevelopment, threats, and danger (Sewpaul, 2007). When students are engaged in reflective dialogue and are asked "where is the Africa that you live in?" they react with surprise, and sometimes with disdain at themselves for their naiveté in buying into dominant constructions. Hall (1985) asserted that

> ideological struggle actually consists of attempting to win some new set of meanings for an existing term or category, or of dis-articulating it from its place in a signifying structure. For example, it is precisely because 'black' is the term which connotes the most despised, the dispossessed, the unenlightened, the uncivilized, the uncultured, the scheming, the incompetent, that it can be contested, transformed and invested with a positive ideological value. (p. 112)

It is toward such ideological contestation, deconstruction, and redefinition that advocates of Afrocentricity and emancipatory social work direct their efforts. This is important, as we know from labelling theory that people come to identify themselves and often behave according to dominant constructs. People might hold onto outmoded and superstitious beliefs and practices if this is what is expected of them. Also, holding onto primordial values is erroneously seen as agency, and as an authentic anti-colonial response, as discussed by Sewpaul, Mdamba, and Seepamore in this book. Yet, paradoxically given the archetypical representations, it is no wonder that education in the Global South is infused with Western ideologies. There is a desire to be seen as being on par with Europeans, and to be European (Kreitzer, 2012). The internalized self-loathing of blackness and the aspiration toward whiteness is cogently described by Fanon (1963, 1967; see also Toni Morrison's poignant novel *The Bluest Eye*). If students have to enter communities with humility enough to engage people in changing cultural traditions that violate human rights and social work values, they need to be well grounded in their own values, identities, and positive conceptualization of self.

Adopting an emancipatory lens to social work, Sewpaul (2007) questioned the pedagogical implications of students' negative constructions of self and of Africa and called for alternative experiences so that such dominant thinking can be disrupted. Deconstruction of dominant ideologies is critical if we are to achieve the kinds of emancipatory goals that Afrocentricity calls for. Educators must use the opportunities provided in the classrooms and create safe spaces to engage students in reflective activities and dialogue that facilitate the inscription of positive values.

Deconstructing Neoliberal Thinking

Each of the chapters in this book proposes ways forward in dealing with human rights violations, including expanding opportunities for education and employment, challenging and changing patriarchy and the hegemonic power of entrenched traditions and values, lobbying for policy and legislative changes, broad-based community education to engender attitudinal and behavioral changes, advocacy, and strategies for reducing poverty. Yet one of the main contributors to poverty and inequality—neoliberal capitalism, as discussed above—is not specifically interrogated. Emancipatory social work calls for all human beings to ask critical questions about the construction of self in the face of the overwhelming legitimating power of neoliberal consumerism. Nyerere (1967) understood this, and while envisioning political, economic, and cultural goals, he emphasized that *Ujamaa* needed to be entrenched in *attitude*; it requires alterations in our conception of humanity, to embrace interdependence and intersubjectivity as does emancipatory social work (IASSW, 2018; Sewpaul & Henrickson, 2019). Given the manufacture of consent and of desire (Leonard, 1997), the market seduces people into believing that their moral worth is determined by their purchasing choices and power (Bauman, 1993; Leonard, 1997). Drawing on the work of Larner (2000) and Steger and Roy (2010), Sewpaul (2015b) conceived of neoliberalism as ideology, as a form of governmentality, and as a policy paradigm—overlapping and mutually reinforcing dimensions, which "penetrate daily consciousness so much so that it is normalized and naturalized, and it is considered necessary for the social order despite the inequality and poverty that it engenders" (p. 463). She points to all our complicity in reproducing neoliberalism, and hierarchies of class, race, and gender. We are also complicit in reproducing hierarchies of language, age, marital status, ethnicity, culture, nationality, sexuality, and mental and physical (dis)abilities.

Yet, as Sewpaul (2014, 2015a) asserted, there is hope, through the use of critically reflexive, consciousness-raising strategies, in people becoming aware of the legitimating power of neoliberal capitalism. Such awareness and its transformative potential rests on critically questioning, challenging, and changing taken-for-granted, commonsense assumptions (Gramsci, 1977; Hahn, 2008; Sewpaul, 2013, 2015b). This is at the heart of emancipatory social work. Social work educators must bring these discourses into the classrooms, and use locally relevant case studies, drama and art, and engage students in exercises such as journal writing and writing of their biographies so that they recognize the impacts of structural determinants, including the ideological control of consciousness by the media and state apparatuses, on their thinking and material conditions of life (Sewpaul, 2013).

Raising critical consciousness, which characterizes emancipatory social work, means examining how intersectional criteria like race, caste, class, gender, language, ethnicity, nationality, (dis)ability, and sexuality combine to constitute sources of advantage and/or disadvantage on our lives (as social work students, educators, researchers, and practitioners) and the lives of people we engage with. In doing so we might be able to better understand and respond to the life circumstances and ideological positioning of the people we work with. But the social work profession is not going to do this alone. The problems facing humankind in the face of the onslaughts of neoliberalism and far-right politics call for far more concerted efforts on a much broader scale. Social workers need to build alliances and bridges across similarities and differences and connect with progressive people's movements on national, regional, and global levels in the ongoing struggle to uphold human dignity and the rights of all peoples of this world (Sewpaul, 2014). But social activism is not going to occur if it is not preceded by developing critical awareness of the legitimating power of societal discourses and practices.

Culture, Education, and Practice

Sometimes law and culture coalesce to violate human rights, as discussed in the case of corporal punishment by Ntshwarang and Sewpaul in chapter 12, but it is applicable to other issues such as sexual orientation. Homophobia, which spans the globe, is defended in the name of religion and culture, punished in some countries by draconian laws that violate human rights. When violating laws and cultures merge, it makes the advocacy efforts of social workers, other professionals, and the citizenry at large more challenging, for change must be directed at both the law and community attitudes and choices. In some instances, there are conflicts between national legislation and customary laws, as in the case of child marriages in some countries. Muchacha, Matsika, and Nhapi in this volume and Werft (2016) cite the cases of Zimbabwe and Malawi respectively, where national law bans the marriage of persons under 18 years of age, but with customary law and/or religious sanction such marriages occur widely.

Having laws that promote and protect human rights does help, but legislation alone is insufficient to protect people against human rights violations that occur in the name of culture. Social workers in Africa, and across the globe, in their role as cultural mediators (IASSW, 2018; Sewpaul, 2014, 2015b) can play important roles in facilitating intercultural dialogue, debate, and constructive confrontation. One of the standards in the Global Standards for Social Work Education and Training (Sewpaul & Jones, 2004) reads: "Ensuring that social work students are schooled in a basic human rights approach" (p. 501), with the following explanatory note:

> Such an approach might facilitate constructive confrontation and change where certain cultural beliefs, values and traditions violate peoples' basic human rights. As culture is socially constructed and dynamic, it is subject to deconstruction and change. Such constructive confrontation, deconstruction and change may be facilitated through a tuning into, and an understanding of particular cultural values, beliefs and traditions and via critical and reflective dialogue with members of the cultural group *vis-à-vis* broader human rights issues. (p. 510)

While it is written in the context of social work education and training, the implications of this for practice are self-evident. Students become practitioners, and they are expected to transfer the knowledge, skills, values, and principles of the profession into the practice context. Social work practitioners, through ongoing professional development, must be consistently aware of the human rights provisions and their applications, or lack thereof, to local contexts, and engage in the same forms of praxis that we engage students in. Furthermore, given the "concealing function of common sense" (Sewpaul, 2013, p. 122), and that we (educators, researchers, and practitioners) are products and producers of our socio-political and cultural worlds, the GSWSEP, which applies to teaching, research, and practice contexts, has specific principles related to this. Principles 4.7 and 4.8 call for the development of awareness of entrapments of one's thinking by dominant socio-political and cultural discourses, which may manifest in a range of prejudices, discriminations, and human rights violations, and for social workers to heighten their own consciousness as well of that of the people they engage with.

Informed by an emancipatory theoretical approach, social work educators, practitioners, and researcher-practitioners can adopt strategies of consciousness raising to challenge taken-for-granted assumptions that are inscribed through dominant socialization and culture (Freire, 1973; Gramcsi, 1977; Sewpaul, 2013, 2015b). Social work education and training is generally designed to equip graduates with the requisite skills in empathy, active listening, facilitation, mediation, and interpersonal relationships. These skills can be used to build bridges across cultures and to engage people in ways that ensure the harmful aspects of culture are confronted, while retaining those that are positive and that allow for intergenerational cultural continuity and human development (Sewpaul, 2014). Social workers must also be courageous to adopt constructive confrontational strategies when necessary, especially when culture threatens people's security, bodily integrity, and life. In this respect it is heartening to note that there are pockets of resistance by social work educators and practitioners in Africa (Sewpaul, 2014), and as writing is a form of resistance, the authors of this text contribute to such resistance.

Practice-Based Research and Learning from Practice

While the classroom constitutes an ideal space to introduce students to critical, post-colonial, and emancipatory theories and research paradigms, and to deconstruct and reconstruct thinking around self and society, it is equally important to learn from practice, through practice-based research, as is so fully discussed in the edited book by Twikirize and Spitzer (2019), reflecting locally specific interventions in Burundi, Kenya, Rwanda, Tanzania, and Uganda. The most compelling examples come from Rwanda, which after the genocide saw *an interventionist state* that, through national dialogues, launched local programs directed at "facilitating people to do things by themselves" (Rutikanga, 2019, p. 73), and the promotion of unity, participatory democracy, and reconciliation on a nation-wide basis (Uwihangana et al., 2019). The role of a facilitative state is critical for sustainable community development, and for wide-scale, national rollouts of programs that have been proven to work. Sewpaul and Hölscher (2007) discuss local interventions in South Africa, in respect of children in very difficult circumstances, where the gains remained constrained on account of lack of government investment in their expansion and continuity.

Through the voices of several authors, the book (Twikirize & Spitzer, 2019) describes various local, culturally relevant approaches based on values such as social cohesion, interdependence, and collective means of dealing with a range of individual and socio-economic problems, drawing on the lived experiences and tacit knowledges of communities, building resilience and self-sufficiency, and respect, unity, and reconciliation—all of which reflect the ethos of *Ubuntu* and *Ujamaa*. Bukuluki and colleagues in this book discuss how practices grounded in positive African values might contribute to the prevention of domestic violence and HIV/AIDS. Conjoining the voices of a "service user/giver" and of a university professor, Sewpaul and Nkosi Ndlovu (2020) describe the transformative and sustaining potential of emancipatory social work and *Ubuntu*, and how HIV+ women shifted from being trapped in trauma, guilt, and secrecy to becoming HIV/AIDS outreach workers, educators, and activists.

One of the identified limitations of the application of indigenous approaches is the reliance on males as the arbiters and leaders in cultural discourse and problem solving. While the exclusion of women, in itself, constitutes a violation of rights, it also perpetuates patriarchal cultures, which are sources of many human rights violations. This is a common theme in all the chapters in this book. Furthermore, the exclusion of women from chieftainship and other leadership positions neglects an enormous resource base that Africa so desperately needs. Werft (2016) highlights the atypical appointment of Theresa Kachindamoto as chief in Malawi. In her position, Kachindamoto annulled over 850 child marriages, suspended chiefs who failed to make this commitment, championed girls' rights to education, and put a ban on sexual initiation rites, where girls as young as seven years of age are taught how to please future husbands, thus exposing them to HIV/AIDS. Reclaiming indigenous approaches in social work education, research, and practice on the African continent does not mean reverting to traditional values and practices that are harmful.

Conclusion

It is difficult to separate the effects of cultural ideological constraints, for example the claims to a primordial essence and an essentialized cultural identity that underlie human rights violations, socio-economic deprivation, and the consumerist ideology engendered by neoliberalism, as each overlaps and constrains the other. Thus, emancipatory social work goals must be directed at developing critical consciousness around the legitimating and normalizing powers of both cultural and neoliberal discourses and practices. The virtues of the we-centred, communitarian ethos, *Ubuntu*, and the distributive justice goals of Afrocentricity must be used in the interests of all people. There is no place in the Afrocentric paradigm, which embraces human dignity, mutuality, reciprocity and respect, for the inferior construction and treatment of women and children, people who do not fit the norms of heterosexuality, and those with mental and physical disabilities, who are often subject to human rights violations.

We concede the power of historical and/or perceived historical continuity in retaining harmful cultural practices, and the deep interconnections made between cultural values and identities. But there are also discontinuities and disruptions; cultural norms and practices wax and wane, take different shapes and forms, and the nature and extent of practices change over time. To conceive of African traditions, values, and beliefs as timeless and primordial is to deny African peoples the capacity for reflexivity, rational thought, and agency—a reinscribing of colonial constructions that Afrocentricity repudiates. Afrocentricity is a transformative project, not the sedimentation of traditions; it is directed at granting agency to African peoples, and is fully aligned with emancipatory social work theory and practice. The core values of Afrocentricity must be used to challenge and change those traditions and customs that violate human rights and human dignity; this is both a privilege and a challenge for the social work profession in Africa. It is human dignity that both social work and Afrocentricity hold as sacrosanct.

REFERENCES

Annan, K. (2006). The causes of conflict and the promotion of durable peace and sustainable development in Africa. In C. Heyns & K. Stefiszyn (Eds.), *Human Rights, peace and justice in Africa: A reader* (pp. 239–243). Pretoria, ZA: Pretoria University Law Press.

Appiah, K. A. (1992). *In my father's house: Africa in the philosophy of culture.* Oxford, UK: Oxford University Press.

Asante, M. K. (2014). Afrocentricity: Toward a new understanding of African thought in the world. In M. K. Asante, Y. Mike, & J. Yin (Eds.), *The global intercultural communication reader* (2nd ed., pp. 101–110). New York, NY: Routledge.

Bauman Z. (1993). *Postmodern ethics.* Oxford, UK: Blackwell Publishing.

Biko, N. M. (1978). *I write what I like* (A. Stubbs, Ed.). Johannesburg, ZA: Heinemann.

Bond, P. (2005). *Elite transition: From apartheid to neoliberalism in South Africa.* Scottsville, ZA: University of KwaZulu-Natal Press.

Cesaire, A. (1972). *Discourse of colonialism.* New York, NY: Monthly Review Press.

Cobbah, J. A. M. (1987). African values and the human rights debate: An African perspective. *Human Rights Quarterly, 9*(3): 309–331.

Dominelli, L. (1996). Deprofessionalizing social work: Anti-oppressive practice, competencies and postmodernism. *British Journal of Social Work, 26,* 153–175.

Dominelli, L. (2008). The new world order, scarcity and injustice: Social work fights back. *Caribbean Journal of Social Work, 6*(7), 6–15.

Donnelly, J. (2006). Cultural relativism and universal human rights. In C. Heyns & K. Stefiszyn (Eds.), *Human Rights, peace and justice in Africa: A reader* (pp 111–121). Pretoria, ZA: Pretoria University Law Press.

Fanon, F. (1963). *The wretched of the earth.* Harmondsworth, UK: Penguin.

Fanon, F. (1967). *Black skin white mask.* New York, NY: Grove Press.

Foueré, M. (2014). Julius Nyerere, Ujamaa, and political morality in contemporary Tanzania. *African Studies Review, 57*(1), 1–24.

Freire, P. (1973). *Education for critical consciousness.* New York, NY: Seabury.

Gramsci, A. (1977). *Selections from political writings 1910–1920.* London, UK: Lawrence & Wishart.

Gyekye, K. (1995). *An essay on African philosophical thought: The Akan conceptual scheme.* Cambridge, UK: Cambridge University Press.

Hahn, N. S. C. (2008). Neoliberal imperialism and pan-African resistance. *Journal of World Systems Research, 13*(2): 142–178.

Hall, S. (1985). Signification, representation, ideology: Althusser and the post-structuralist debates. *Critical Studies in Mass Communication, 2,* 91–144.

Hallen, B. (2002). *A short history of African philosophy.* Bloomington, IN: Indiana University Press.

Henrickson, M., & Fouché, C. (2017). *Vulnerability and marginality in human services.* Surrey, UK: Routledge.

Ibhawoh, B., & Dibua, J. I. (2003). Deconstructing Ujamaa: The legacy of Julius Neyerere in the quest for social and economic development in Africa. *African Journal of Political Science, 8*(1): 59–83.

IASSW. (2018). *Global social work statement of ethical principles.* https://www.iassw-aiets. org/2018/04/18/global-social-work-statement-of-ethical-principles-iassw/IASSW/ IFSW. (2014). *Global definition of social work.* https://www.iassw-aiets.org/global-definition-of-social-work-review-of-the-global-definition/

IASSW/IFSW/ICSW. (2012). *Global agenda for social work and social development commitment to action.* https://www.iassw-aiets.org/wp-content/uploads/2017/01/ Global-Agenda-English.pdf

Keynes, J. M. (1933). National self-sufficiency. *Yale Review, 22*(4): 755–769. https://www. mtholyoke.edu/acad/intrel/interwar/Keynes.htm

Kreitzer, L. (2012). *Social work in Africa: Exploring culturally relevant education and practice in Ghana.* Calgary, AB: University of Calgary Press.

Kumah-Abiwa, F. (2016). Beyond intellectual construct to policy ideas: The case of the Afrocentric paradigm. *Africology: The Journal of Pan-African Studies, 9*(2): 7–27.

Larner, W. (2000). Neo-liberalism: policy, ideology, governmentality. *Studies in Political Economy, 63,* 5–26.

Leonard, P. (1997). *Postmodern welfare: Reconstructing an emancipatory project.* London, UK: Sage.

Levinas, E. (1985) *Ethics and infinity.* Pittsburgh, PA: Duquesne University Press.

Makgoba, M., & Seepe, S. (2004). Knowledge and identity: An African vision of higher education transformation. In S. Seepe (Ed.), *Towards an African identity in higher education* (pp. 13–57). Pretoria, ZA: Vista University and Scottsville Media.

Makinde, M. A. (1988). African culture and moral systems: A philosophical study. *Second Order 1*(2): 1–27.

Mandela, N. (1995). *Long walk to freedom: An autobiography of Nelson Mandela.* Boston, MA: Little, Brown.

Mazama, A. (2001). The Afrocentric paradigm: Contours and definitions. *Journal of Black Studies, 31*(4): 387–405.

Metz T. (2014). Harmonizing global ethics in the future: A proposal to add south and east to west. *Journal of Global Ethics, 10*(2): 146–155.

Nyerere, J. K. (1967). *Freedom and unity, Uhuru na Ujoma: A selection from writings and speeches 1952-1965.* London, UK: Oxford University Press.

Opoku, R. (2017). *Gendered violence: Patterns and causes of women-to-women violence in the Lake Zone regions of Tanzania, East Africa*. Tampere, FI: University of Tampere Press.

Parmar, S. L. (1975). Self-reliant development in an interdependent world. In G. F. Erb & V. Kallab, (Eds.), *Beyond dependency: The developing world speaks out* (pp. 2–27). Washington DC: Overseas Development Council.

Rutikanga, C. (2019). A social work analysis of home-grown solutions and poverty reduction in Rwanda: The traditional approach of *Ubudehe*. In J. M. Twikirize & H. Spitzer (Eds.), *Social work practice in Africa: Indigenous and innovative approaches* (pp. 61–80). Kampala, UG: Fountain Publishers.

Samoff, J. (1990). Modernizing a socialist vision: Education in Tanzania. In M. Carnoy & J. Samoff (Eds.), *Education and social transition in the Third World* (pp. 209–274). Princeton. NJ: Princeton University Press.

Sen, A. (1999). *Development as freedom*. Oxford, UK: Oxford University Press.

Serequebehan, T. (2000). *Our heritage*. New York, NY: Rowman & Littlefield.

Sewpaul, V. (2005). Feminism and globalisation: The promise of Beijing and neoliberal capitalism in Africa. *Agenda, 19* (64): 104–113.

Sewpaul, V. (2007). Power, discourse and ideology: Challenging essentialist notions of race and identity in institutions of higher learning in South Africa. *Social Work/ Maatskaplike Werk, 43*(1): 16–27.

Sewpaul, V. (2010). Professionalism, postmodern ethics and global standards for social work education and training. *Social Work/Maatskaplike Werk 46*(3): 253–262.

Sewpaul, V. (2013). Inscribed in our blood: Confronting and challenging the ideology of sexism and racism. *Affilia: Journal of Women and Social Work, 28*(2): 116–125.

Sewpaul, V. (2014). Social work and human rights: An African perspective. In S. Hessle (Ed.), *Human rights and social equality: Challenges* (pp. 13–28). Surrey, UK: Ashgate.

Sewpaul, V. (2015a). Politics with soul: Social work and the legacy of Nelson Mandela. *International Social Work, 59*(6), 697–708. https://doi.org/10.1177/0020872815594226

Sewpaul, V. (2015b). Neoliberalism. In J. Wright (Ed.), *International encyclopedia of the social and behavioral sciences* (2nd ed., Vol. 16, pp. 462–468). Amsterdam, NL: Elsevier.

Sewpaul, V. (2016). The West and the Rest divide: Culture, human rights and social work. *Journal of Human Rights and Social Work, 1*, 30–39.

Sewpaul, V., & Hölscher, D. (2004). *Social work in times of neoliberalism: A postmodern discourse*, Pretoria, ZA: Van Schaik.

Sewpaul, V., & Hölscher, D. (2007). Against the odds: Community-based interventions for children in difficult circumstances. In L. D. Dominelli (Ed.), *Revitalising communities* (pp. 193–206). Hampshire, UK: Ashgate.

Sewpaul, V., & Henrickson, M. (2019). The (r)evolution and decolonization of social work ethics: The Global Social Work Statement of Ethical Principles (GSWSEP). *International Social Work, 62*(6), 1469–1481. https://doi.org/10.1177/0020872819846238

Sewpaul, V., & Jones, D. (2004). Global standards for social work education and training. *Social Work Education, 23*(5): 493–513.

Sewpaul, V., & Ndlovu, N. (2020). Emancipatory, relationship-based and deliberative collective action: The power of the small group in shifting from adversity to hope, activism and development. *Czech and Slovak Social Work, 20*(1), 108–122.

Shai, K. B. (2018). US foreign policy towards Ghana and Tanzania: An Afrocentric view. *Strategic Review for Southern Africa, 40*(2): 52–66.

Sogolo, G. S. (1993). *Foundations in African philosophy: A definitive analysis of conceptual issues in African thought.* Ibadan, NG: University of Ibadan Press.

Steger, M. B., & Roy, R. K. (2010). Neoliberalism: A very short history. New York, NY: Oxford University Press.

Twikirize, J. M., & Spitzer, H. (Eds.). (2019). *Social work practice in Africa: Indigenous and innovative approaches.* Kampala, UG: Fountain.

Uwihangana, C., Hakizamungu, A., & Bangwanubusa, T. (2019). *Umugoro w'Ababyeyi:* An innovative social work approach to socio-economic wellbeing in Rwanda. In J. M. Twikirize & H. Spitzer (Eds.), *Social work practice in Africa: Indigenous and innovative approaches* (pp. 81–94). Kampala, UG: Fountain.

Vitali, A., Hunt, K., & Thorp V. F. (2018). *Trump referred to Haiti and African nations as "shithole" countries.* https://www.nbcnews.com/politics/white-house/trump-referred-haiti-african-countries-shithole-nations-n836946

Werft, M. (2016, April 7). *Meet the brave female chief who stopped 850 child marriages in Malawi. Global Citizen.* https://www.globalcitizen.org/en/content/malawi-chief-woman-ends-sex-initiation-and-child-m/

Williams, L. O., & Sewpaul, V. (2004). Modernism, postmodernism and global standards setting. *Social Work Education, 23*(5): 555–565.

CONTRIBUTORS

ZIBLIM ABUKARI is an Associate Professor and the Program Director of the BSW program in the Department of Social Work at Westfield State University in Massachusetts, US.

ALICE BOATENG is a Senior Lecturer at the Department of Social Work, University of Ghana. She completed her PhD at Brown School of Social Work, St Louis, Missouri, US. Her research focuses on women and children's issues.

PAUL BUKULUKI, PhD is an Associate Professor in the Department of Social Work and Social Administration, Makerere University, Uganda. He is a Social Worker and Medical Anthropologist. His specialty is social norm change research and programming in child protection and prevention of violence against women and children.

JULIE DROLET is Professor in the Faculty of Social Work at the University of Calgary's Central and Northern Alberta Region in Edmonton. Her research focus is in International social work, disaster recovery and climate change, as well as social development, social protection, immigrant settlement and integration, and social work field education. She has many years of social work practice and policy experience in Africa.

MEL GRAY, Emeritus Professor of Social Work at the University of Newcastle, Australia has an extensive, internationally recognised track record in social work research and scholarship. Her work embraces the diversity of perspectives in International Social Work, decolonising methodologies, and the shared struggle for effective indigenous, culturally relevant social work interventions. Her roots in Africa, and ongoing quest for an Afrocentric perspective, culminated in *The Handbook of Social Work and Social Development in Africa* (Routledge, 2017).

LINDA KREITZER, PhD is a Professor at the University of Calgary, Canada. She is the author of *Social Work in Africa: Exploring Culturally Relevant Education and Practice in Ghana* (University of Calgary Press, 2012), which highlights her PhD work in Ghana. She has co-edited two other books. She is a member of the Association of Schools of Social Work in Africa. Her current research pertains to curriculum issues in Africa.

RONALD LUWANGULA is a Lecturer in the Department of Social Work and Social Administration, Makerere University, Uganda. He holds a PhD in Children's Social Protection Rights from Alpen Adria University Klagenfurt, Austria, a Master's in Social Work and Human Rights from the University of Gothenburg, Sweden, and a Bachelor of Social Work and Social Administration from Makerere University, Uganda.

ABEL BLESSING MATSIKA is an independent consultant based in Zimbabwe. He is currently finalising his PhD thesis on Intimate Partner Violence and Social Work in Zimbabwe.

MANQOBA VICTOR MDAMBA is a qualified, registered Social Worker, working in Cape Town for the NGO Yabonga, working with families and children affected and infected by HIV/AIDS. He completed his Bachelor of Social Work at the University of KwaZulu-Natal. He has volunteered for various social work initiatives, such as the social work military and social work students' associations.

MUNYARADZI MUCHACHA is a qualified and registered social worker, with over six years of practice experience, working in Zimbabwe, the United Kingdom, and Australia. He has previously taught at the University of Zimbabwe.

JACOB RUGARE MUGUMBATE started teaching social work at Bindura University in Zimbabwe and now teaches at the University of Wollongong, Australia. He trained in Zimbabwe and has a PhD from the University of Newcastle. He is involved in epilepsy work in Africa and globally.

DR. RONARD MUKUYE holds a PhD in Social and Cultural Anthropology from University of Vienna, Austria, and an MA in Development Studies from the International Institute of Social Studies, Netherlands. He is currently the Country Programme Support Officer for the United Nations Office for Project Services (Cities Alliance) in Uganda. His main areas of research include children and childhood, culture, social protection, health, and sustainable urban development.

Juliana Naumo Akoryo is a culture, gender, intangible cultural heritage, and community development specialist. She is a founding member of the Organization of Indigenous Peoples of Africa with over twenty-nine years of experience in the formulation, design, and implementation of cultural and creative industry programmes. She was the contact person for the 2003 and the 2005 UNESCO Conventions.

Tatenda Nhapi is an Independent researcher affiliated to the Erasmus Mundus MA Advanced Development in Social Work—a joint Programme between the University of Lincoln, England, Aalborg University, Denmark, Technical University of Lisbon, Portugal, University of Paris Ouest Nantere La Defense, France, and Warsaw University, Poland. Tatenda has published in the areas of social security, social work, and developmental social work.

Aloysious Nnyombi is a PhD candidate in Social and Cultural Anthropology at the University of Vienna, Austria. His research focus includes HIV/AIDS and gender-based violence.

Poloko Nuggert Ntshwarang is Senior Lecturer in the Department of Social Work at the University of Botswana. She holds a PhD in social work from the University of KwaZulu-Natal, South Africa. Dr Ntshwarang's research focus is parenting issues, child protection, family and children's well-being, health, and gender issues. She has published on issues related to adolescents and children.

Augusta Yetunde Olaore, PhD, LMSW, is an Associate Professor at Babcock University, Nigeria, an Adjunct Professor at Azusa Pacific University, US, and the pioneering Chair of the Department of Social Work at Babcock University, Nigeria.

Israel Bamidele Olaore, PhD, is an associate professor of Educational Leadership and Religious Education. He is currently the Head of School at the Glendale Adventist Academy, US.

Tanusha Raniga is Professor in the Department of Social Work and Community Development at the University of Johannesburg, South Africa. She has published widely on feminisation of poverty, social protection policy, and community development.

SHAHANA RASOOL is Professor in the Department of Social Work and Community Development at University of Johannesburg, South Africa. She has published in the area of gender-based violence, decoloniality, and help-seeking. She is the Vice-president of the Association of Schools of Social work in Africa (ASSWA).

BOITUMELO SEEPAMORE is a lecturer in the discipline of social work at the University of KwaZulu-Natal, South Africa. Her 2018 article in the *Advances in Gender Research Journal* was based on the subject close to her heart—mothering and parenting within marginalised spaces and communities. She has also co-edited the *Routledge Handbook on Postcolonial Social Work*.

YANIA SEID-MEKIYE holds a PhD in social work and social development. Her research interests include gender and diversity with a particular focus on married Muslim women experiences in marital relationship. She currently works as State/Deputy Minister of Development and Administration sector at Ministry of Innovation and Technology, Ethiopia.

VISHANTHIE SEWPAUL is Emeritus Professor at University of KwaZulu Natal, South Africa and a Professor ii at University of Stavanger, Norway. She is a widely published, internationally recognised scholar and an awardee of three honorary doctoral degrees. She chaired the Global Standards for Social Work Education and Training Committee (2004), the Global Social Work Definition Committee (2014), and the Global Social Work Statement of Ethical Principles Taskforce (2018) on behalf of the IASSW.

CYNTHIA A. SOTTIE is an Associate Professor of Social Work at Booth University College, Canada, and a former head of the Department of Social Work at the University of Ghana. She has an MSW from West Virginia University, US, and a PhD from Queen's University Belfast, Northern Ireland.

EUNICE TUMWEBAZE possesses twenty years' experience in development and policy work, majoring in culture, gender, and community empowerment at the national and sub-national level. She has a Master of Science in equality studies from University College Dublin, Ireland. Her research is in several areas including social norms, working mothers and parenting.

INDEX

Author Index

Abramson, 155, 163
Addis, 156, 162,
Adejumobi, 5, 9, 21, 42, 43
Adnan, 130, 144
Adzoye, 110, 111, 122
Agbanu, 110, 122
Ahmad, 259, 270
Airhihenbuwa, 237, 253
Akinbi, 49, 50, 58, 64
Akpabli-Honu, 110, 111, 122
Akujobi, 67, 80, 82
Alewo, 49, 50, 59, 60, 64
Al-Hibri, 129, 130, 132, 144
Alldred, 68, 79, 8, 82
Althusser, 30, 37, 40, 43, 268, 270, 292
Ame, 106, 114, 122
Ameh, 110, 111, 122
Annan, 5, 21, 278, 282, 292
Ansah-Koi, 187, 204
Ansell, 25, 32, 38, 43
Appiah, 191, 204, 276, 292
Applebaum, 220, 233
Asante, 4, 6, 7, 21, 282, 283, 284, 292
Askew, 226, 234, 239, 253
Asomah, 110, 122
Atansah, 119, 120, 122
Attoh, 60, 64
Ayodele, 47, 49, 50, 64

Babbie, 260, 270
Baker, 86, 89, 90, 101
Banda, 119, 120, 122
Barlas, 127, 129, 130, 132, 133, 136, 137, 140, 144
Barnard, 7, 21
Barnes, 37, 43
Baskind, 86, 87, 88, 89, 93, 101
Bauman, 42, 43, 277, 286, 292
Baumrind, 79, 82
Beech, 157, 162
Bennett, 79, 82
Berg, 218, 219, 233
Berggren, 214, 226, 229, 230, 233

Biko, 4, 5, 6, 21, 283, 292
Bilyeu, 110, 111, 122
Birbeck, 86, 87, 88, 89, 93, 101
Bitensky, 258, 270,271
Boakye-Boateng, 185, 204
Boccagni, 76, 79, 82
Boikhutso, 267, 271
Bond, 278, 281, 282
Bourdillon, 174, 175,181
Bowlby, 71, 82
Boyden, 173, 174, 180
Bradshaw, 258, 259, 266, 270
British Broadcasting Corporation, 197, 204
Brody, 37, 43
Bruun, 238, 253
Bukuluki, 14, 19, 209, 237, 254, 279, 290

Calvert, 90, 101
Casale, 33, 44
Cesaire, 283, 292
Chavunduka, 86, 101
Chawane, 6, 7, 21
Chimombo, 194, 195, 204
Chireshe, 31, 43
Chirwa, 190, 204
Chitando, 175, 180, 181
Chukwuokolo, 5, 21
Chung, 10, 21
Clerk, 195, 196, 204
Cobbah, 9, 10, 21, 283, 292
Collins, 68, 69, 80, 82
Coniavitis, 95, 96, 101
Contreras, 69, 76, 82
Cooke, 105, 122, 192, 204
Cooper, 50, 58, 59, 64
Corbin, 51, 65
Cox, 8, 23
Creswell, 127, 144
Currie, 151, 162

Dahl, 95, 102, 223, 233
Danermark, 95, 96, 101
de Boer 89, 101

Dei, 4, 21, 22
Dekker, 89, 90, 101
De Waal, 151, 162
Dibua, 280, 281, 282, 293
Dixon-Woods, 215, 233
Dolphyne, 106, 107, 108, 122
Dominelli, 276, 278, 292, 294
Donnelly, 212, 232, 233, 277, 266, 270, 277, 292
Doucet, 226, 227, 229, 232, 233
Dovlo, 110, 111, 122, 123
Drolet, 15, 51, 65, 105, 241
Duggan, 86, 93, 101
Dunne, 195, 204
Durojaye, 49, 58, 64
Durrant, 258, 259, 269, 270

Edemikpong, 107, 122
Elger, 89, 90, 92, 101
Elisheva, 223, 233
Ellison, 258, 270
Enwereji, 59, 60, 64
Ewelukwa, 49, 63, 64

Fairclough, 30, 43, 73, 82
Fanon, 2, 4, 5, 6, 7, 11, 22, 281, 283, 284, 285, 292
Fashina, 6, 22
Ferguson, 86, 88, 101
Figueroa, 176, 180
Finke, 223, 224, 233
Firestone, 159, 160, 163
Fiske, 12, 22, 205
Foster, 193, 202
Fouché, 276, 293
Foueré, 280, 292
Fraser, 68, 70, 82, 85, 95, 96, 100, 101, 102
Freire, 37, 39, 41, 43, 289, 292
Frimpong-Manso, 186, 205
Frizelle, 67, 68, 69, 78, 82
Fromm-Reichmann, 71, 82

Garcia, 89, 103
Geertz, 149, 162
Genyi, 50, 64
Gershoff, 258, 259, 270, 271
Ghana Statistical Service, 112, 122, 196, 197, 205
Gilbert, 33, 43, 70, 74, 82, 205
Gillespie, 69, 83
Giroux, 39, 40, 41, 43

Glaser, 51, 64
Glover, 111, 122
Gondolf, 155,162
Goody, 186, 187, 205
Gostin, 211, 234
Gramsci, 37, 39, 40, 41, 43, 286, 292
Green, 86, 88, 102, 272
Griffith, 69, 76, 82
Gruenbaum, 221, 234
Gudyanga, 258, 259, 271
Gyekye, 281, 292

Hahn, 278, 281, 282, 286, 292
Haight, 107, 108, 123
Hall, 39, 40, 41, 43, 284, 292
Hallen, 3, 4, 6, 7, 22, 275, 276, 281, 293
Hallfors, 170, 171, 172, 180, 181
Harms Smith, 4, 22
Hassan, 133, 145
Hatch, 133, 145
Hayes, 68, 82
Haynes, 10, 21
Hays, 68, 70, 81, 83
Heine, 199, 205
Helman, 237, 253
Henrickson, 276, 278, 286, 293, 295
Heymann, 79, 83
Hölscher, 276, 290, 294
Hugman, 12, 22, 175, 180
Hunter, 28, 31, 33, 37, 43, 103

Ibhawoh, 280, 281, 282, 293
Ibisomi, 48, 64
Ife, 12, 13, 22
Isiugo-Abanihe, 48, 65, 186, 187, 188, 205

Jackson, 148, 163
Jacques, 269, 271
Jawad, 126, 133, 136, 138, 140, 145
Jenk, 189, 195, 205
Jewkes, 80, 83, 151, 162, 163
Jones, 12, 23, 39, 45, 233, 273, 274, 288, 295
Jotia, 267, 271
Julius, 258, 262, 264, 269, 271
Juma, 61, 64

Kalichi, 89, 101
Kaplan, 84, 221, 233, 234
Keddie, 126, 145
Keesbury, 239, 253
Keikelame, 87, 102

Kell, 67, 69, 78, 80, 82
Keynes, 280, 293
Kirmayer, 47, 64
Kitayama, 199, 206
Kizilhan, 220, 234
Kleinman, 1, 3, 22, 213, 234
Klot, 36, 43
Knoema, 125, 145
Kometsi, 37, 43
Korang-Okrah, 107, 108, 123
Kreitzer, 1, 4, 5, 17, 23, 125, 203, 205, 273, 285, 293
Kruger, 69, 83
Kufogbe, 110
Kumah-Abiwu, 4, 22, 283, 293
Kuyini, 186, 205
Kwafo, 110, 123

Laird, 167, 172, 173, 180, 185, 188, 189, 190, 195, 201, 203, 205, 206
Lansford, 257, 258, 259, 271
Larner, 286, 293
Larsen, 39, 45
Lawrence, 87, 102
Leonard, 280, 286, 293
Levinas, 277, 293
LeVine, 191, 206
Limann, 106, 123
Lister, 148, 162
Lubombo, 175, 181
Lucas, 201, 202, 203, 206

Machingura, 170, 177, 181
Macleod, 69, 73, 78, 83
Madziva, 76, 78, 83
Magazi, 88, 102
Maguranyanga, 169, 170, 171, 173, 177, 179, 181
Mahalik, 156, 162
Maharaj, 80, 83
Makama, 48, 58, 65
Makgoba, 10, 22, 283, 293
Makinde, 276, 293
Malacrida, 69, 83
Mandela, 7, 12, 22, 283, 293
Mandelbaum, 149, 162
Manful, 184, 189, 199, 200, 206
Mann, 211, 234
Marcus, 199, 206
Mathews, 81, 83, 157, 159, 162, 163
Matsika, 105, 165, 168, 175, 178, 181, 279, 287

Maundeni, 204, 269, 271
Mawere, 28, 29, 41, 44
Mayo Clinic, 245, 253
Mazama, 284, 293
Mazrui, 26, 36, 44
Mbugua, 191, 206
McGregor, 147, 163
Meintjes, 81, 83
Melchiorre, 168, 181
Merla, 77, 83
Metalsky, 155, 163
Metz, 276, 293
Meyer, 73, 82, 83, 84
Midgley, 4, 22
Millman, 79, 83
Mir-Hosseini, 127, 145
Mofolo, 251, 253
Monaghan, 188, 195, 206
Monyooe, 37, 44
Morrell, 37, 43, 44, 80, 83
Moscardino, 48, 65
Mostafa, 226, 234
Moyo, 237, 253
Mpofu, 170, 180, 181
Muchacha, 18, 105, 165, 168, 172, 174, 175, 178, 181, 279, 287
Mudege, 48, 64
Mughees, 87, 103
Mugumbate, 16, 85, 89, 90, 94, 103, 280
Mullaly, 260, 271
Mupedziswa, 7, 22, 182
Mupotsa, 26, 29, 31, 32, 35, 44
Murray, 26, 44
Mushi, 86, 87, 92, 93, 106
Mutanana, 86, 103
Mutara, 86, 103
Mwamwenda, 37, 44
Mwansa, 4, 5, 22, 23
Mweru, 263, 264, 269, 272
Myers, 174, 175, 181

Nathane, 4, 22
Ndlovu, 290, 295
Ndofirepi, 185, 206
Nemukuyu, 172, 181
Neuman, 207, 260, 272
Newlands, 177, 181
Newton, 89, 103
Nguyen, 36, 43
Njue, 226, 234
Nkosi, 26, 27, 31, 32, 35, 36, 37, 38, 44

Norval, 252, 253
Ntini, 69, 70, 73, 74, 84
Ntoimo, 48, 65
Nukunya, 110, 111, 123
Nyanguru, 94, 103
Nyangweso, 213, 221, 234
Nyanzi, 58, 65
Nyerere, 280, 281, 286, 292, 293
Nyongesa, 108, 123

Okyere, 196, 206
Olaore, 15, 47, 51, 65, 105, 241
Olong, 49, 50, 59, 60, 64
Olowu, 190, 206
Oluoch, 108, 123
Onwauchi, 185, 190, 206
Opoku, 37, 38, 44, 279, 294
Oye Lithur, 113, 123
Oyeniyim, 49, 65

Palitza, 252, 253
Para-Mallam, 48, 62, 65
Parmar, 282, 294
Parreñas, 79, 84
Parsons, 269, 272
Patton, 128, 145
Pawar, 8, 23
Pendergast, 147, 163
Penn, 188, 195, 207
Perry, 108, 123
Pew-Templeton Research Center, 49, 65
Phoenix, 69, 70, 71, 84
Pilon, 186, 187, 188, 207
Porter, 193, 207
Posel, 26, 27, 29, 31, 32, 33, 38, 44

Querido, 79, 84

Rasool, 17, 147, 153, 156, 163
Ratele, 161, 163
Refaat, 229, 234
Rempel, 260, 272
Renzaho, 258, 272
Reynolds, 12, 23
Richter, 34, 43, 44
Roald, 127, 145
Robins, 252, 253
Robson, 110, 111, 123
Roy, 286, 295
Rozmus, 87, 102
Rubin, 149, 163

Rudwick, 26, 27, 29, 31, 32, 38, 44
Russell, 159, 163
Rutikanga, 289, 294

Säävälä, 152, 163
Sachs, 213, 232, 234
Sackey, 194, 207
Saheeh International, 132, 133, 143, 144, 145
Said, 27, 44
Salisbury, 148, 163
Samoff, 282, 294
Sarpong, 114, 118, 123
Sayre, 188, 207
Schmidt, 89, 90, 92, 101
Schumm, 133, 145
Schwartz, 71, 84
Scott, 89, 103
Sebonego, 261, 272
Seepe, 10, 22, 283, 293
Sekatawa, 251, 252, 254
Sen, 11, 23, 29, 42, 44, 281, 294
Sengendo, 251, 252, 254
Serequebehan, 278, 294
Serra, 187, 207
Serran, 159, 160, 163
Sewpaul, 1, 4, 6, 7, 9, 10, 12, 13, 14, 15, 20, 25,
    29, 30, 33, 34, 37, 38, 39, 41, 42, 45, 67, 69,
    70, 72, 73, 74, 80, 83, 84, 255, 267, 268,
    269, 273, 274, 276, 277, 278, 279, 280, 282,
    283, 284, 285, 286, 287, 288, 289, 290, 294
Shai, 278, 281, 282, 295
Shell-Duncan, 226, 228, 234
Shope, 33, 45
Shorvon, 85, 88, 89, 103
Shumba, 185, 206, 259, 272
Sibanda, 167, 168, 169, 171, 172, 174, 181
Smith, 59, 65, 259, 266, 272
Sogolo, 276, 295
Sono, 9, 23
Sossou, 58, 65, 107, 123
Sovran, 238, 254
Spencer-Oatey, 2, 23
Spitzer, 22, 289, 290, 294, 295
Spock, 71, 84
Staub-Bernasconi, 197, 198, 207
Steger, 286, 295
Stengel, 7, 23
Stoltz, 95, 102
Strauss, 23, 51, 64, 65
Sudarkasa, 67, 69, 70, 80, 84
Suleman, 156, 163

Swartz, 83, 87, 102
Syed, 136, 138, 145

Tafa, 259, 272
The Africa Report, 116, 123
Theron, 49, 65
Thorpe, 26, 45
Tierney, 14, 23
Tiruneh, 237, 254
Toolis, 258, 272
Tsanga, 26, 45
Twikirize, 22, 289, 290, 294, 295
Twum-Danso, 114, 117, 124, 166, 175, 181, 205,
     206, 207

Uwihangana, 289, 295

Vetten, 161, 163
Vitali, 284, 295
Vloeberghs, 220, 235

Wadud, 127, 129, 130, 132, 137, 140, 141, 145
Wagner, 26, 36, 45
Walker, 33, 45, 67, 68, 80, 84, 148, 163
Watts, 87, 88, 93, 99, 103
Wax, 14, 24
Webster, 237, 253
Weiner, 155, 163
Weis , 258, 272
Wells, 159, 163
Werft, 287, 290, 295
Wessells, 176, 182
Whitehorn, 220, 235
Williams, 276, 277, 295
Willig, 95, 102
Winkler, 87, 103
Winnicott, 71, 84
Wodak, 73, 82, 84
Wood, 151, 163,
Woollett, 71, 84
Wyatt, 174, 182

Yarbrough, 26, 32, 33, 35, 45
Ylvisaker, 71, 72, 84

Zeleza, 10, 24, 29, 45
Zontini, 76, 78, 83

Subject Index

Africa: cultures 3, 10, 29, 242; Diaspora 5, 7, 282; heritage 8, 21, humanism 6, 7; identities 6, 283; traditional religion 49,169, 170

African (Banjul) Charter on Human and Peoples Rights, 11, 15, 58, 60, 114, 115, 166, 183, 184, 190, 191, 193, 200, 203, 220, 227, 239

African Charter on the Rights and Welfare of the Child, 19, 166, 183, 190, 191, 203, 255

African Union, 11

Afrocentricity and Afrocentric values, 3, 5-11, 20, 81, 99, 190, 275-291

Akan ethnic group, 107-108

Allah, 87, 88, 127, 131, 132, 133, 143, 144

Alur cultural institution, 237-259

ancestors and ancestral spirits, 26, 55, 57, 86

anti-colonialism, 3, 11, 28, 285

Apostolic sects, 167-179

Asian people and context, 8, 11, 33

Basotho group, 74

Beijing Declaration and Platform for Action, 114

best interests of the child,15, 68, 79, 188

biomedical model, 88-90

biopsychosocial model, 34, 89-91

Black Consciousness Movement, 5, 21

body beautification, 20, 229, 244-245

bodily integrity, 13, 18, 161, 275, 279, 289

Botswana: botho, 7; corporal punishment, 255-272; Children's Act, 256, 261, 263-264; Education Act, 266; kgotla, 269; Penal Code, 256; Tswana traditions, 261

bride price and wealth, 14, 25, 28, 37-38, 59, 61-63, 108, 241, 243, 246, 252, 279

British Association of Social Workers, 202, 203

burial rites, 49, 52-54, 61, 106

Burkina Faso: female genital mutilation and cutting, 120; kinship foster care, 187; traditional practices, 115

caregivers and caregiving, 68-76, 78, 80, 189, 259

Charter of the United Nations, 239

children: born out of wedlock, 26, 74; child care, 68, 69, 70, 111, 166, 169; construction of childhood, 19, 185; child bearing, 67; exploitation, 16; fostering, 19, 184, 186, 187, 188, 202; labour, 167, 184, 192, 194, 195, 196, 203, 279; marriage, 18, 105, 171, 279, 287, 290; Child Marriage Model Law, 177; protection, 18, 166-179, 184, 189, 191, 250, 268; rearing, 67-75, 188, 189, 269; rights, 18, 165, 166, 176, 184, 267; survival, 189; vulnerability, 19, 186, 250

childbirth, 67, 224, 228

childhood: Eurocentric and Western construction, 166-167, 184, 189, 195; Ghanaian construction, 185; early development, 188; experiences and co-dependence, 266; onset epilepsy, 92; socio-cultural constructions, 279; universalization, 166, 185

Christianity, 49, 86, 125, 170, 171, 261

civil rights, 9, 11, 15, 38, 141, 188, 279, 281

civil society, 119, 166, 177, 220, 240

clitoridectomy, 108, 118, 209

collective: action and response, 121, 290; caring, 8, 9; 29, 80; child-rearing, 75, 190; decision-making, 18, 176; dialogue, 231; responsibility, 7, 8, 9, 29, 274; values, 190; vocation, 8; wellbeing, 61; wisdom, 59

collectivism, 9, 10, 28, 29

colonial: administration, 27; assault on humanity, 5; attitudes, 16; constructions, 291; dispossession, 28; history, 5, 169, 172, 186, 278; legacies, 4, 29, 41, 63; power, 198; rule, 105; thinking, 283

colonialism, 3, 4, 5, 10, 27-29, 41, 170, 184, 193, 203, 278, 281-284

common sense assumptions, 14, 26, 30, 33-34, 37, 40, 267-268, 286, 288-289

community education and engagement, 15, 17,18, 39-42, 61, 98, 100, 115, 118, 119, 173-179, 201, 251-252, 257, 268-270, 285, 287-290
conflict and human rights violations, 5, 12,16, 18, 117, 170
conflict resolution, 202, 249
Congo: bomoto, 7; Niger-Congo language family, 105
constitutional rights, 18, 161
Convention on the Elimination of All Forms of Discrimination against Women (CEDAW), 61, 114, 125, 168
Convention on the Rights of the Child (CRC): 19, 20, 114, 166, 183-185, 188-191, 193-196, 199, 203, 220, 255-256
Core values/principles: 11, 81, 188, 198, 203, 252, 273-275, 278, 291
Corporal punishment (CP): 20, 255-270, 287
Critical Discourse Analysis: 72
cultural: annihilation 4, attitudes, 90, 193, 194, 200; assimilation, 40; conceit, 10; 11; difference, 13; dimensions, 237; diversity, 10, 12, 13, 61, 97, 211, 212, 213, 273; epistemologies, 2; mediators, 13, 39, 268, 277, 288; norms, 4, 19, 30, 68, 127, 169, 217, 238, 239, 240, 249, 251, 252, 278, 291; ontology, 47; practices, 5, 7, 11-16, 37-38, 47-52, 57-, 58-63, 89, 97, 105-106, 110, 117-122, 128, 168-169, 179, 186, 200, 213, 241, 247, 256-257, 268, 291; relativism, 13, 212, 232, 277; sensitivity, 13
customary law: court, 60, 61; laws, 62, 63, 168, 287; practices, 50, 62
Customs, 3, 49, 54, 107, 109, 118, 127, 185, 258, 291

death: asset distribution, 250; in customary marriage, 49; and female ritual bondage, 110-112; grieving period, 49; punishment, 56, 58, 60; and female genital mutilation and cutting, 218, 220, 232; widow inheritance, 20, 61, 241, 242; rites and rituals, 49, 50, 52-54, 58, 61, 63, 106-108, 238
democracy: capitalism, 282; colonial influence, 5, democratic participation, 9, 96; democracy and socio-economic development 10, ideals and practices 11; 267; nation, 105, people-centered social

democracy, 6, 280, 281, 289; non-racial, 7; socialist, 282
demons, 87, 88
dialogue: community, 18, 34, 61,118-119, 167, 176-177, 179, 231, 268, 283; intercultural, 39, 288; in multicultural relations, 7; reflective and reflexivity, 15, 39, 41, 269, 284-285
dichotomy and dichotomies, 10, 29, 35, 175, 274
disability: intersection with other social criteria, 6; perspective, 90-91; People's Organization, 98; services, 16, 90-94; and social justice, 96; social model, 91
disadvantages: gender, 35, 120, 139; economic, 95; and epilepsy, 91, 99, 100; injustice, 95, 96; Global South, 10; intersectional criteria, 287
discourses: dominant, 31, 32, 37, 38, 40, 70, 72, 78, 80, 270, 284, 285, 288; contested, 26, 32; femininities and masculinities, 38; ideological, 40; intensive mothering, 16; illobolo, 25-45; mode of practice, 30; multiple, 3; multicultural, 6; normalized, 29; orders of, 30; power, 36; relativistic, 12; subordination, 28
divorce, 60, 134, 135, 186, 187
domestic violence and violence against women, 17, 28, 36, 109, 115, 147, 148, 149, 150, 154-161, 175, 290
domestic workers, 15-16, 67-84
dowry, 63, 139, 242, 243

Eastern culture, 10
economic: benefits 55, 57; Economic Structural Adjustment Programs, 174; circumstances, 32, 68, 279; distributive justice, 95, 202, 279, 282, 291; exploitation, 11, 96; necessity, 15; redistribution, 99; security, 50, 194
emancipation, 9-10, 11, 15, 26, 40, 63
emancipatory social work, 11, 12, 13, 20, 25, 39, 40, 268, 273-276, 279, 282-289
environmental rights, 11
epilepsy, 16, 85 -10, 280
equality, 9, 18, 31, 35, 38, 58, 59, 60-63, 80, 106, 114, 126, 148, 149, 151, 161, 165, 177, 178, 197, 211, 212, 231, 248, 251, 278, 280
ethics, 6, 51, 111, 198, 203, 229-230, 259, 275-276, 281

Ethiopia: Constitution 125; harmful practices against women, 115; Islam and women's rights, 125-146

ethnic: diversity 48; groups, 5, 38, 48, 51, 54, 105, 107, 109-110, 125, 239; identification, 9, 42

Eurocentrism, 4, 6, 10, 71, 166, 189, 276, 283

Europe, 5, 7, 10, 29, 186, 278, 282

Ewe ethnic group, 107, 110-111

exploitation: children, 16, 117, 165, 167-168, 191-192, 195, 203, 212, 255; economic, 11, 96; women, 80

faith and faith based organisations, 8, 14, 87, 88, 133, 176, 177, 201, 261

family: conflict, 16; extended, 8, 27, 35, 52-54, 59, 106, 108, 141, 186, 191; honour, 37, 112, 245, 247, 252; nuclear, 72, 108, 188; Norwegian, 71; planning, 171; property and inheritance 136, 138, 341, 136, 138, 241; relationships 17, 79, 128, 190; type and structure, 6, 20, 70, 81, 259-261, 267; universality, 47; unity, 7; wellbeing, 11; 15, 50, 199

fathers and fatherhood, 28, 29, 30, 34, 37, 48, 74, 137, 139, 185, 250

female genital mutilation/cutting, 16, 19, 37-38, 106-120, 167, 209-232, 279

female ritual bondage (troxovi system), 110-112, 114, 119-120

female-headed households: 33, 34, 261

femicide, 157, 160

femininity and feminism, 31, 33, 41, 67, 95, 147

fertility, 33, 67, 109, 111, 224

Fiasidi (wife or slave of a deity),110

focus group discussions, 19, 51, 72, 215, 226, 229-230, 240

foster care and fostering: crisis, 186, 187; domestic, 186, 187; educational; 186, 188; kinship, 186; mothers, 69; non-kinship, 186; pre-colonial traditional, 19, 184-186

Fon ethnic group110

freedom: from abuse and exploitation, 165, 167; of expression and association 18, 148, 151; of movement 18, 148, 154, 160

Ga ethnic group, 107, 110

Gambia: female genital mutilation and cutting, 120, 220

gender: bias, 56, 57, 126; equality, 31, 35, 38, 62, 80, 106, 126, 149, 161, 177, 212, 231, 248, 251; inequality, 31, 35, 58, 62, 126, 129, 136, 251; parity, 193, 194; relations, 18, 128, 141, 142, 152, 169, 250, 252; stereotypes, 62, 127, 194; gender-based violence, 19, 20, 150, 165, 177, 237-252

Ghana: Action Aid, 116; Association of Social Workers, 203; Baptist Convention, 116; child labour, 183-208; Constitution 114-115, 192; criminal code 110, 113, 115; Department of Social Welfare, 192; Education Service, 195; harmful cultural practices, 105-124; National Association of Teachers,193; National Commission on Children, 191; NGO Coalition on the Rights of the Child (GNCRC) 193, 205; child laws, 19

Global Agenda for Social Work and Social Development, 12, 198, 273

Global Campaign against Epilepsy, 90-91, 99

Global Definition of Social Work, 12, 22, 198, 273-275

Global Initiative to End All Corporal Punishment of Children (GIEACPC), 256-258, 264, 267-268, 271

Global Social Work Statement of Ethical Principles (GSWSEP), 12, 13, 273, 275, 277, 278, 288

Global South, 4, 85, 165-167, 173, 278-279, 285,

Global Standards on Social Work Education and Training, 12, 23, 39, 45, 198, 273 -275, 288

God, 86, 87, 110, 111, 127, 135, 170, 227, 276

hadiths, 130, 139, 140, 228

harm reduction, 26, 221, 224, 226, 230,

harmful cultural and traditional practices, 16, 17, 42, 47, 50, 105-124, 165, 168-169, 175, 209-213, 231-232, 257, 268, 279-280, 290-291

healing, 20, 86, 87, 93, 97-98, 109, 141, 170, 176, 218, 244

health-care professionals and providers, 19, 209, 214, 221, 226, 227, 229, 231, 232,

hegemony: counter-hegemonic, 267; Eurocentric, 4; ideological, 40, 41; patriarchal, 147, 285; Western, 6, 10, 189, 267

HIV/AIDS, 19, 20, 29, 36, 108, 177, 187, 237-242, 247, 290

human agency, 2, 6, 11, 30, 35, 39, 40,41, 63, 73, 152, 155, 285, 291 human dignity, 3, 9, 11, 18-19, 38, 58, 60, 81, 108, 131, 135, 148, 150-151, 157-158, 160-161; 175, 197, 198, 203, 210-211, 247, 256-259, 267, 274-275, 277-278, 287, 291

human rights violations, 3, 5, 9, 13, 26, 29, 116, 128, 273, 275, 279, 285, 288-291

Human Rights Watch, 167, 171, 177

Humanity, 2, 5-7, 10-11, 81, 121, 139, 161, 278, 286

IASSW, 12-13, 81, 269, 273, 275, 277, 286, 288

IASSW/IFSW, 12, 273, 275

IASSW/ICSW/IFSW, 12, 273

ideology and ideologies, 4, 11, 30, 40, 68, 75, 79, 156, 267-268, 285-286, 291

Igbos ethnic group, 48, 51

ilobolo, 14, 15, I25 - 42

imams, 88, 228

imperialism, 4-5, 27, 278,

Indigenous: African values, 11; African intellect, 276; Afrocentric social care practices, 15, 50, 58, 63; churches, 169; communication tools, 62; perspectives on epilepsy, 85-88; epistemologies, 276; knowledge and beliefs, 47, 274; methods, 198; limitations of Indigenous approaches, 290

infibulation, 109, 209-210, 213, 216, 226, 228-230,

inheritance: practices, 20, 49, 50, 54, 59; rights 17, 127, 128, 138, 139, 140

intergenerational: cultural continuity, 42, 289; cycles of poverty, 34, 188; socio-economic status, 194; transmission of culture, 2; patterns of corporal punishment, 267-268

International Classification of Functioning, Disability and Health, 90

International Covenant on Civil and Political Rights, 220

International Covenant on Economic, Social and Cultural Rights, 220

International Federation of Social Workers (IFSW), 184, 197, 198

International Federation of Women Lawyers, 62

international human rights, 15-16, 39, 62, 63, 106, 118, 121, 166-168, 183, 220, 239

International Labour Organization, 196

International League Against Epilepsy, 90

International Money Fund (IMF), 188, 280-281

intersectionality: political economy, culture, and human rights, 3, 95; race, class, and gender, 16, 68, 81; culture, religion, and women's rights, 17, 125-145; lens, 72; multiple social criteria, 6, 287; violence against children and violence against women, 217

intersubjectivity, 2, 3, 286

isiZulu, 14, 15, 25-26, 30-31, 33, 72

Islam: intersection between culture and religion, 17, 56, 125-146; polygamy, 133-136; Islamic scriptures, 126, 143

justice: criminal justice reform, 202; distributive, 279, 282, 291; environmental and climate, 278; natural 60-61; juvenile 184, 191; recourse to, 16, 92, 94, 100; restorative, 7; social, 9, 12, 14, 16, 25, 41,42, 61, 91, 92, 94-96, 99, 100, 120, 165, 175, 178, 180, 198, 203, 269, 273, 274, 282; in Islam, 129, 131, 133, 139- 144

Kenya: collective child rearing practices, 190; self-help 91; corporal punishment, 264, 269; locally specific interventions, 289

Kwanzaa, 21, 280

Lesotho: distance parenting, 74, 76; bohali (bridewealth), 25

Local: culture, customs, and traditions, 3, 10, 18, 47, 50, 175, 179, 185, 188, 244, 274, 276; group affiliation, 3; languages and cultures 5, 110, 166, 212, 260; socio-economic circumstances 18, 166, 175; solutions, 198, 200, 203, 231, 274, 277, 286, 288, 289

Malawi: Eurocentric imposition, 185; child marriage, 287, 290; girl's education, 194-195; Indigenous healing methods, 86-87; umunthu, 7

marginalization: advocacy, 13,39; epilepsy, 87, 90; non-participation, 96; widows, 107; women, 63, 68, 70, 78, 79, 169

marriage: child, 18, 105, 112-120, 165-182, 191, 279, 287, 290; childless, 54; civil, 49; cultural practices, 15, 16, 41, 47-66, 242; customary, 25, 63; delayed, 26, 34;

infidelity in, 15, 47, 55-63; in Islam, 125-146; non-consensual, 242-243, 251; polygamous, 17, 55-59, 113, 127-128, 133-136, 221, 242, 251; polygynous, 113; white wedding, 35

masculinities, 38, 80, 147, 148, 157

maternal mortalities, 165, 175

midwives, 19, 214, 215, 221, 224-232

migrants and migration, 28, 78-79, 109, 111

modernity, 27, 28, 31, 63

moral: arc, 9; claim, 6; codes, 170, 185; degradation, 29; development, 258; dilemma, 226; hazards, 183; imperative, 247; obligation, 11; positive value, 68, 80; questions, 212; reasoning, 3; right, 232; self, 277; relativism, 13, 277; worth, 286

Morocco: beliefs about epilepsy, 87; Indigenous healing methods, 86

mothers and mothering: blaming, 71, 78, 79; disabilities, 69; distance, 16, 67-84; good mother, 36, 68, 76; incarcerated, 69; identities, 68,74; intensive, 16, 67-71, 76-78; othermothering, 15, 67-69, 72, 75; same sex, 69; shared, 69; self-regulatory, 78; single, 26, 30, 69, 73; transnational, 77; working, 69, 70

motherhood: conceptualization, 15, 16; fertility and motherhood, 33,67; unmarried, 28, 32-34; socio-cultural constructions, 67-84; unemployment, 32-34

multicultural, 6, 7

Multiple Indicator Cluster Survey, 112

Multiple Indicator Monitoring Survey, 171

Muslims, 17, 49, 126-142, 228

naming ceremonies, 74

neoliberalism and neoliberal capitalism, 4, 15, 20, 275, 278, 280-282, 285-287, 291

Nguni groups, 69

Nigeria: Constitution 60; ethnic groups, 51; female ritual bondage, 110-111; marital cultural practices, 47-66; gender inequality, 47-66; mutual aid, 201; Ubuntu, 61; women's empowerment, 62

non-discrimination, 58, 63, 114, 115, 188, 198, 211, 232, 278

normalization: harm, 12; corporal punishment, 256, 258, 261, 263-267; cultural and neoliberal discourses, 291; distant mothering, 76, 80; illobo, 26,

28-31; oppression, 37; female genital mutilation and cutting, 38, 229; social workers, 269; violation of women's rights, 143

norms: core identities, 2; corporal punishment, 257-258, 263-266; dominant masculinity, 238; heterosexuality, 291; middle-class, 71; positive social norms, 249-251; socio-cultural, religious, and traditional, 4, 11, 15, 28, 30, 38, 40-41, 68, 80, 107, 117, 127, 139, 165, 169, 173, 200, 237; 239-241, 278; 291; social norm change, 209, 212, 216-217, 221, 229-232; tribal groups, 50

oppressed and oppressors, 7, 13, 142, 161, 283

oppression, 5-6, 26, 31, 35, 37-39, 201, 269, 281, 283

oral tradition, 51, 111

Organization of African Unity, 11, 15, 19, 58, 114, 239

orphans, 133, 187, 250

parents and parenting: authoritative, 79; culturally entrenched parenting practices, 255-272; distance, 15, 16, 67-84; education, 98, 100, 189, 194; conscious positive parenting, 20, 257; female-parent families, 20; intensive, 80, 81; migrant, 79; parental versus children's rights and responsibilities, 261-263; single, 70, 81; two parent families, 20, 34

participation: barriers to, 68, 90, 96, 100; community, 190, 195; leaders, 18, 176-178; parity of, 96, 99, 101, 280-281; party politics, 141; policy making, 201-202

patriarchy and patriarchal culture, 10, 15, 17, 35, 37, 38, 48, 53, 63, 68, 70, 107, 127, 130, 133, 135, 142, 143, 147, 148, 156, 161, 248, 250, 251, 252, 279

political rights, 9, 11, 188, 220

positive cultural resources, 20, 238, 240, 246, 249, 252

post-colonial: critique, 29; dangers, 281; intellectual, 2; theories and theorising, 274, 289; status, 280

poverty: free market ideologies, 4, 15, 278; 285, 286; and conflicts, 5; and human rights violations, 18, 19, 117, 118, 192, 196; and ilobolo, 26, 28, 32, 34, 39; and race, 70, 80; and teenage pregnancies, 73; and distant mothering, 75; treatment gap, 89; and epilepsy, 99, 280; and child marriages, 112, 113, 167, 169, 171, 172, 174, 178, 179, 279; uneven access to education, 187, 193, 194; intergenerational transmission, 188, reduction, 192, 197, 202

power: colonial, 27, 198, 278; dynamics, 223-225, 232; and gender, 17, 18, 37, 38, 119, 137; and language, 41, 62, 73; and privilege, 7, 30; patriarchal, 35, 63, 126, 129, 136, 147, 163, 238, 248, 150, 252; parental, 259, 262, 270; supernatural, 88

primordial essence, 32, 39, 41, 291

privilege, 7, 8, 30, 39, 63, 70, 76, 81, 147, 283, 291

pronatalist culture, 48

property and inheritance rights, 14, 15, 17, 47, 52, 54, 61, 127, 128, 136, 138, 139, 140,

Prophet Mohamed (PBUH), 88, 227

Protocol to the African Charter on Human and Peoples' Rights on the Rights of Women in Africa, 58, 60, 115, 220, 227

provider role, 34, 37, 249

psychosocial issues, 34, 88, 90

public social welfare,16, 92, 93

Quran, 17, 87, 88, 126, 128, 129, 130, 131, 132, 133, 135, 136, 138, 139, 140, 141, 142, 143, 144

race: Afrocentricity, 6, 279; discrimination, 190-191, 211; intersectional criterion, 16, 40, 67-68, 81, 286-287; ontological power, 67; thinking, 284; socio-political and cultural construct, 67

racism, 70, 284

radical: Marxist leaning, 12, 95; views 29; religious doctrine, 170; developmental social work, 178, changes, 189; cultural relativism, 232

re-infibulation, 110, 213, 216, 226, 228, 229, 230

religion: and colonialism, 4, 5, 283; Islam, 125-146; justification for harmful practices 16, 25-45, 47-65, 106-117, 167, 169; leaders, 119, 121, 176-177, 216, 224, 227-231; multiple universes of discourse, 3; mweya, 170-171,179; perspectives on epilepsy, 85-89; regulation of religious

healing, 98; reconciling religious and scientific discourses, 276; respect for diversity, 275

representation: social justice, 95; political 96; rights based approach 97-100, women 141

resistance: anti-colonial, 3, 6; to change, 26; to power and authority, 73, 152, 177, 178, 289; to universalized childhood, 185

respect: for authority, 8, 131, 176, 179, 185, 190, 231, 247; for the dead, 49; for diversities, 9, 12, 13, 96, 117; for human dignity, 38; for human rights, 5, 116, 211; mutual, 250; for persons, 6, 19, 29, 60, 118, 188

responsibilities: in child marriage, 112, 113,117; children's, 166, 203; collective, 8, 9, 11, 29, 274; and freedom, 40; government, 62, 257; in Islamic marriage, 129, 132, 133, 137, 138, 139, 142; parental versus children's, 261-263, 270; productive and reproductive, 35; supernatural interference, 86; traditional aunties, 247; in troxovi, 111; Ujima, 7; in wife inheritance, 49, 52, 59; women and child rearing, 69, 70, 73, 78, 79, 80

rights-based approach, 96, 97, 150, 212, 214, 232

rite of passage, 37, 223, 224

rituals, 35, 41, 49, 53, 63, 88, 106, 107, 108, 120, 185, 275

Rwanda: ethnic identification, 9; genocide, 9; interventionist state, 289

self-help: groups, 201; projects, 91

sex: age of consent, 112, 113, 172; food for sex, 152; same sex, 69; unprotected, 38; work, 167,

sexism, 26, 25, 41, 221; and discrimination, 35; malignant, 26

sexual: control, 221; desire, 134, 219; exploitation, 114; female ritual bondage, 110-111; functioning risks, 219; harassment, 195; heterosexual, 68, 71, 149; high risk behaviour, 226; identity, 6; infidelity, 160; intercourse, 35, 109; jealousy, 159; male pleasure, 109; minorities, 95; misconduct, 195; orientation, 6, 40, 81, 237, 287; partners, 56, 59; objects and property, 134, 157; and reproductive health rights, 209, 211; services, 26; violation, 150, 156

sexual and reproductive health rights, 209, 211, 212, 230, 231
Sharia, 137, 138, 139
Shona, 7, 25, 28
slave women, 69
slavery, 69, 106, 282
social policy, 10, 42, 90, 148, 201, 202
social and group solidarity, 6, 9, 63, 190, 281-282
social work education, 2, 4, 10, 12, 15, 19, 39, 40, 50, 184, 198, 199, 200, 201, 273, 274, 288, 289, 290
socio-cultural constructions, 27, 39, 41, 67, 68, 239, 279, 288
socio-economic circumstances, realities, and injustices, 2, 3, 8, 10, 11, 15, 17, 18, 20, 26, 27, 32-33, 38, 40, 80-81, 91, 95, 126, 129, 136, 139, 141, 166, 167, 171, 174-175, 179, 194, 199, 202, 209, 231, 261, 267, 273, 279, 290, 291
Sotho groups, 69
South Africa: apartheid, 7, 27, 28, 149, 281; Black Consciousness Movement, 5; Commission on Gender Equality, 35; Constitution, 148, 150-151; Customary Marriages Act, 25, 74; distance parenting, 67-84; domestic violence, 147-164; domestic workers, 67-84; Employment Equity Act, 90-91; Epilepsy South Africa, 90-91; ilobolo, 25-46; post-apartheid, 149, 281; Truth and Reconciliation Commission, 7; Ubuntu, 7
South African Development Community, 177
Spirit led churches, 169
spirits, 47, 55, 57, 87, 88, 257, 282
status: gender, 50, 70, 125, 128, 134, 137, 147, 223; and ilobolo, 27-28; intersectional criterion, 6, 68, 197; motherhood, 73; refugee, 191; socio-economic, 20, 95, 135, 192, 194, 261
stereotypes: gender and gender roles, 30, 37, 62, 127, 194, 238; deconstruction, 41; racial, 30; reproduction of, 30
structural constraints and influences, 40, 67, 71, 81, 90, 91, 279
Sub-Saharan Africa, 165, 170, 184, 185, 193, 196, 201
supernatural forces, 86, 237
Sustainable Development Goals, 211, 212, 231, 267

Tanzania: bumuntu, 7; corporal punishment, 256; Indigenous healing, 86; Nyumba Ntobhu, 38; Ujamaa, 280
traditional: activities, 49; beliefs, 19; communities, 8, 9; healers, 86, 87, 97; healing practices, 244; mourning practices, 106; subordination, 28

Ubuntu, 7-9, 12, 61, 80, 99, 175, 258, 273, 275, 277-278, 290-291
Uganda: AIDS Commission, 238; gender-based violence, 237-254; HIV/AIDS, 237-254; Umuntu, 7
Ujamaa, 8, 280, 282, 286, 290
UN Centre for Human Rights, 198
UN Fund for Population Activities, 115, 165, 166, 167, 169
UN Office of the High Commission for Human Rights, 106
UN Women, 238
UN World Declaration on the Survival, Protection and Development of Children, 255
UNICEF, 106, 109-110, 115, 165, 169-173, 176-177, 192, 197, 215- 217, 221-222, 228, 231, 259
United Nations Commission on Human Rights, 214
United Nations Development Program, 92, 107, 119, 192, 193
United Nations Education, Scientific and Cultural Organization, 36, 237, 240, 252,
United Nations Treaty Monitoring Bodies, 214
Universal Declaration of Human Rights, 59, 61, 113, 125, 168, 220, 239

virgins and virginity, 109-111, 224, 246, 247, 248

Western archetypes, culture, and hegemony, 4, 6-7, 10-11, 14, 28-29, 47, 88, 97, 111, 167, 175, 187-189, 195, 201, 257, 282-285
widows: cleansing, 38; inheritance, 14, 16, 20, 49, 50, 52, 106, 108, 241, 251; transfer, 49, 52, 53, 62
widowhood rites, 14, 16, 48, 49, 58, 106, 107, 108
witch camps, 116
witchcraft, 87, 116
women: in Law and Development in Africa [WiLDAF], 113; Consortium of Nigeria,

62; oppression, 26, 31; rights, 15, 17, 58, 62, 63, 126, 127, 128, 130, 131, 133, 136, 139, 140, 143, 148, 150, 151, 161, 162, 191, 226; status, 128, 134; women-centred networks, 69

World Bank, 188, 189, 280-281

World Declaration on the Survival, Protection and Development of Children, 272

World Health Organization, 85, 88-, 89-93, 98, 100, 109-110, 115, 120, 209-218, 220, 229, 231

Yorubas, 48, 51

Zimbabwe: child marriages, 165-182; Constitution, 172; epilepsy misrecognition, 85-104; hunu, 7; lobola, 25; roora, 25; Shona culture, 28

Zion Christian Churches, 171

CPSIA information can be obtained
at www.ICGtesting.com
Printed in the USA
LVHW012135020921
696794LV00023B/2848

9 781773 851822